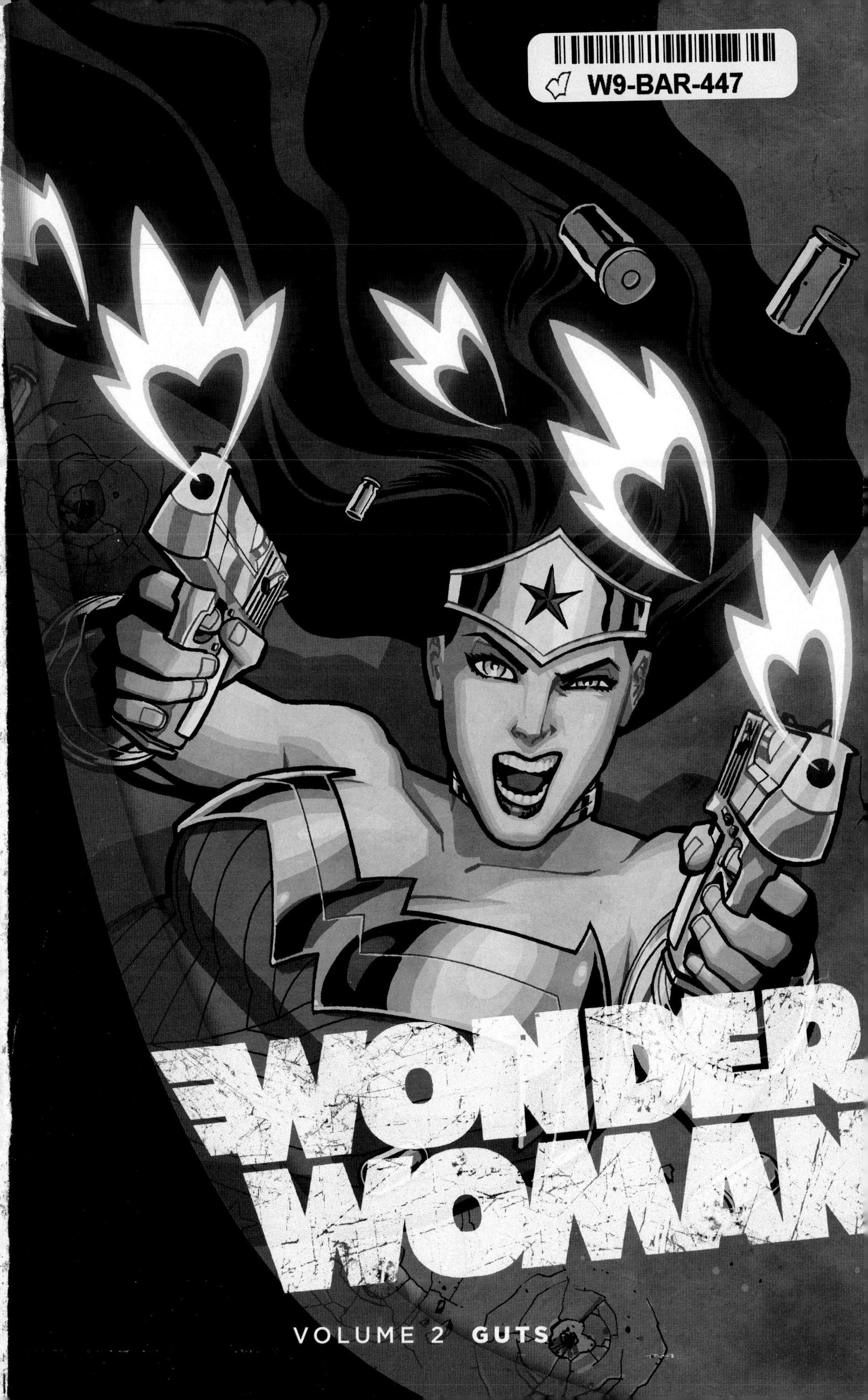
WONDER
WOMAN
VOLUME 2 GUTS

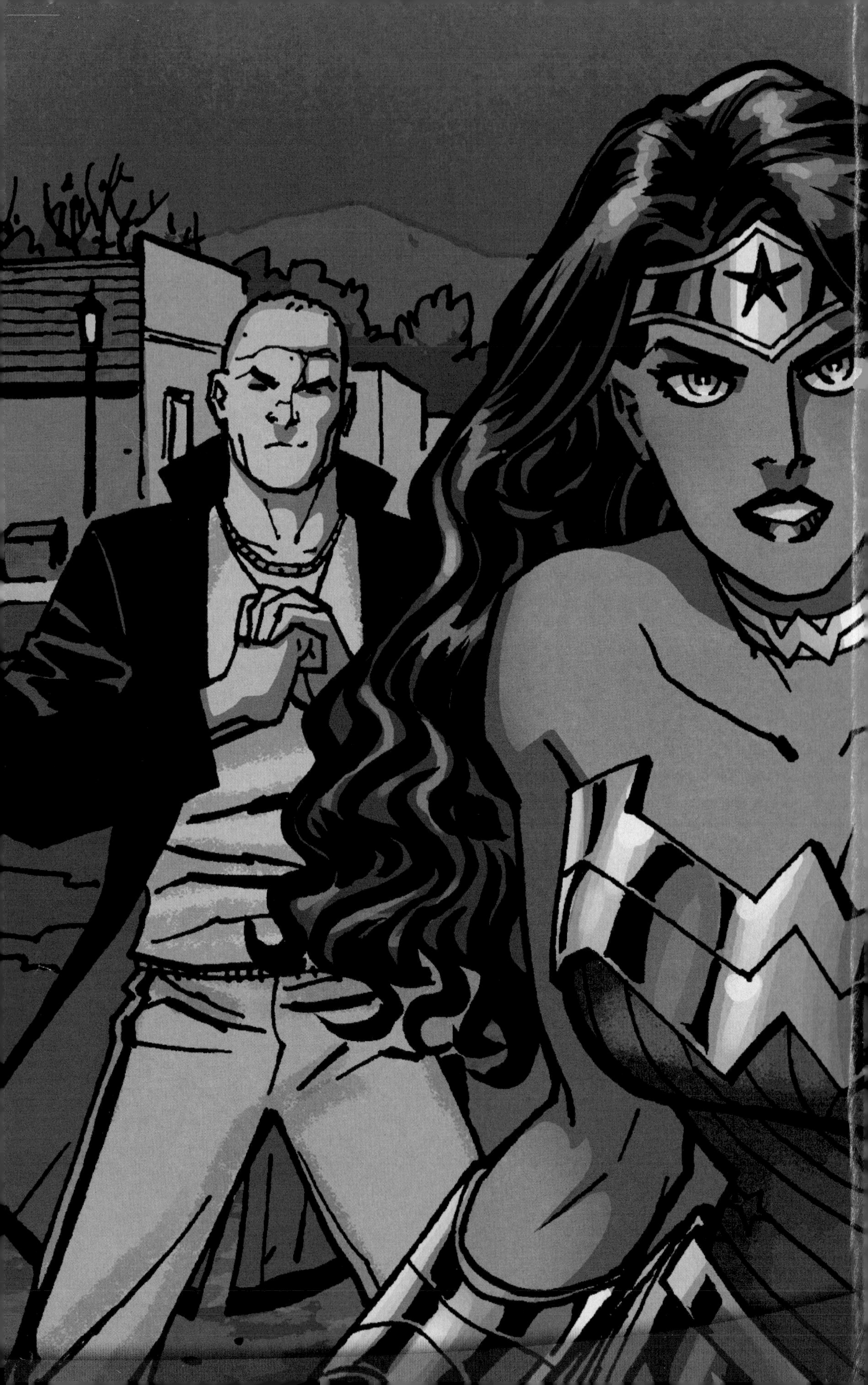

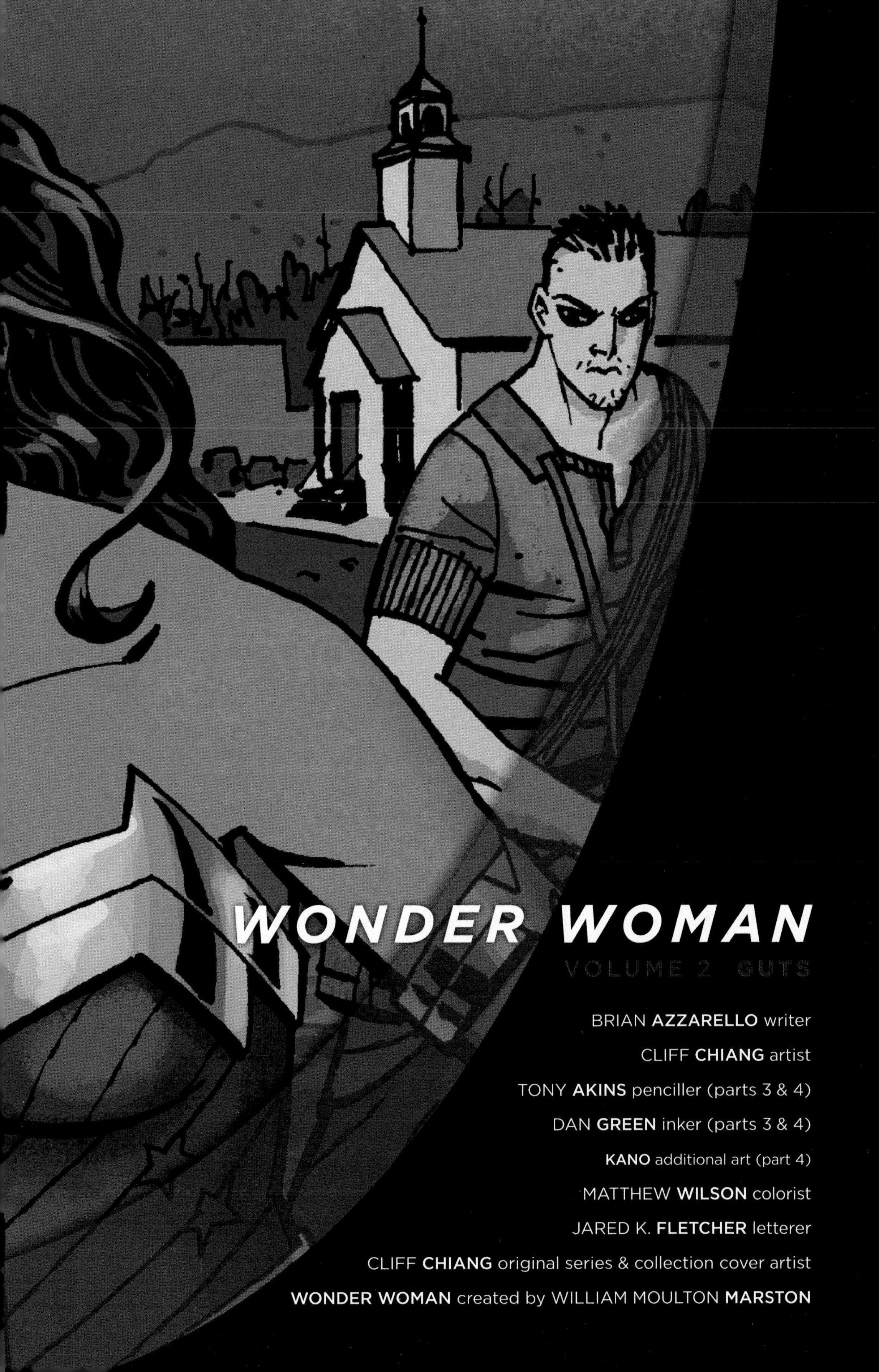

WONDER WOMAN

VOLUME 2 GUTS

BRIAN **AZZARELLO** writer

CLIFF **CHIANG** artist

TONY **AKINS** penciller (parts 3 & 4)

DAN **GREEN** inker (parts 3 & 4)

KANO additional art (part 4)

MATTHEW **WILSON** colorist

JARED K. **FLETCHER** letterer

CLIFF **CHIANG** original series & collection cover artist

WONDER WOMAN created by WILLIAM MOULTON **MARSTON**

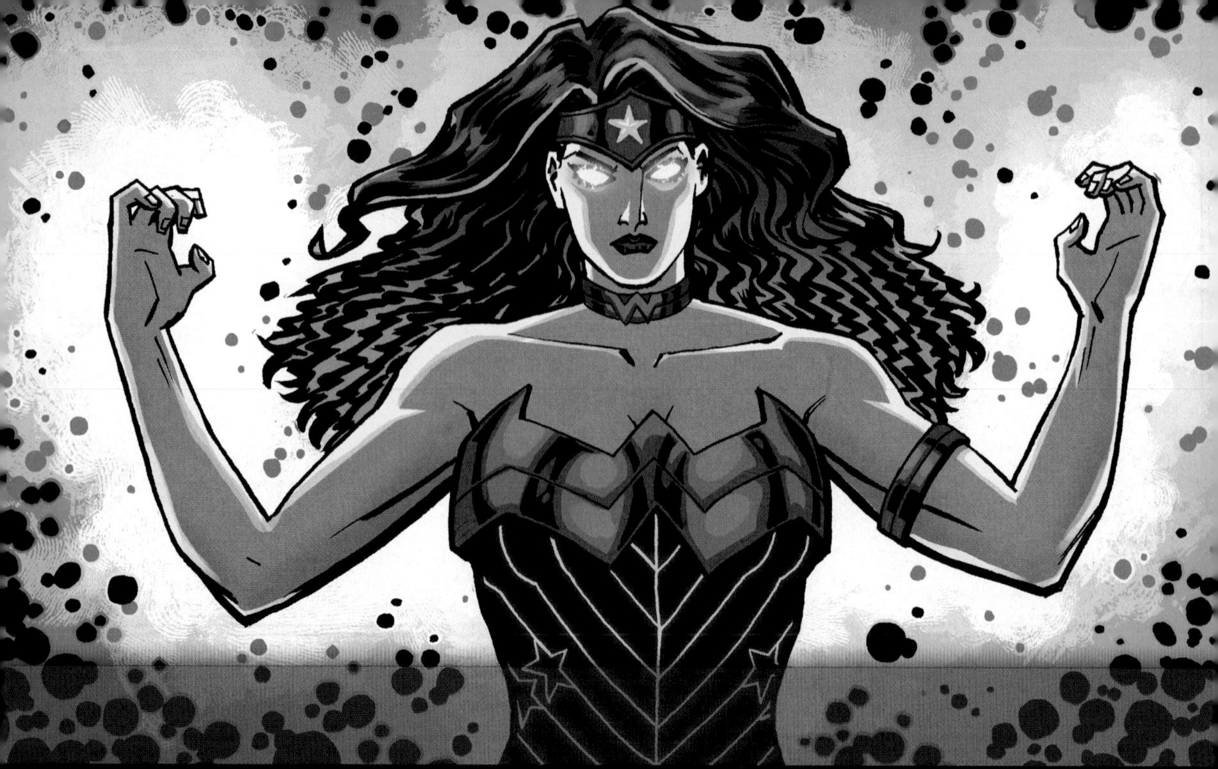

MATT IDELSON Editor – Original Series CHRIS CONROY Associate Editor – Original Series
ROBIN WILDMAN Editor ROBBIN BROSTERMAN Design Director – Books
ROBBIE BIEDERMAN Publication Design

BOB HARRAS Senior VP – Editor-in-Chief, DC Comics

DIANE NELSON President DAN DIDIO and JIM LEE Co-Publishers
GEOFF JOHNS Chief Creative Officer
JOHN ROOD Executive VP – Sales, Marketing and Business Development
AMY GENKINS Senior VP – Business and Legal Affairs NAIRI GARDINER Senior VP – Finance
JEFF BOISON VP – Publishing Planning MARK CHIARELLO VP – Art Direction and Design
JOHN CUNNINGHAM VP – Marketing TERRI CUNNINGHAM VP – Editorial Administration
ALISON GILL Senior VP – Manufacturing and Operations HANK KANALZ Senior VP – Vertigo & Integrated Publishing
JAY KOGAN VP – Business and Legal Affairs, Publishing JACK MAHAN VP – Business Affairs, Talent
NICK NAPOLITANO VP – Manufacturing Administration SUE POHJA VP – Book Sales
COURTNEY SIMMONS Senior VP – Publicity BOB WAYNE Senior VP – Sales

WONDER WOMAN VOLUME 2: GUTS

DC Comics, 1700 Broadway, New York, NY 10019
A Warner Bros. Entertainment Company.
Printed by RR Donnelley, Salem, VA, USA. 8/9/13. First Printing.

ISBN: 978-1-4012-3810-0

Library of Congress Cataloging-in-Publication Data

Azzarello, Brian.
Wonder Woman. Volume 2, Guts / Brian Azzarello, Cliff Chiang, Tony Akins.
p. cm.
"Originally published in single magazine form in Wonder Woman 7-12."
ISBN 978-1-4012-3809-4
1. Graphic novels. I. Chiang, Cliff. II. Akins, Tony. III. Title. IV. Title: Guts.
PN6728.W6A98 2012
741.5'973—dc23
2012032150

SUSTAINABLE FORESTRY INITIATIVE
Certified Chain of Custody
At Least 20% Certified Forest Content
www.sfiprogram.org
SFI-01042
APPLIES TO TEXT STOCK ONLY

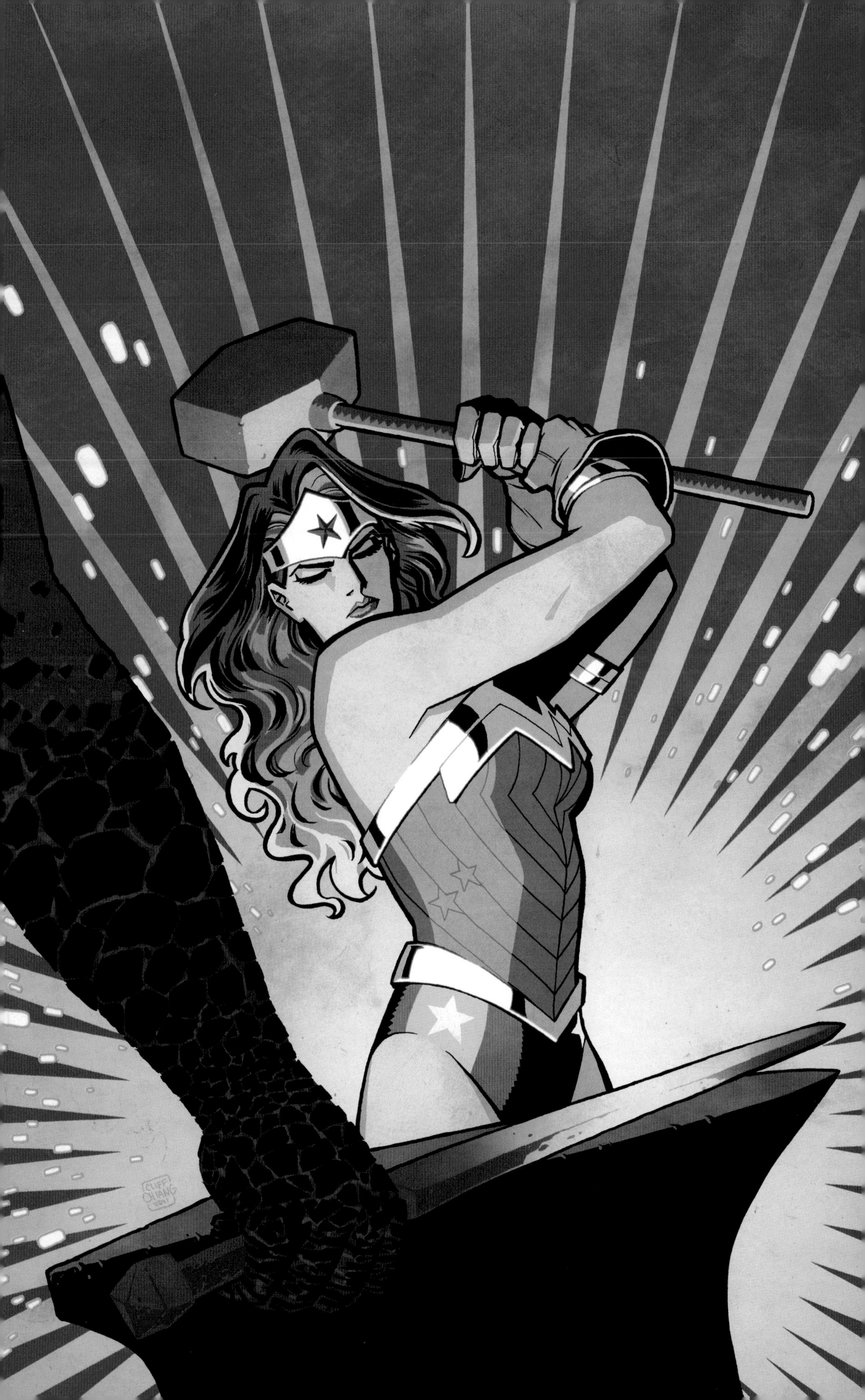
CLIFF CHIANG 2011

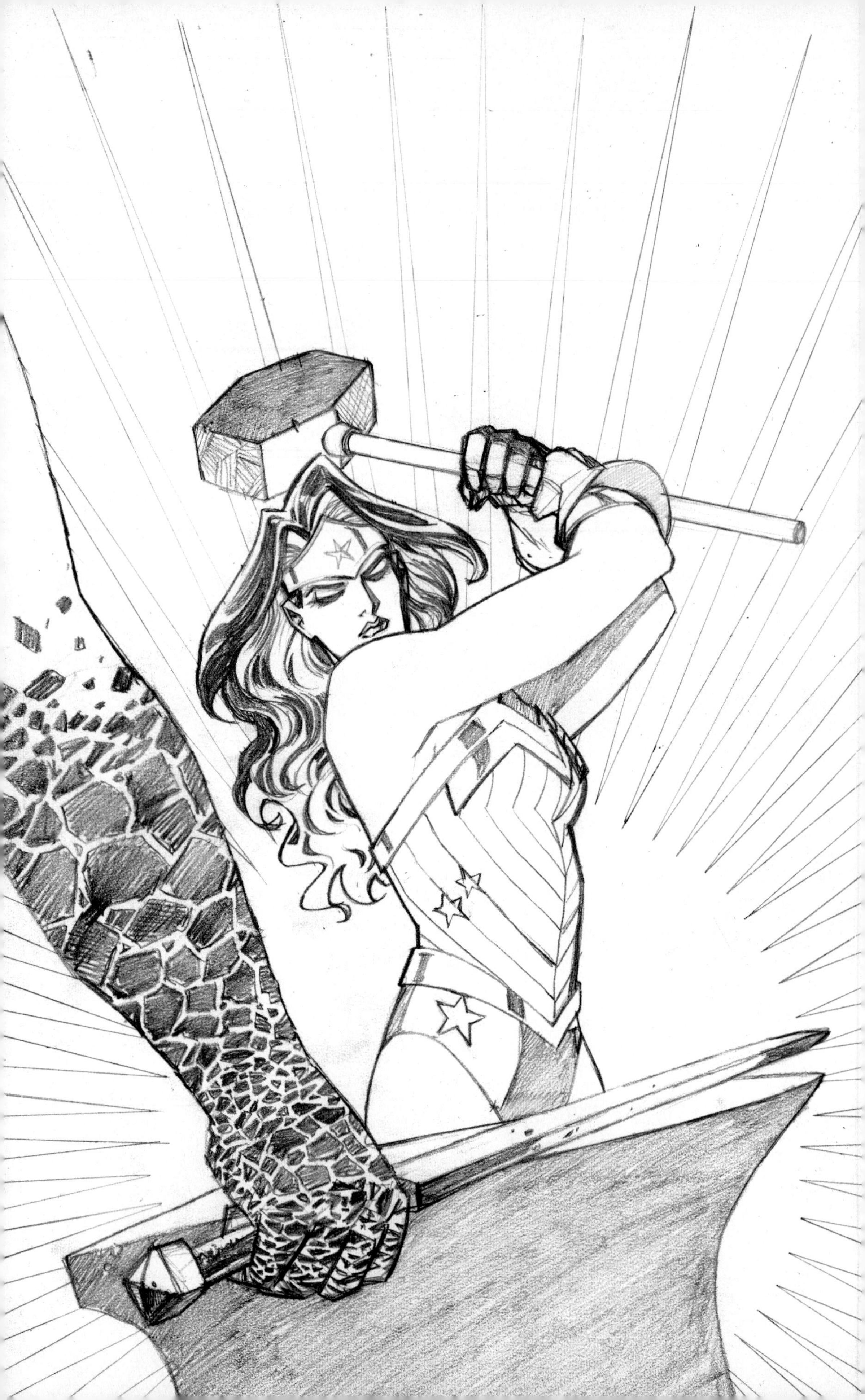

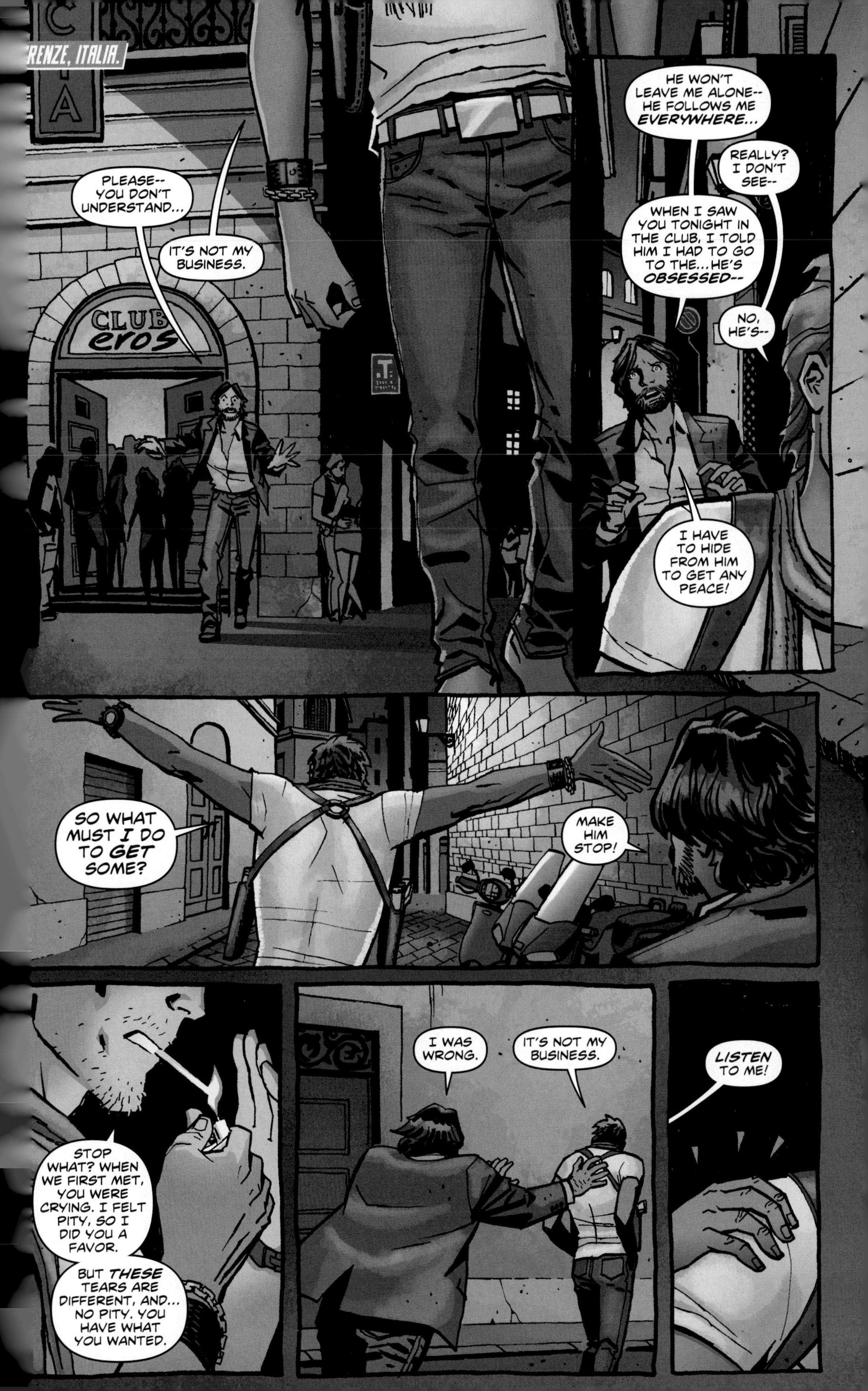

...RENZE, ITALIA.
CLUB eros
PLEASE-- YOU DON'T UNDERSTAND...
IT'S NOT MY BUSINESS.
HE WON'T LEAVE ME ALONE-- HE FOLLOWS ME EVERYWHERE...
REALLY? I DON'T SEE--
WHEN I SAW YOU TONIGHT IN THE CLUB, I TOLD HIM I HAD TO GO TO THE...HE'S OBSESSED--
NO, HE'S--
I HAVE TO HIDE FROM HIM TO GET ANY PEACE!
SO WHAT MUST I DO TO GET SOME?
MAKE HIM STOP!
STOP WHAT? WHEN WE FIRST MET, YOU WERE CRYING. I FELT PITY, SO I DID YOU A FAVOR.
BUT THESE TEARS ARE DIFFERENT, AND... NO PITY. YOU HAVE WHAT YOU WANTED.
I WAS WRONG.
IT'S NOT MY BUSINESS.
LISTEN TO ME!

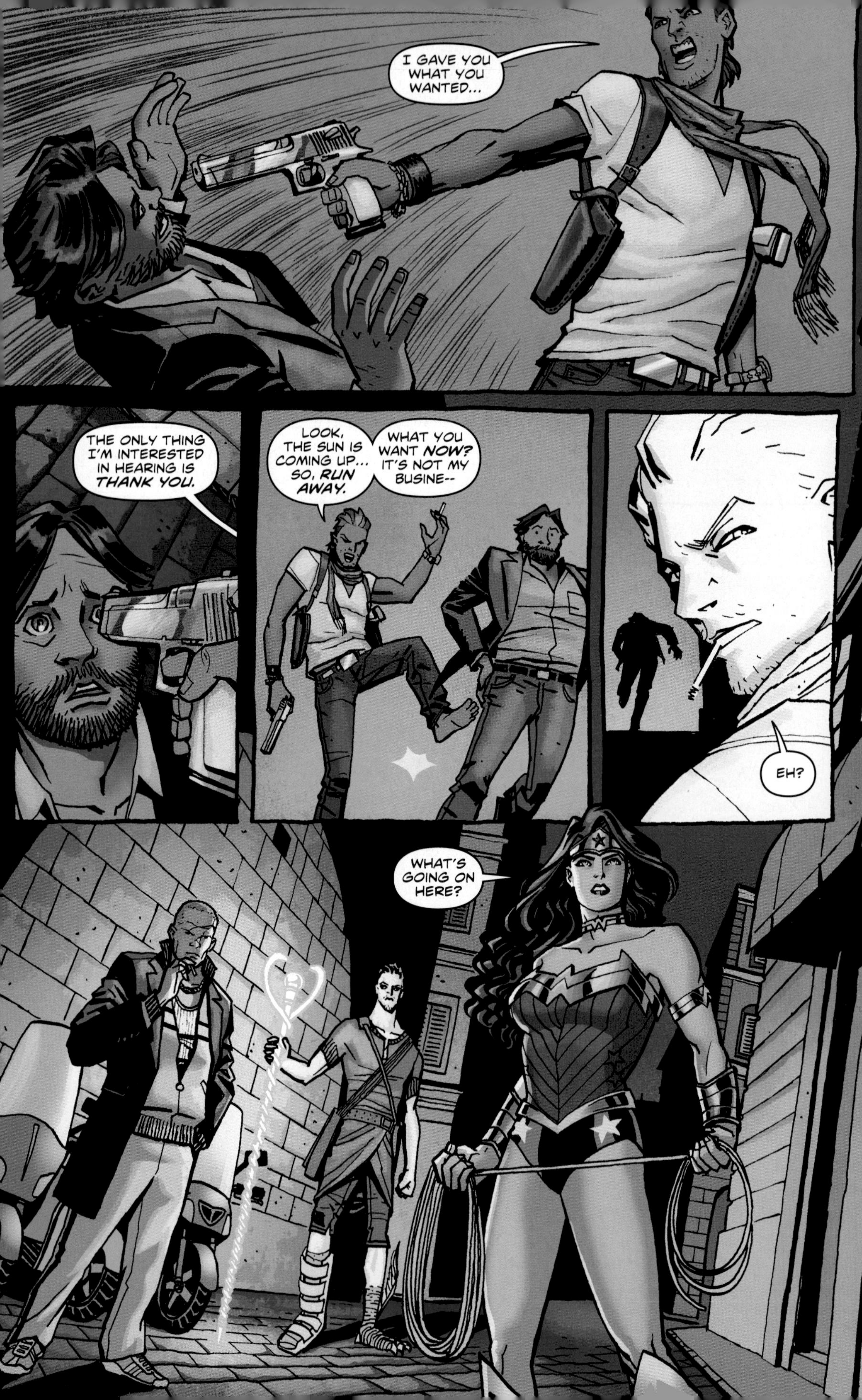
I GAVE YOU WHAT YOU WANTED...
THE ONLY THING I'M INTERESTED IN HEARING IS *THANK YOU.*
WHAT YOU WANT *NOW?* IT'S NOT MY BUSINE--
LOOK, THE SUN IS COMING UP... SO, *RUN AWAY.*
EH?
WHAT'S GOING ON HERE?

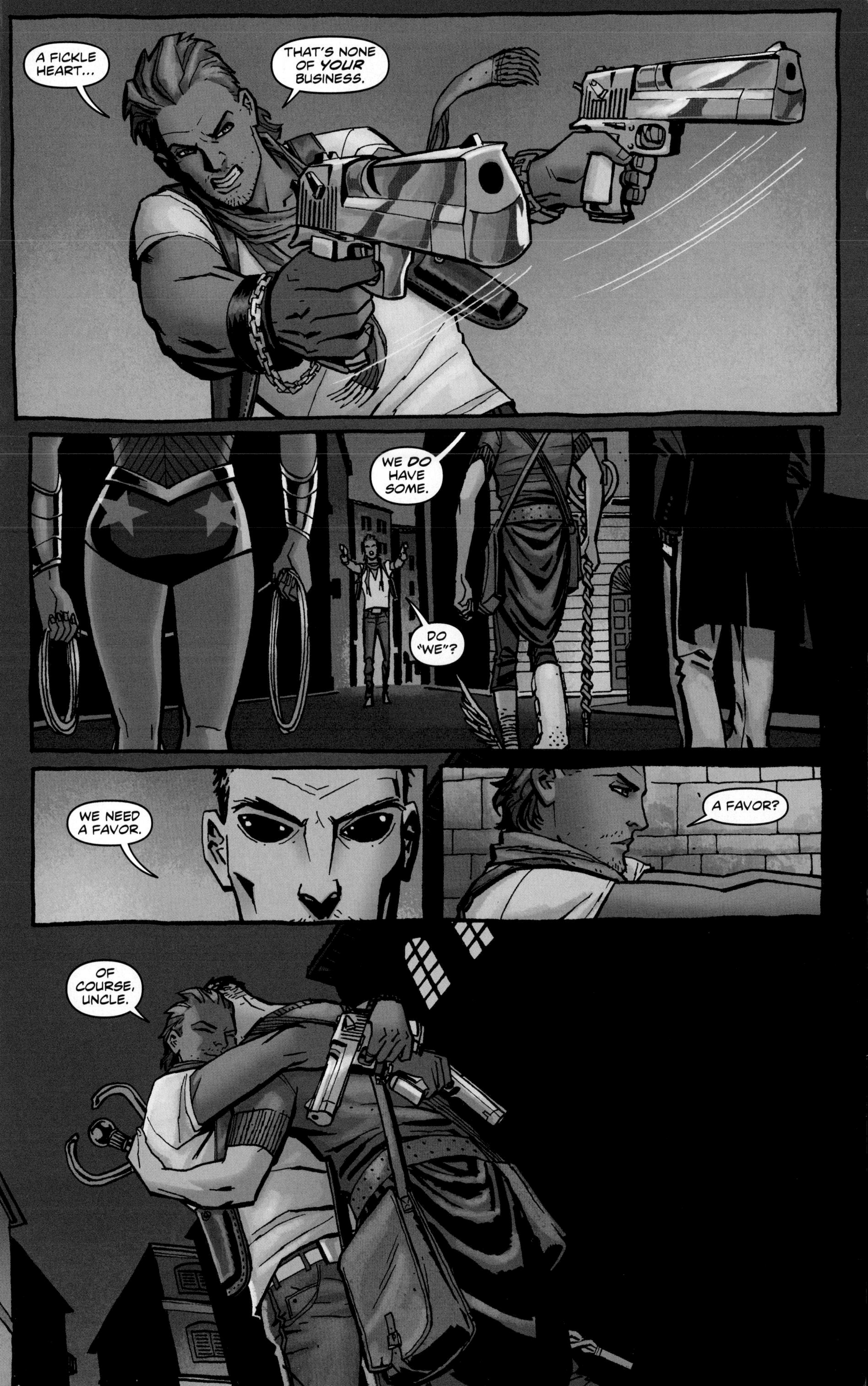
A FICKLE HEART...
THAT'S NONE OF YOUR BUSINESS.
WE DO HAVE SOME.
DO "WE"?
WE NEED A FAVOR.
A FAVOR?
OF COURSE, UNCLE.

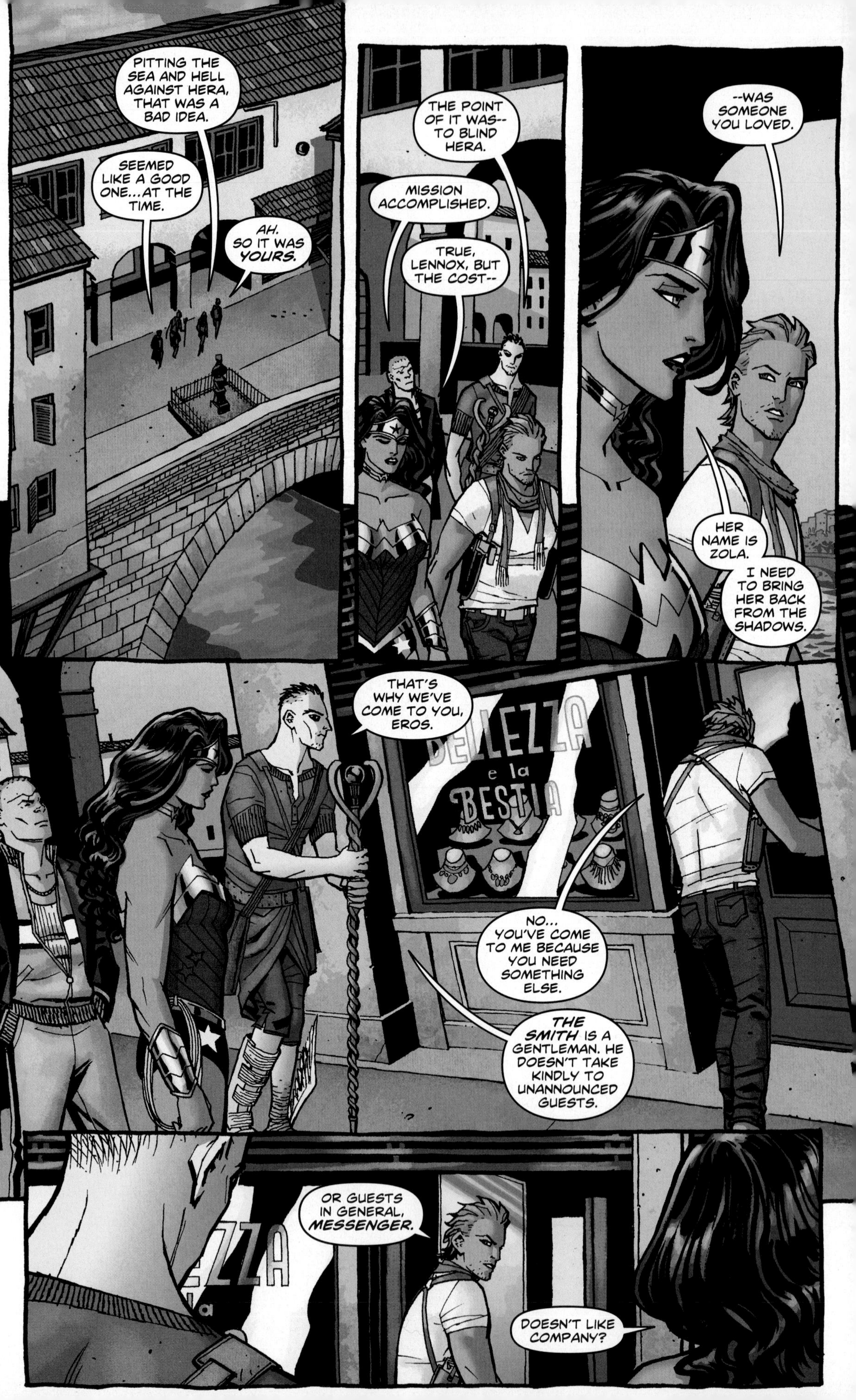
PITTING THE SEA AND HELL AGAINST HERA, THAT WAS A BAD IDEA.
SEEMED LIKE A GOOD ONE...AT THE TIME.
AH. SO IT WAS *YOURS*.
THE POINT OF IT WAS-- TO BLIND HERA.
MISSION ACCOMPLISHED.
TRUE, LENNOX, BUT THE COST--
--WAS SOMEONE YOU LOVED.
HER NAME IS ZOLA.
I NEED TO BRING HER BACK FROM THE SHADOWS.
THAT'S WHY WE'VE COME TO YOU, EROS.
BELLEZZA e la BESTIA
NO... YOU'VE COME TO ME BECAUSE YOU NEED SOMETHING ELSE.
THE SMITH IS A GENTLEMAN. HE DOESN'T TAKE KINDLY TO UNANNOUNCED GUESTS.
OR GUESTS IN GENERAL, *MESSENGER*.
DOESN'T LIKE COMPANY?

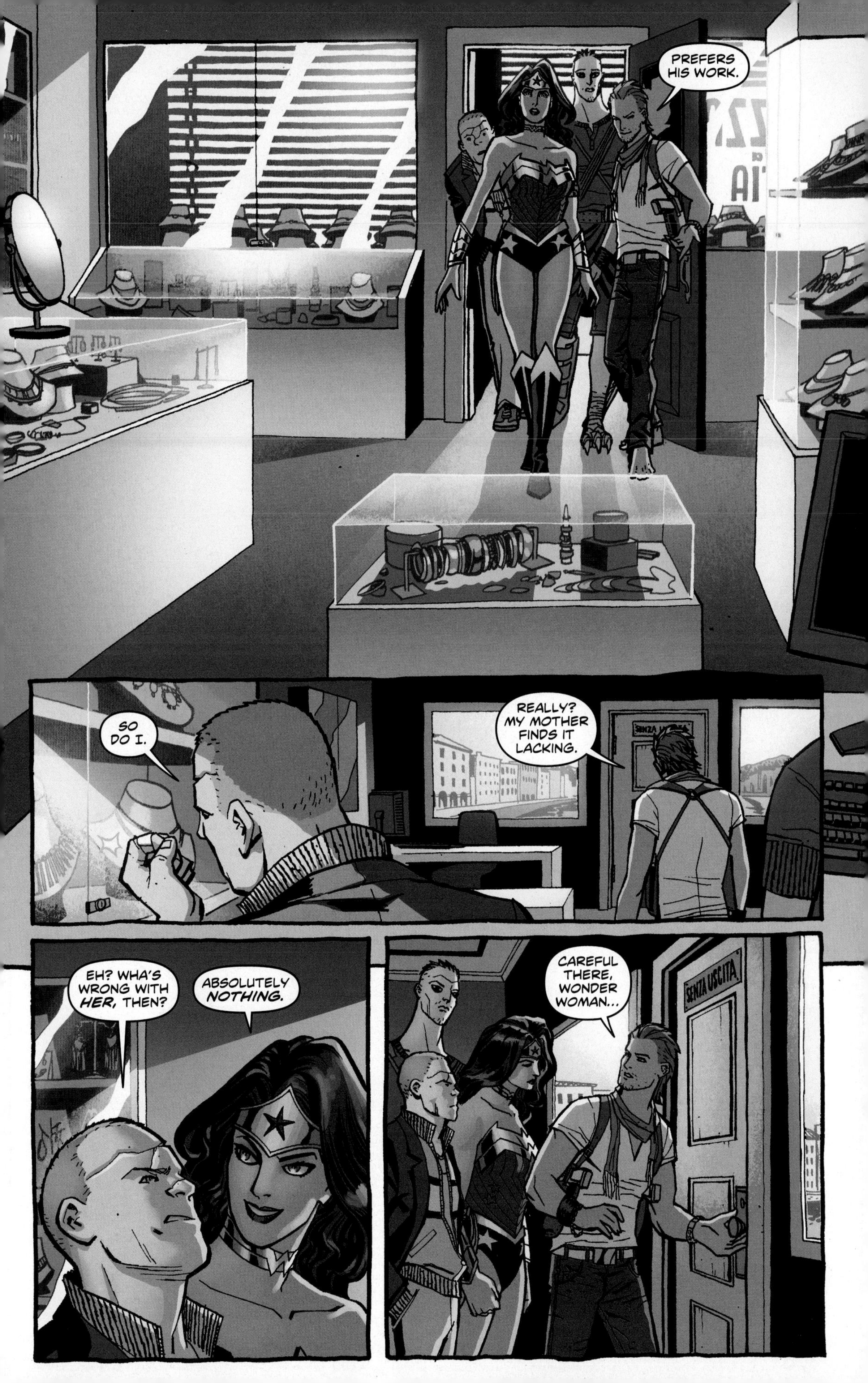
PREFERS HIS WORK.
SO DO I.
REALLY? MY MOTHER FINDS IT LACKING.
EH? WHA'S WRONG WITH *HER*, THEN?
ABSOLUTELY *NOTHING*.
CAREFUL THERE, WONDER WOMAN...
SENZA USCITA

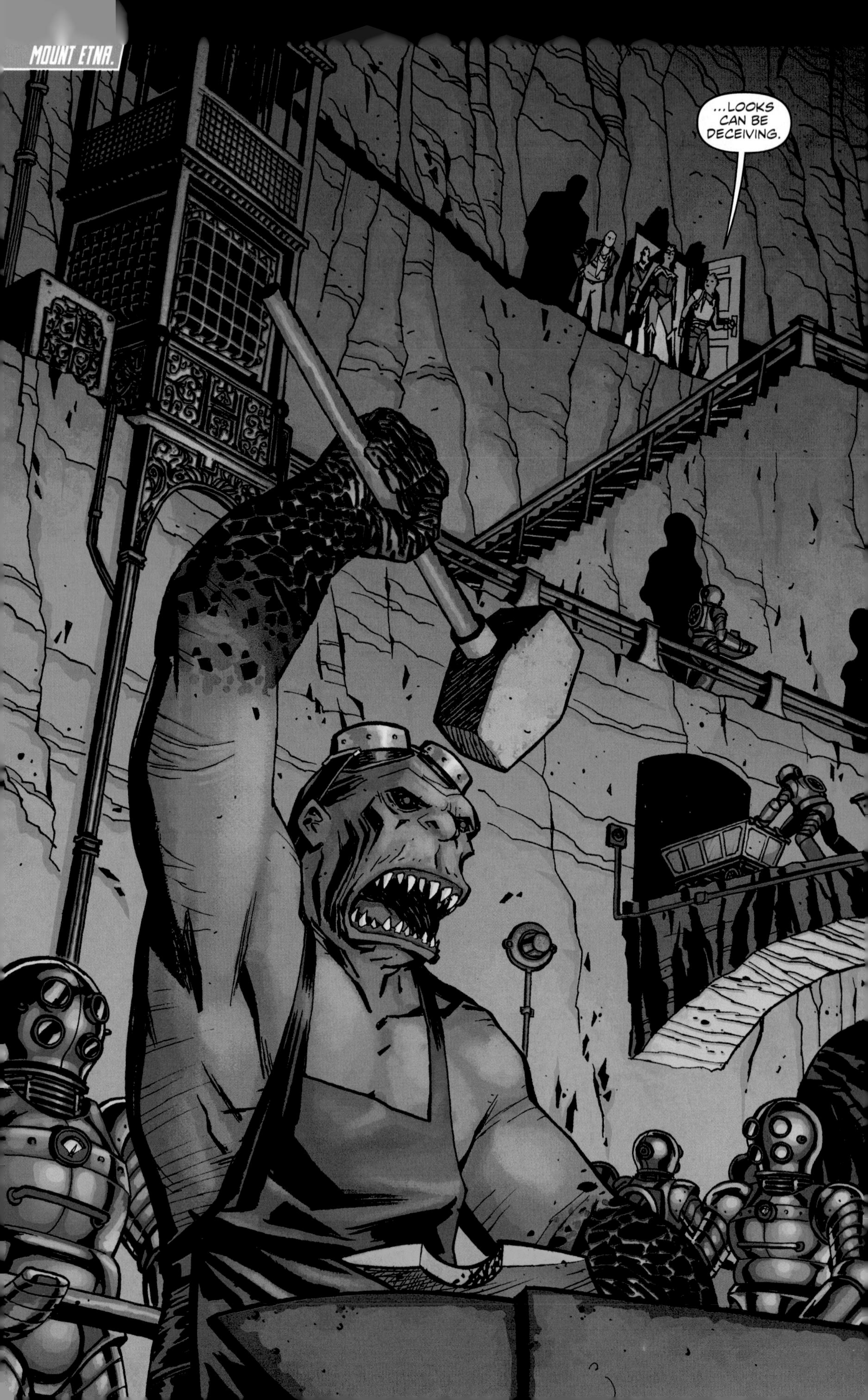
MOUNT ETNA.
...LOOKS CAN BE DECEIVING.

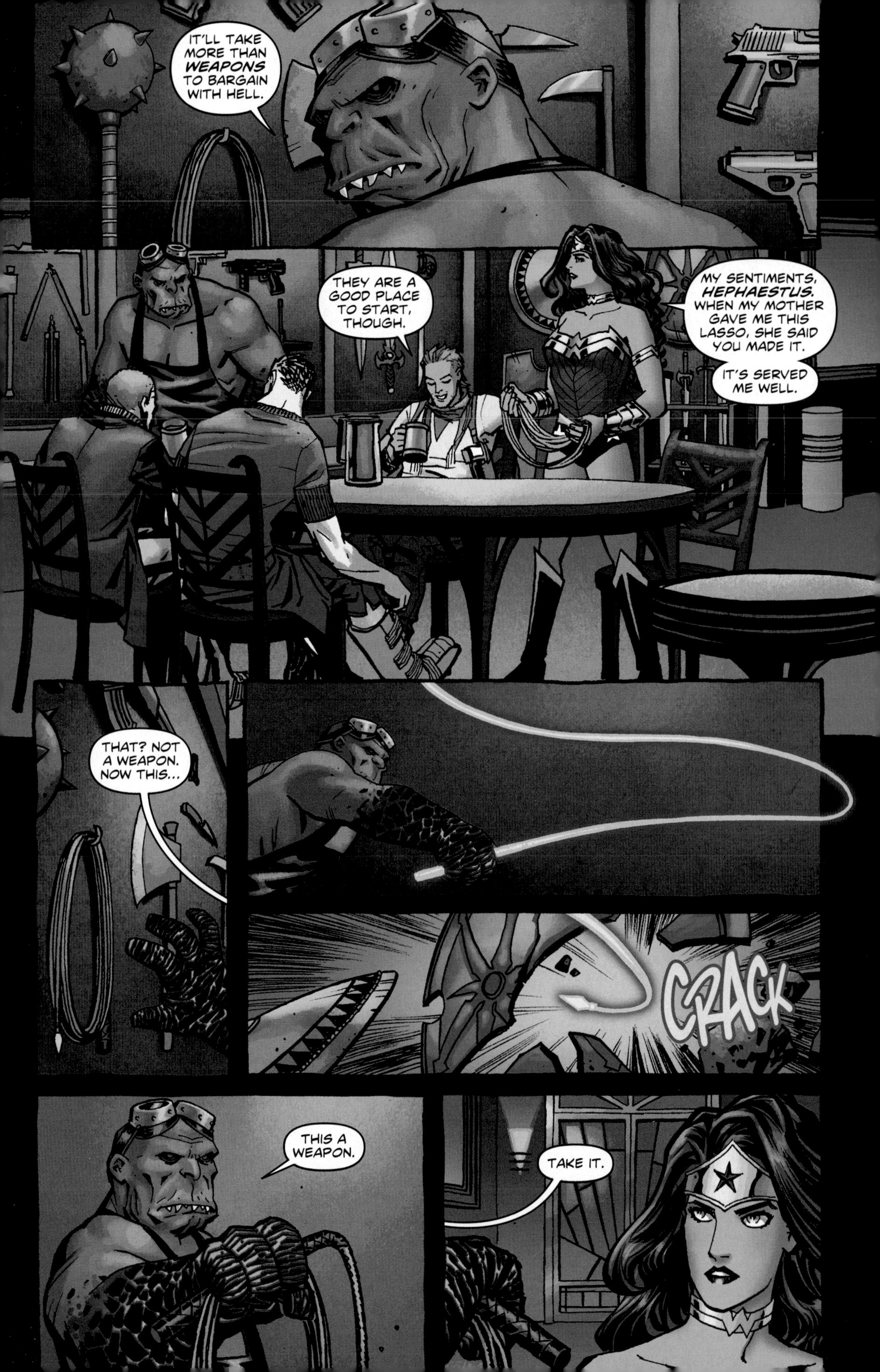
IT'LL TAKE MORE THAN WEAPONS TO BARGAIN WITH HELL.
THEY ARE A GOOD PLACE TO START, THOUGH.
MY SENTIMENTS, HEPHAESTUS. WHEN MY MOTHER GAVE ME THIS LASSO, SHE SAID YOU MADE IT.
IT'S SERVED ME WELL.
THAT? NOT A WEAPON. NOW THIS...
CRACK
THIS A WEAPON.
TAKE IT.

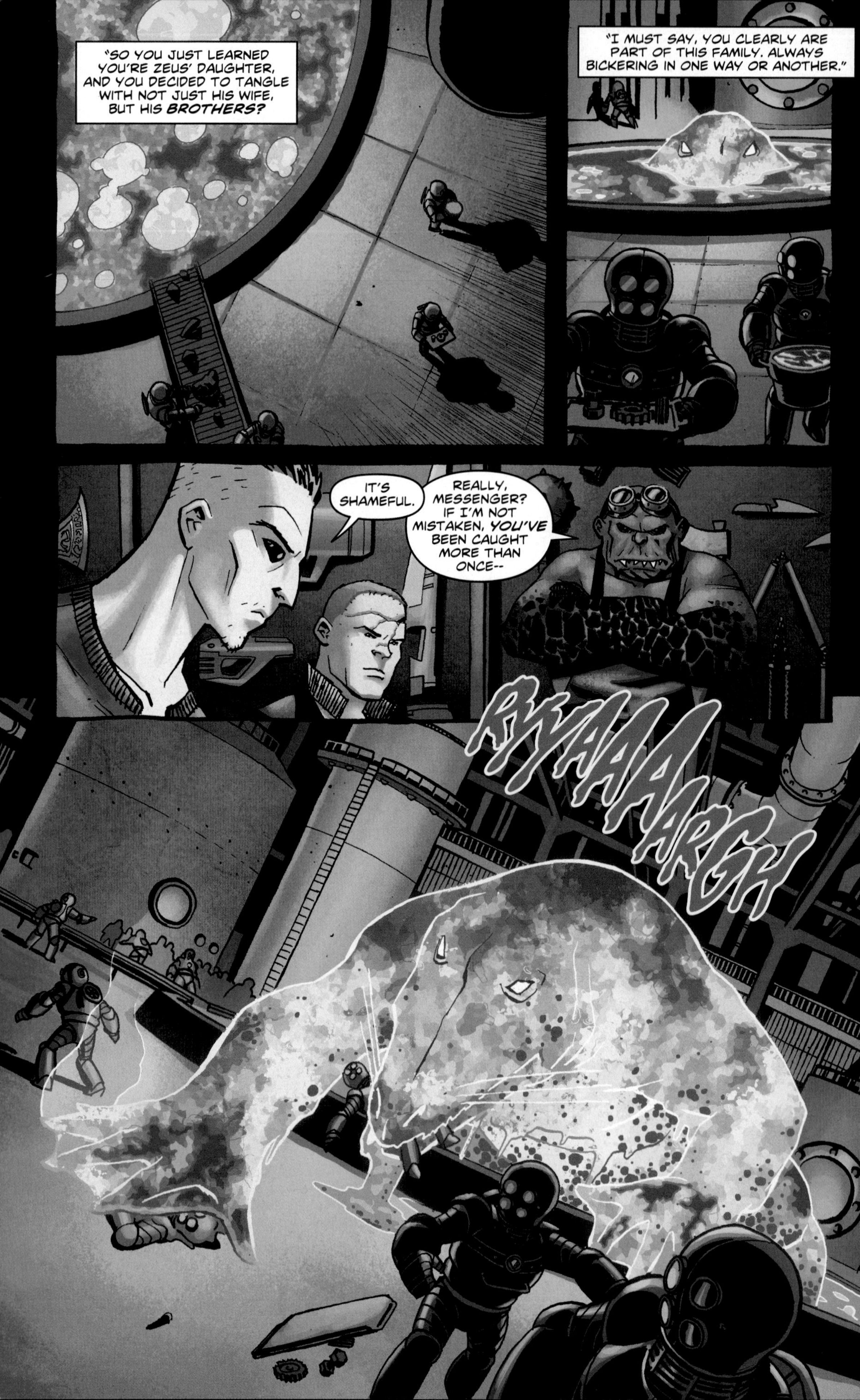
"SO YOU JUST LEARNED YOU'RE ZEUS' DAUGHTER, AND YOU DECIDED TO TANGLE WITH NOT JUST HIS WIFE, BUT HIS BROTHERS?
"I MUST SAY, YOU CLEARLY ARE PART OF THIS FAMILY. ALWAYS BICKERING IN ONE WAY OR ANOTHER."
IT'S SHAMEFUL.
REALLY, MESSENGER? IF I'M NOT MISTAKEN, YOU'VE BEEN CAUGHT MORE THAN ONCE--
RYYAAAAARGH

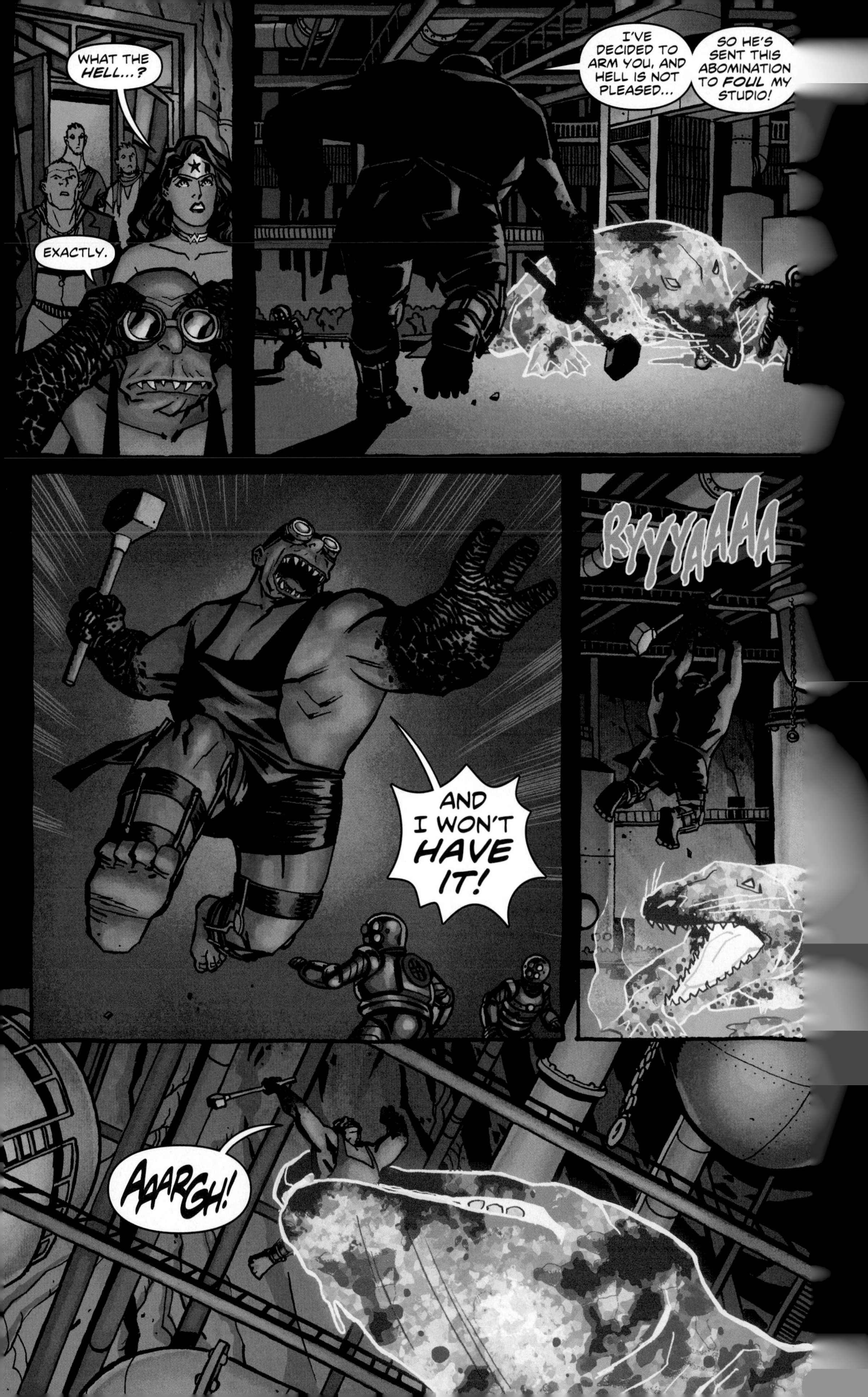
WHAT THE HELL...?
EXACTLY.
I'VE DECIDED TO ARM YOU, AND HELL IS NOT PLEASED...
SO HE'S SENT THIS ABOMINATION TO FOUL MY STUDIO!
AND I WON'T HAVE IT!
RYYYAAAA
AAARGH!

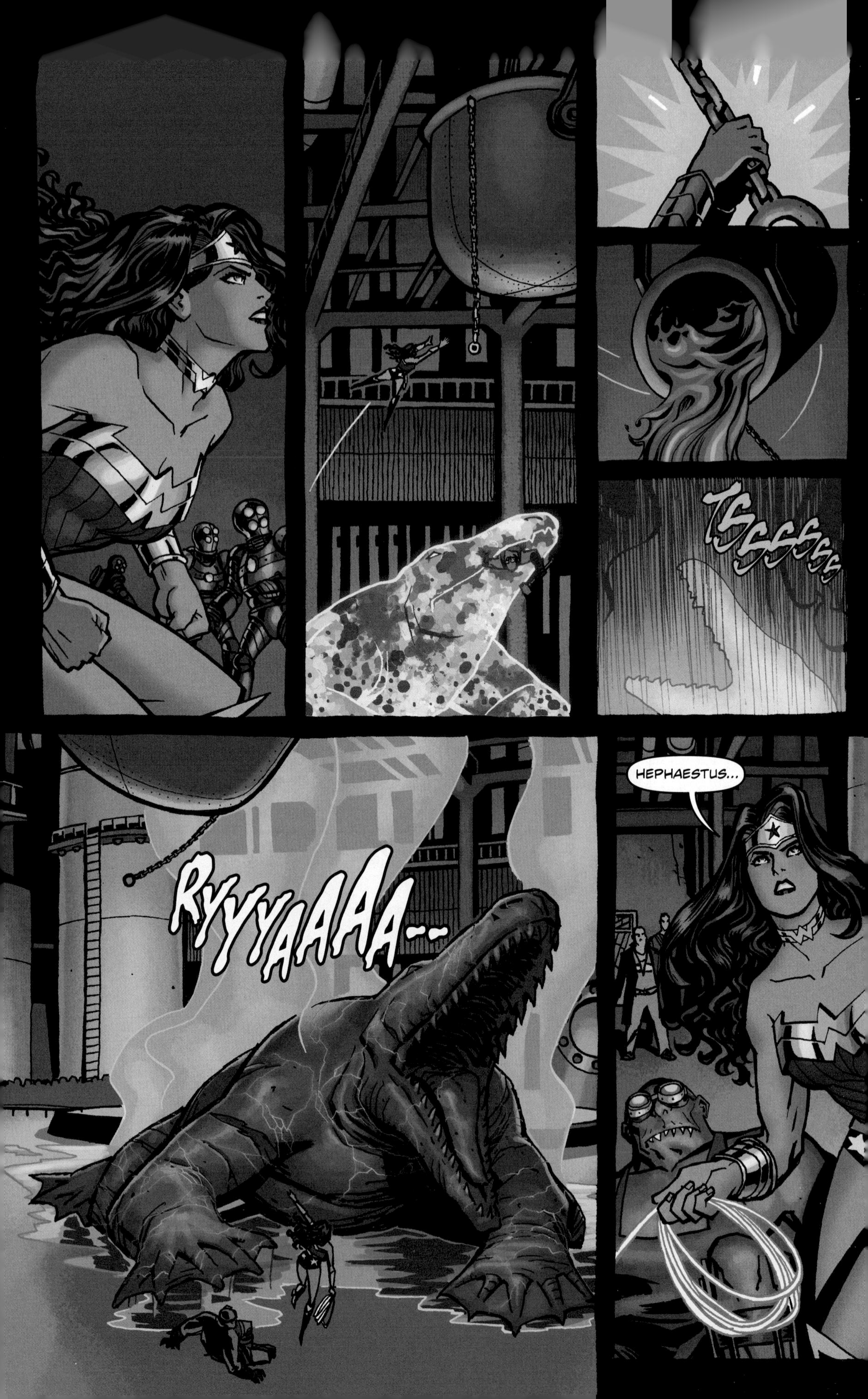
TSSSSSS
RYYYAAAA--
HEPHAESTUS...

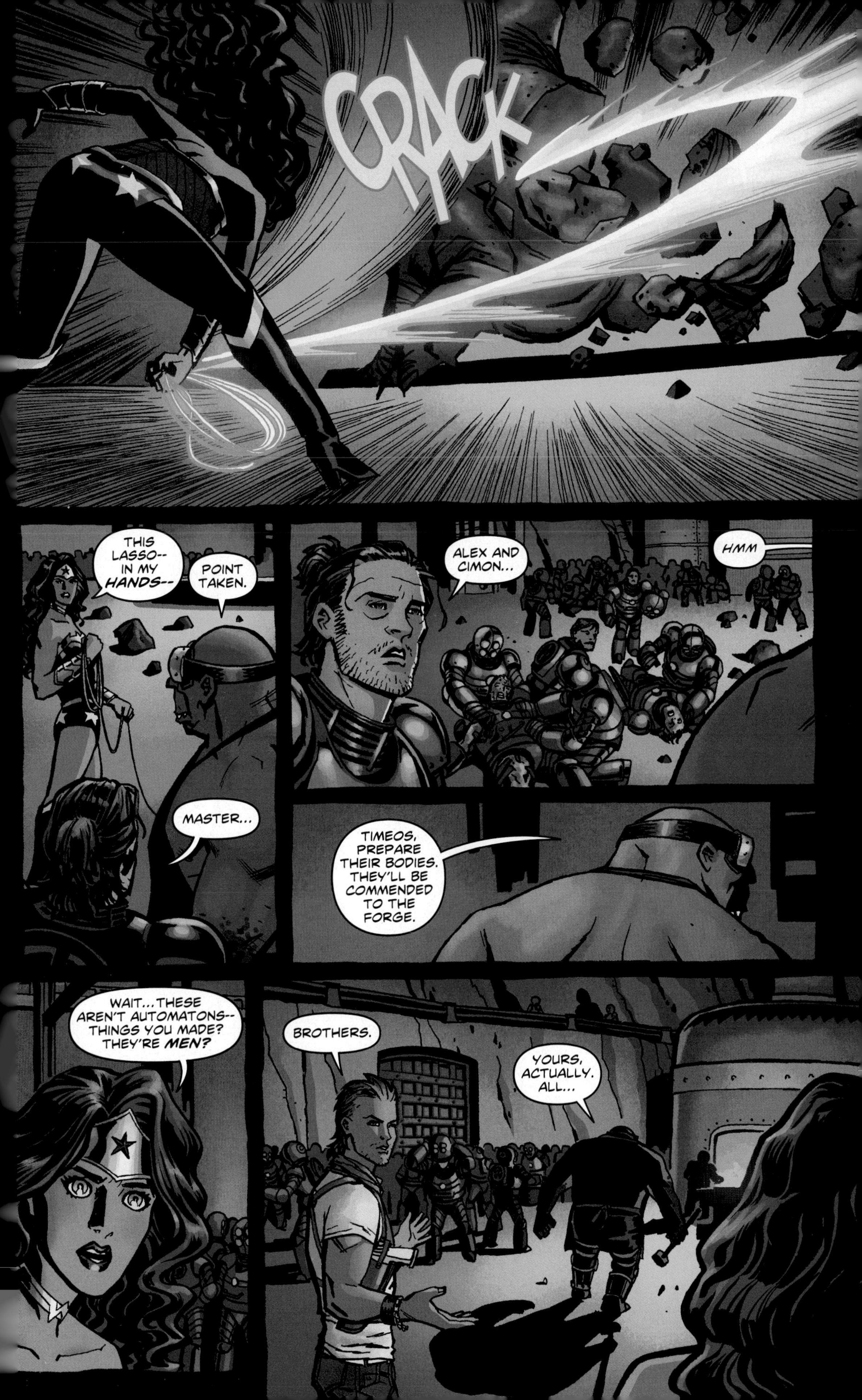
CRACK
THIS LASSO-- IN MY *HANDS--*
POINT TAKEN.
MASTER...
ALEX AND CIMON...
HMM
TIMEOS, PREPARE THEIR BODIES. THEY'LL BE COMMENDED TO THE FORGE.
WAIT... THESE AREN'T AUTOMATONS-- THINGS YOU MADE? THEY'RE *MEN?*
BROTHERS.
YOURS, ACTUALLY. ALL...

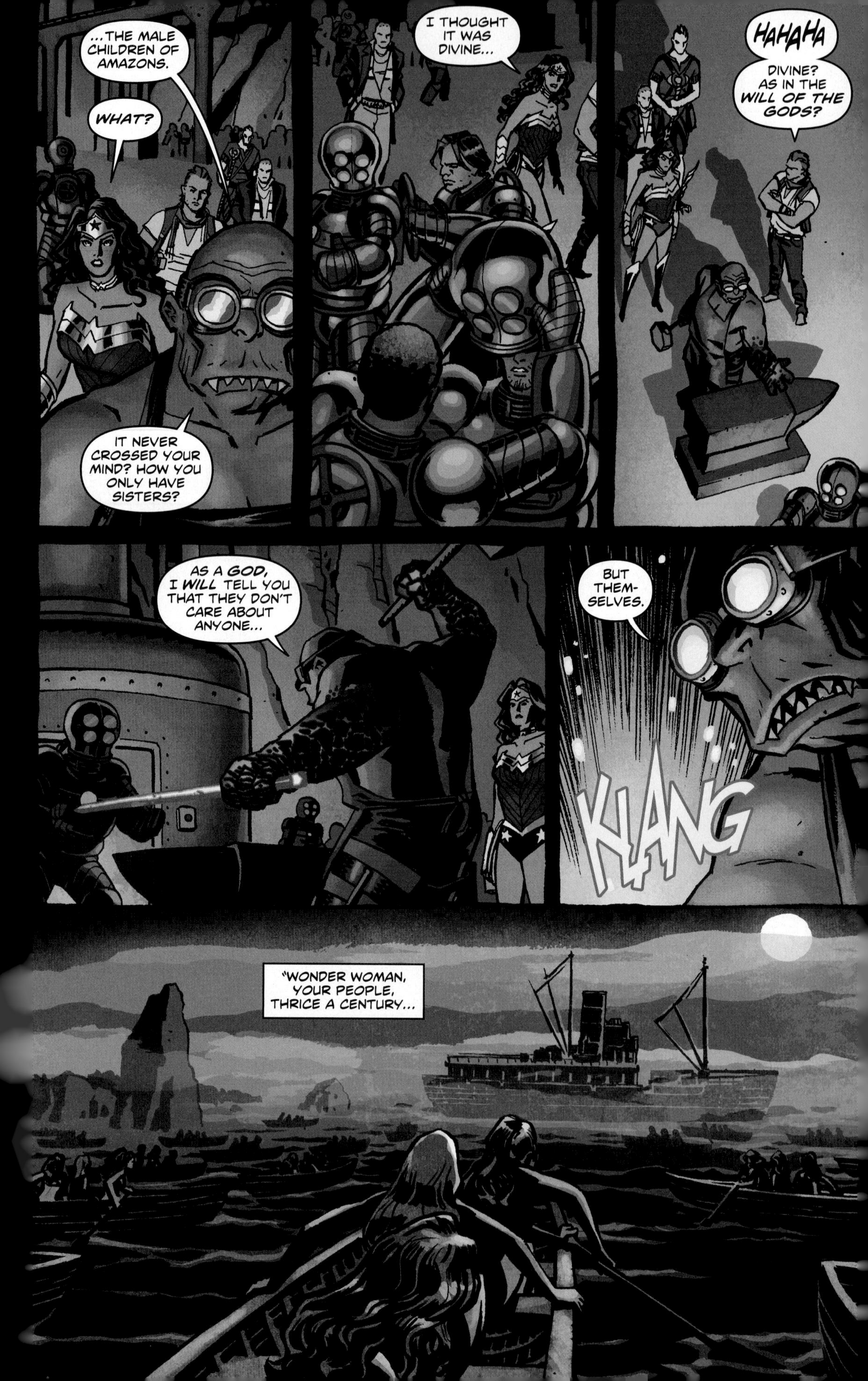
...THE MALE CHILDREN OF AMAZONS.
WHAT?
IT NEVER CROSSED YOUR MIND? HOW YOU ONLY HAVE SISTERS?
I THOUGHT IT WAS DIVINE...
HAHAHA
DIVINE? AS IN THE WILL OF THE GODS?
AS A GOD, I WILL TELL YOU THAT THEY DON'T CARE ABOUT ANYONE...
BUT THEM-SELVES.
KLANG
"WONDER WOMAN, YOUR PEOPLE, THRICE A CENTURY...

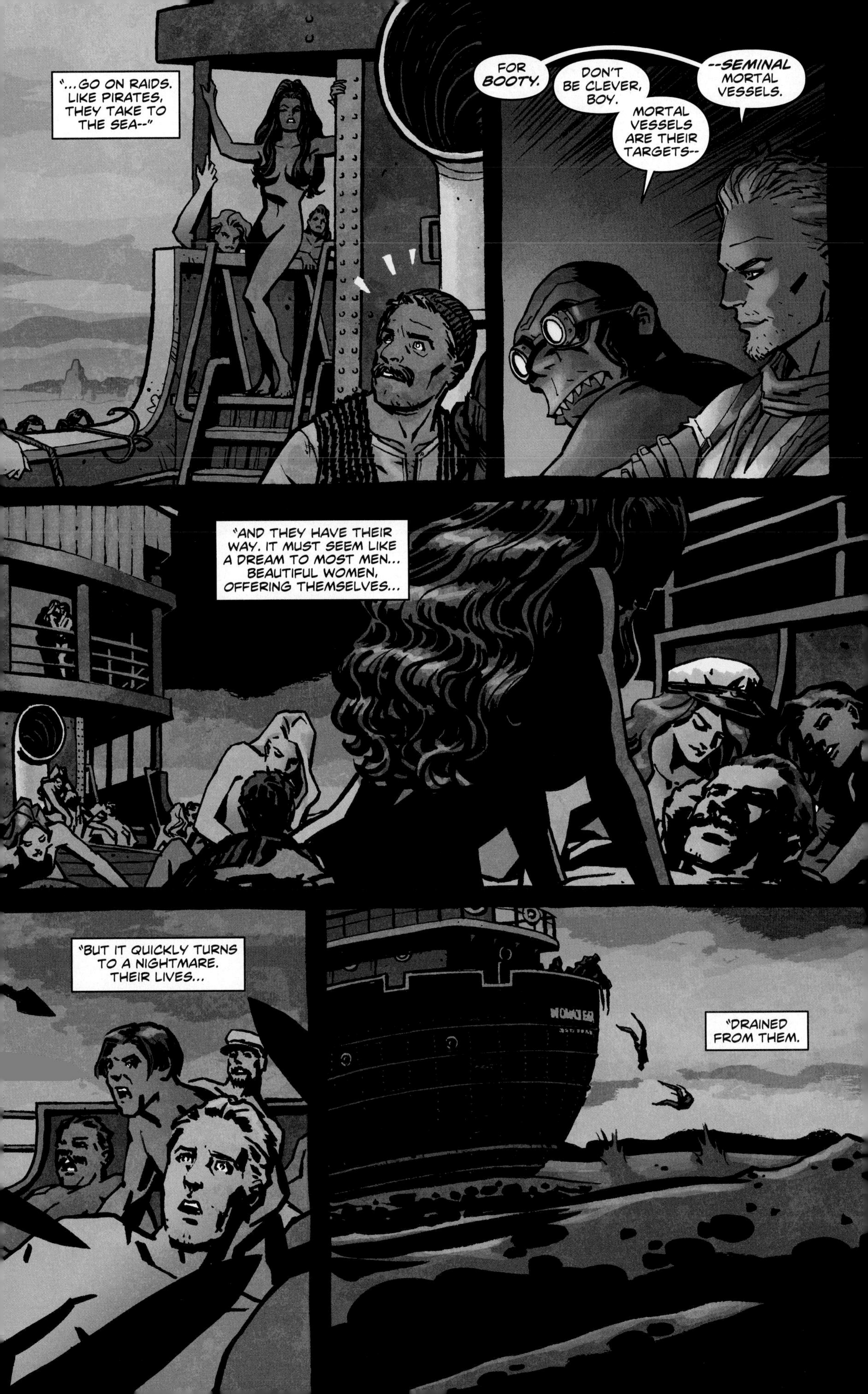
"...GO ON RAIDS. LIKE PIRATES, THEY TAKE TO THE SEA--"
FOR BOOTY.
DON'T BE CLEVER, BOY.
MORTAL VESSELS ARE THEIR TARGETS--
--SEMINAL MORTAL VESSELS.
"AND THEY HAVE THEIR WAY. IT MUST SEEM LIKE A DREAM TO MOST MEN... BEAUTIFUL WOMEN, OFFERING THEMSELVES...
"BUT IT QUICKLY TURNS TO A NIGHTMARE. THEIR LIVES...
"DRAINED FROM THEM.

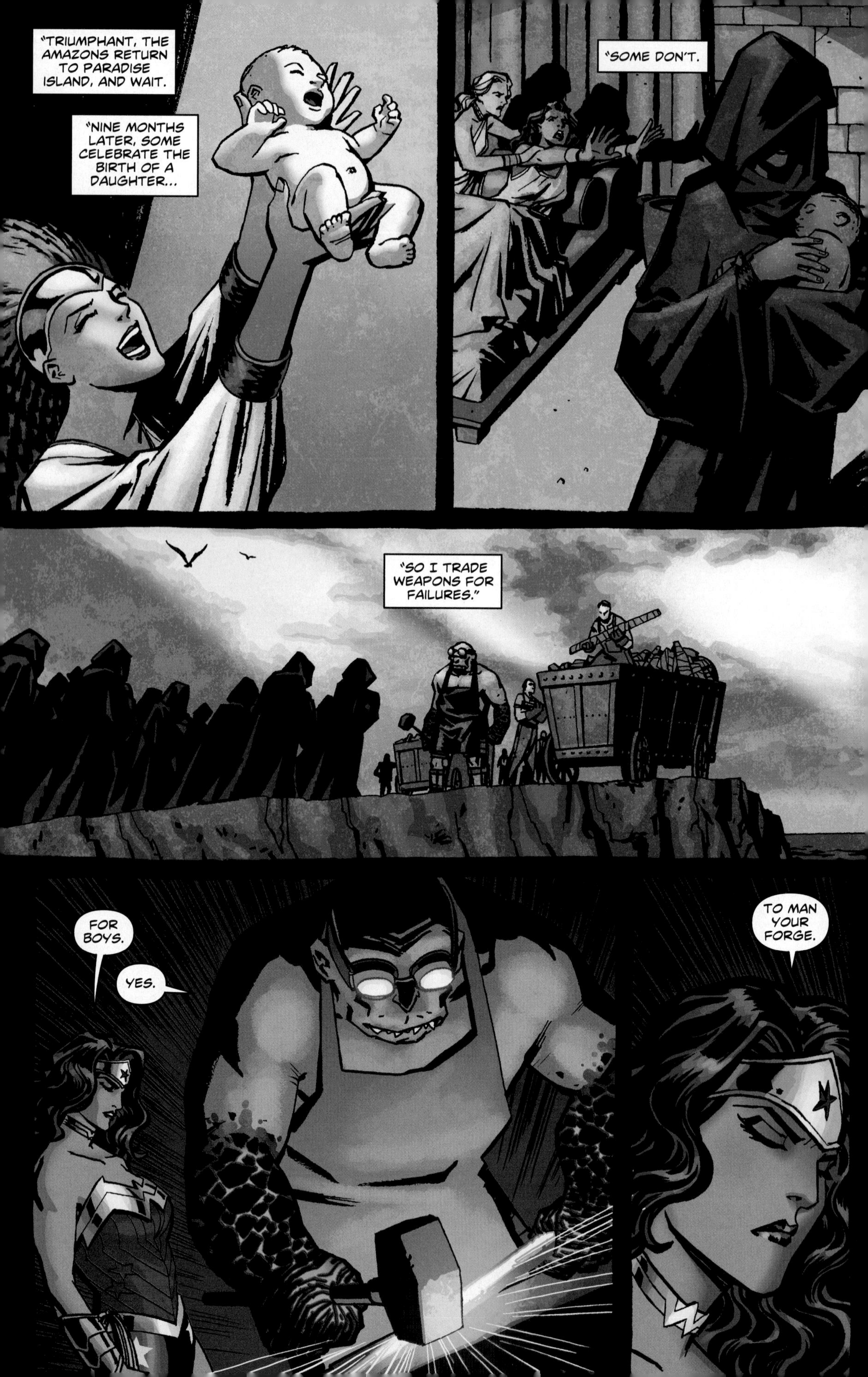
"TRIUMPHANT, THE AMAZONS RETURN TO PARADISE ISLAND, AND WAIT.
"NINE MONTHS LATER, SOME CELEBRATE THE BIRTH OF A DAUGHTER...
"SOME DON'T.
"SO I TRADE WEAPONS FOR FAILURES."
FOR BOYS.
YES.
TO MAN YOUR FORGE.

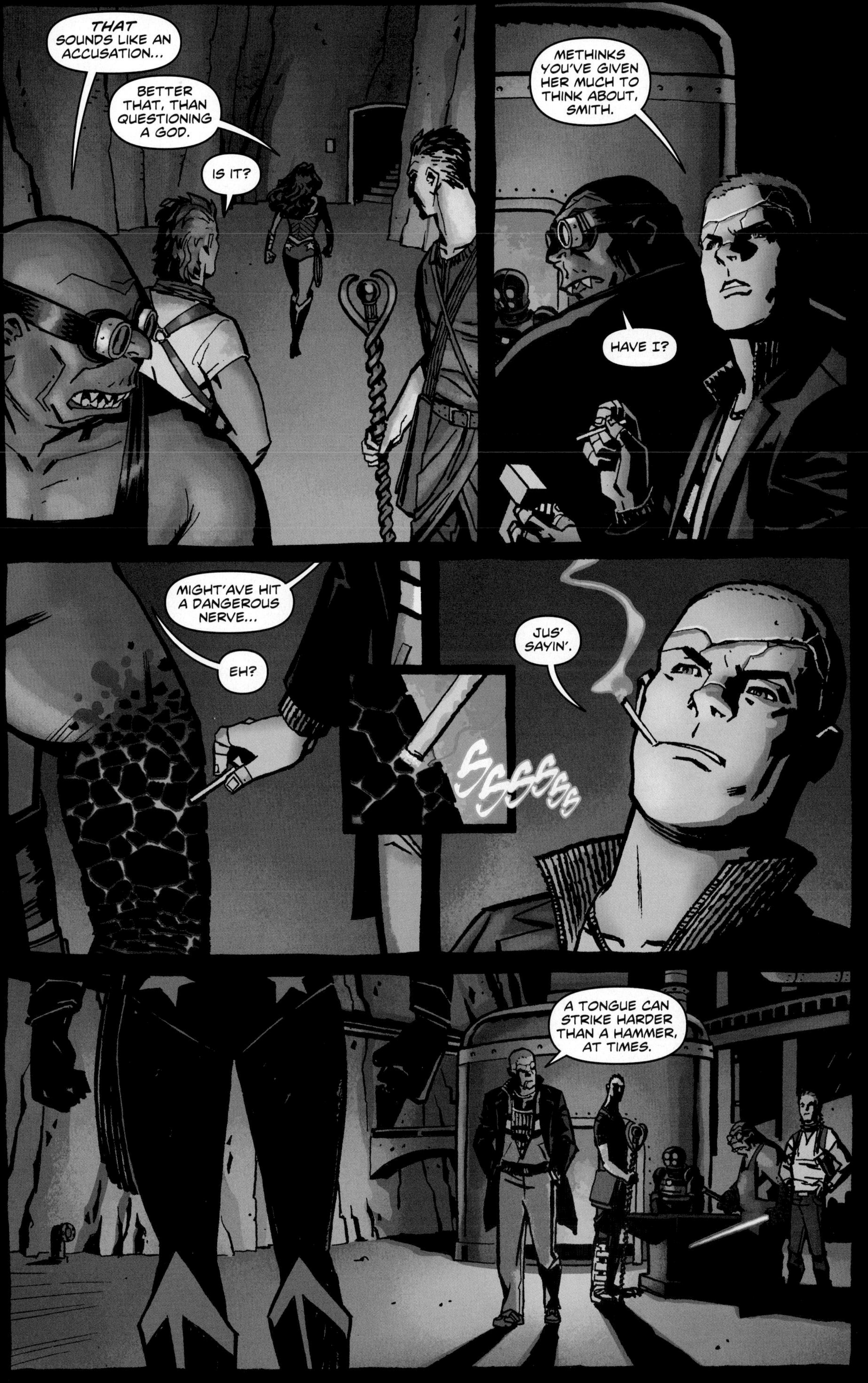
THAT SOUNDS LIKE AN ACCUSATION...
BETTER THAT, THAN QUESTIONING A GOD.
IS IT?
METHINKS YOU'VE GIVEN HER MUCH TO THINK ABOUT, SMITH.
HAVE I?
MIGHT'AVE HIT A DANGEROUS NERVE...
EH?
JUS' SAYIN'.
SSSSSS
A TONGUE CAN STRIKE HARDER THAN A HAMMER, AT TIMES.

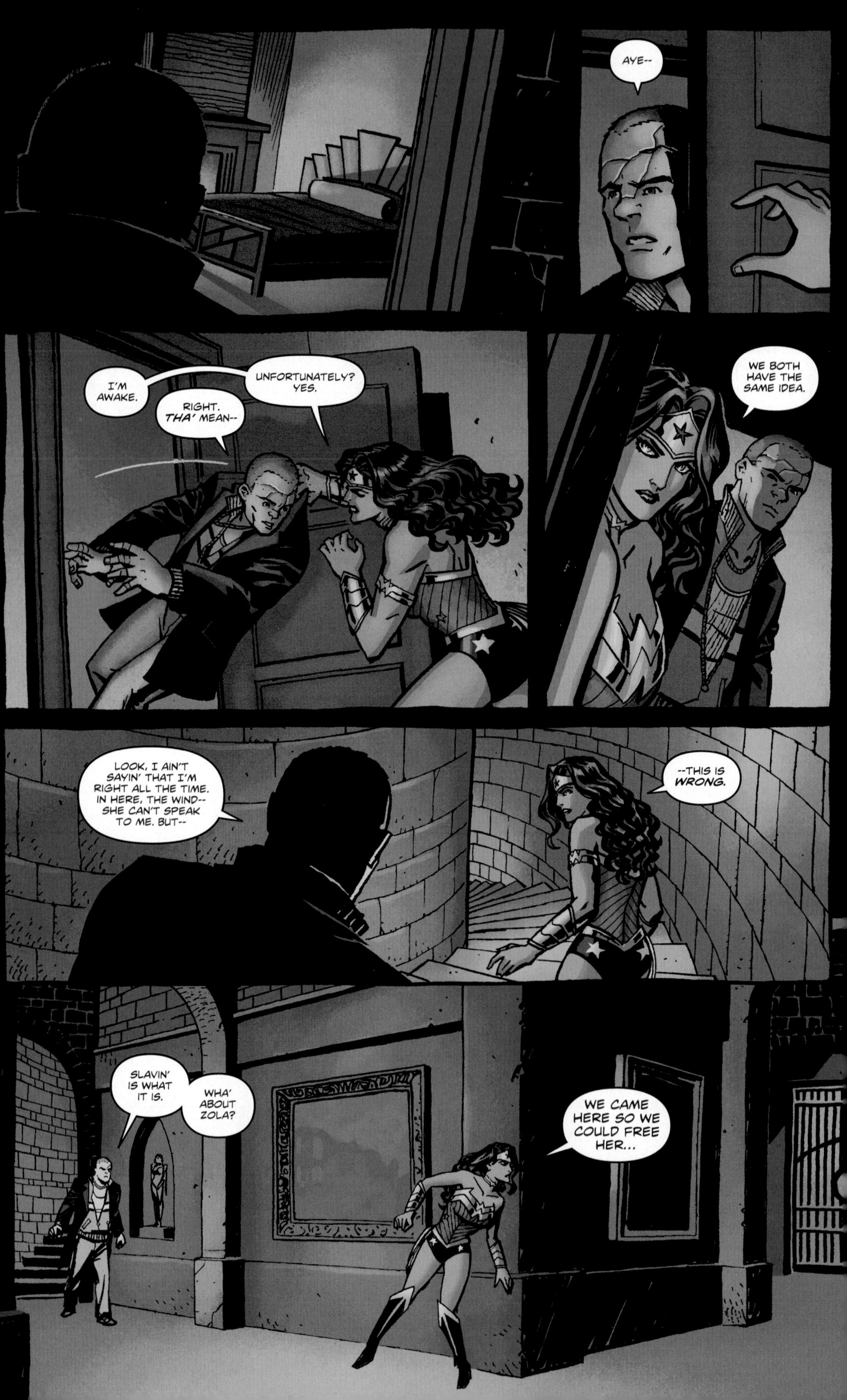
AYE--
I'M AWAKE.
UNFORTUNATELY? YES.
RIGHT. THA' MEAN--
WE BOTH HAVE THE SAME IDEA.
LOOK, I AIN'T SAYIN' THAT I'M RIGHT ALL THE TIME. IN HERE, THE WIND-- SHE CAN'T SPEAK TO ME. BUT--
--THIS IS WRONG.
SLAVIN' IS WHAT IT IS.
WHA' ABOUT ZOLA?
WE CAME HERE SO WE COULD FREE HER...

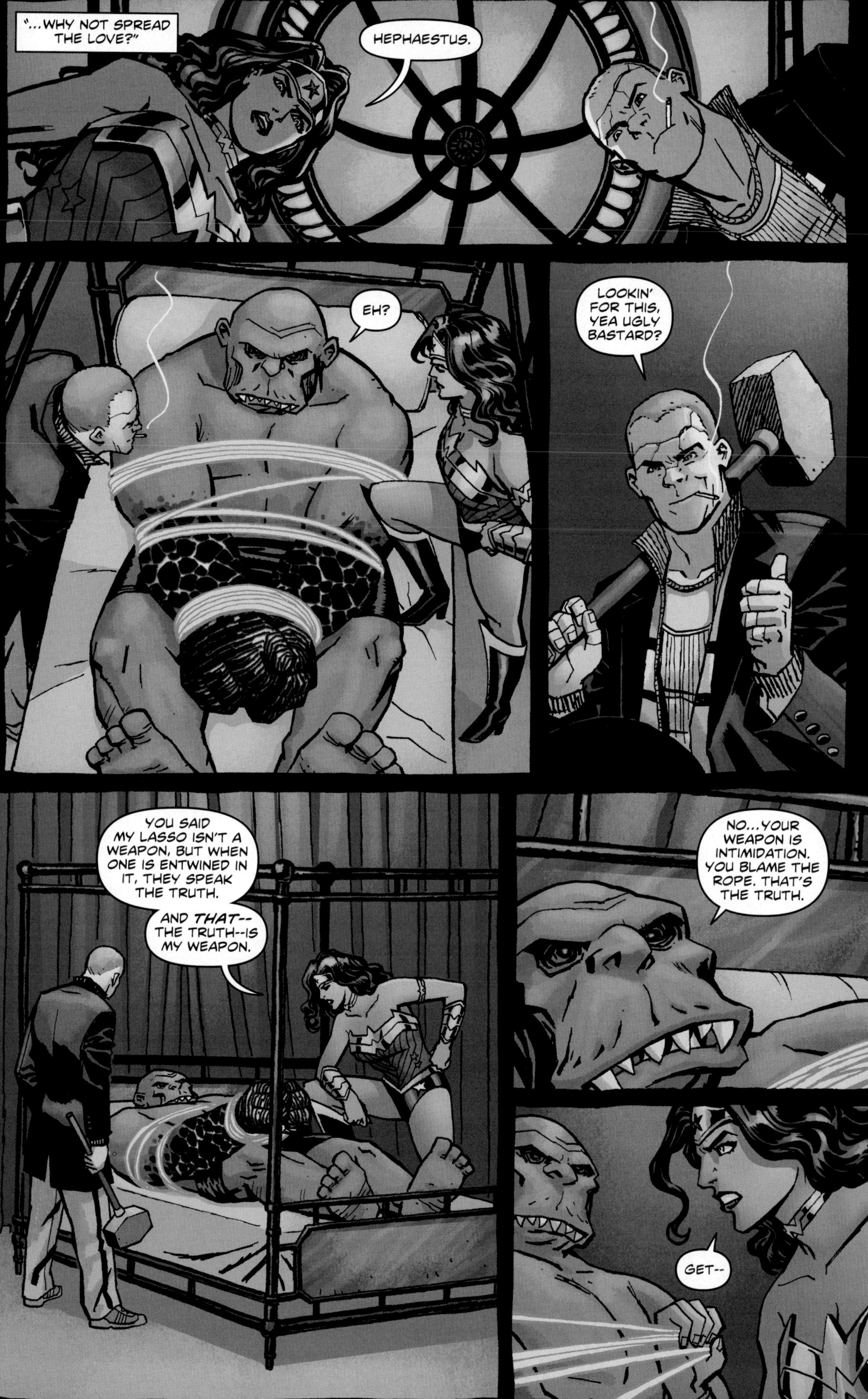
"...WHY NOT SPREAD THE LOVE?"
HEPHAESTUS.
EH?
LOOKIN' FOR THIS, YEA UGLY BASTARD?
YOU SAID MY LASSO ISN'T A WEAPON, BUT WHEN ONE IS ENTWINED IN IT, THEY SPEAK THE TRUTH.
AND THAT-- THE TRUTH--IS MY WEAPON.
NO...YOUR WEAPON IS INTIMIDATION. YOU BLAME THE ROPE. THAT'S THE TRUTH.
GET--

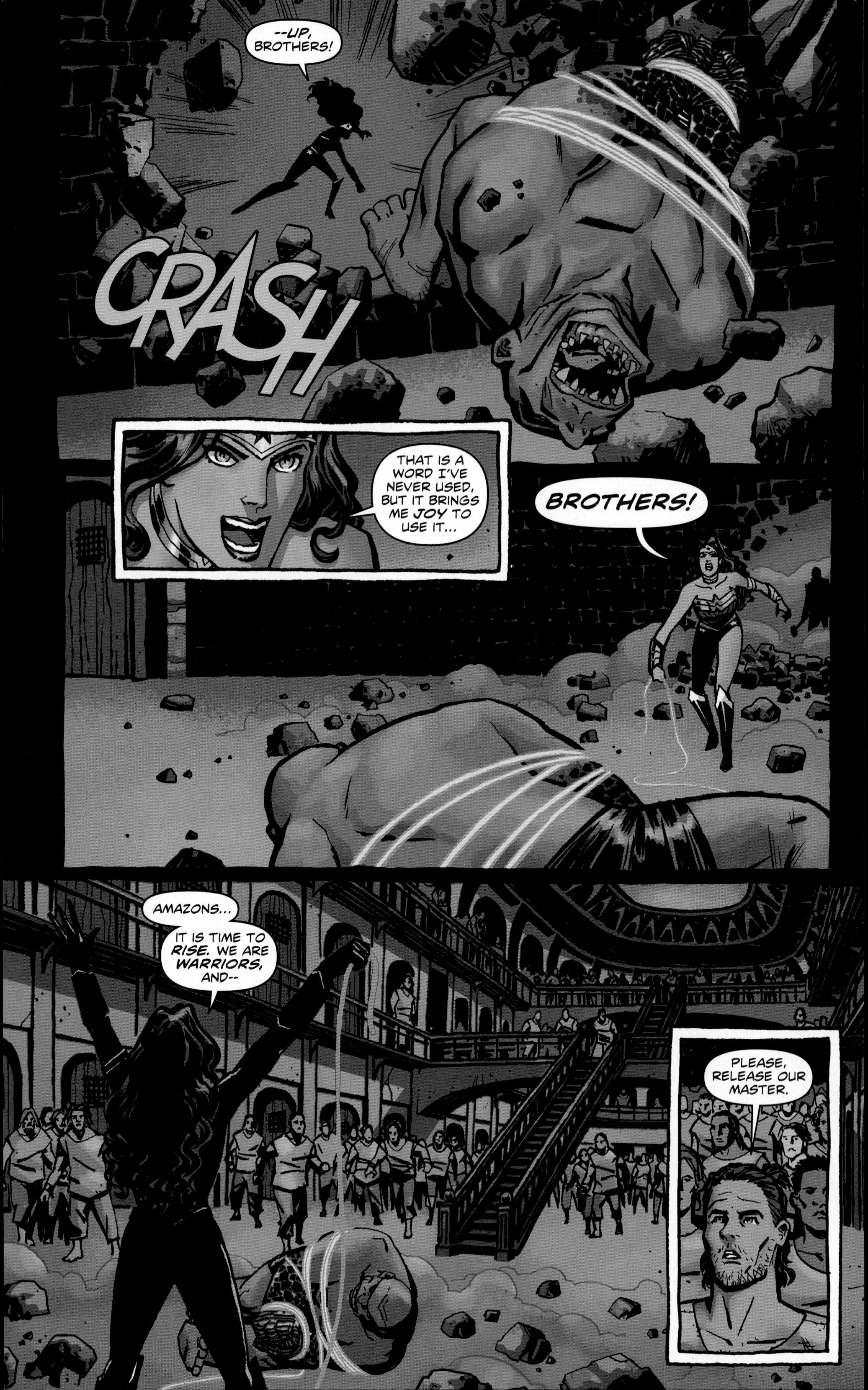
--UP, BROTHERS!
CRASH
THAT IS A WORD I'VE NEVER USED, BUT IT BRINGS ME JOY TO USE IT...
BROTHERS!
AMAZONS...
IT IS TIME TO RISE. WE ARE WARRIORS, AND--
PLEASE, RELEASE OUR MASTER.

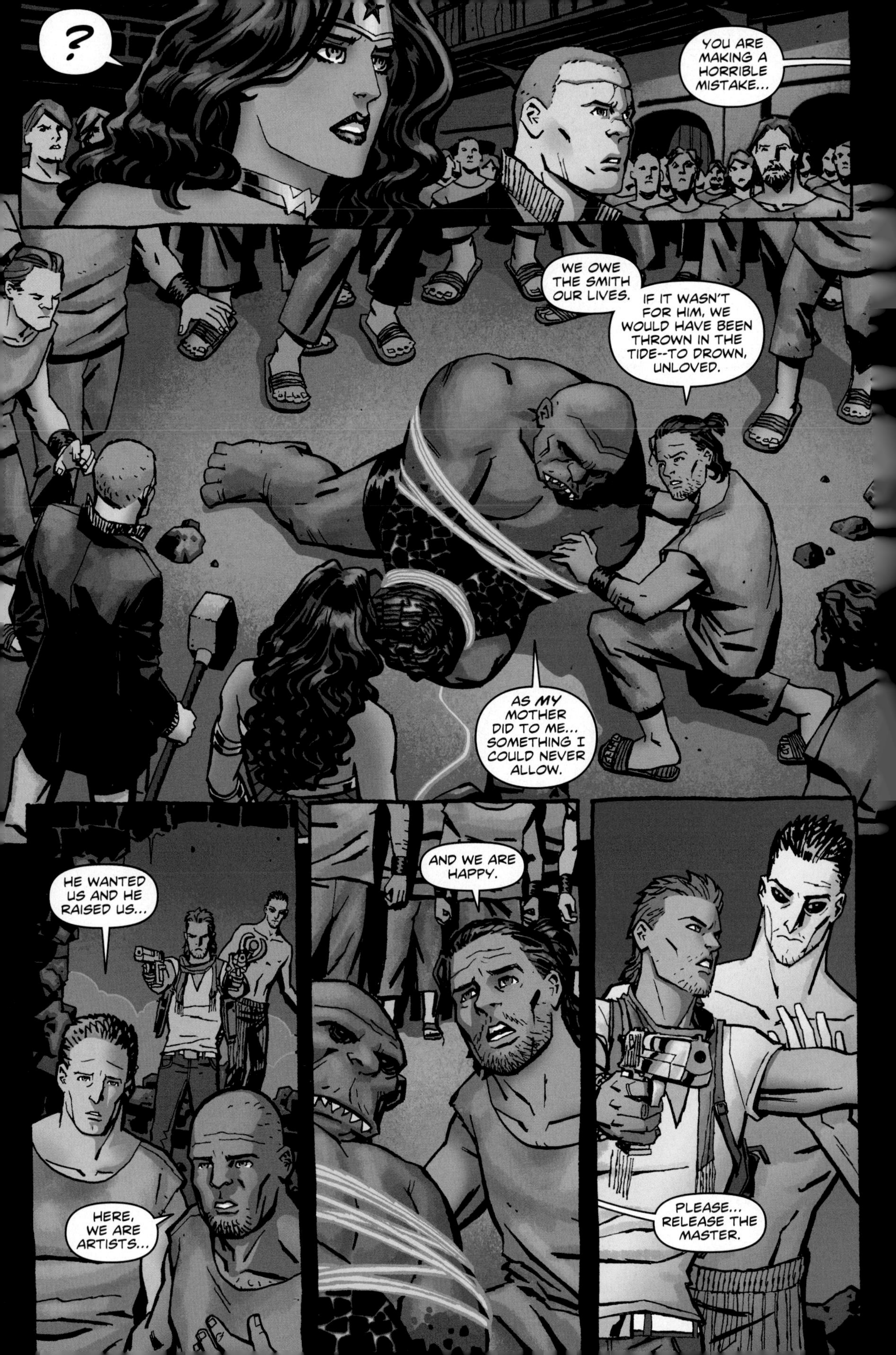
?
YOU ARE MAKING A HORRIBLE MISTAKE...
WE OWE THE SMITH OUR LIVES.
IF IT WASN'T FOR HIM, WE WOULD HAVE BEEN THROWN IN THE TIDE--TO DROWN, UNLOVED.
AS *MY* MOTHER DID TO ME... SOMETHING I COULD NEVER ALLOW.
HE WANTED US AND HE RAISED US...
HERE, WE ARE ARTISTS...
AND WE ARE HAPPY.
PLEASE... RELEASE THE MASTER.

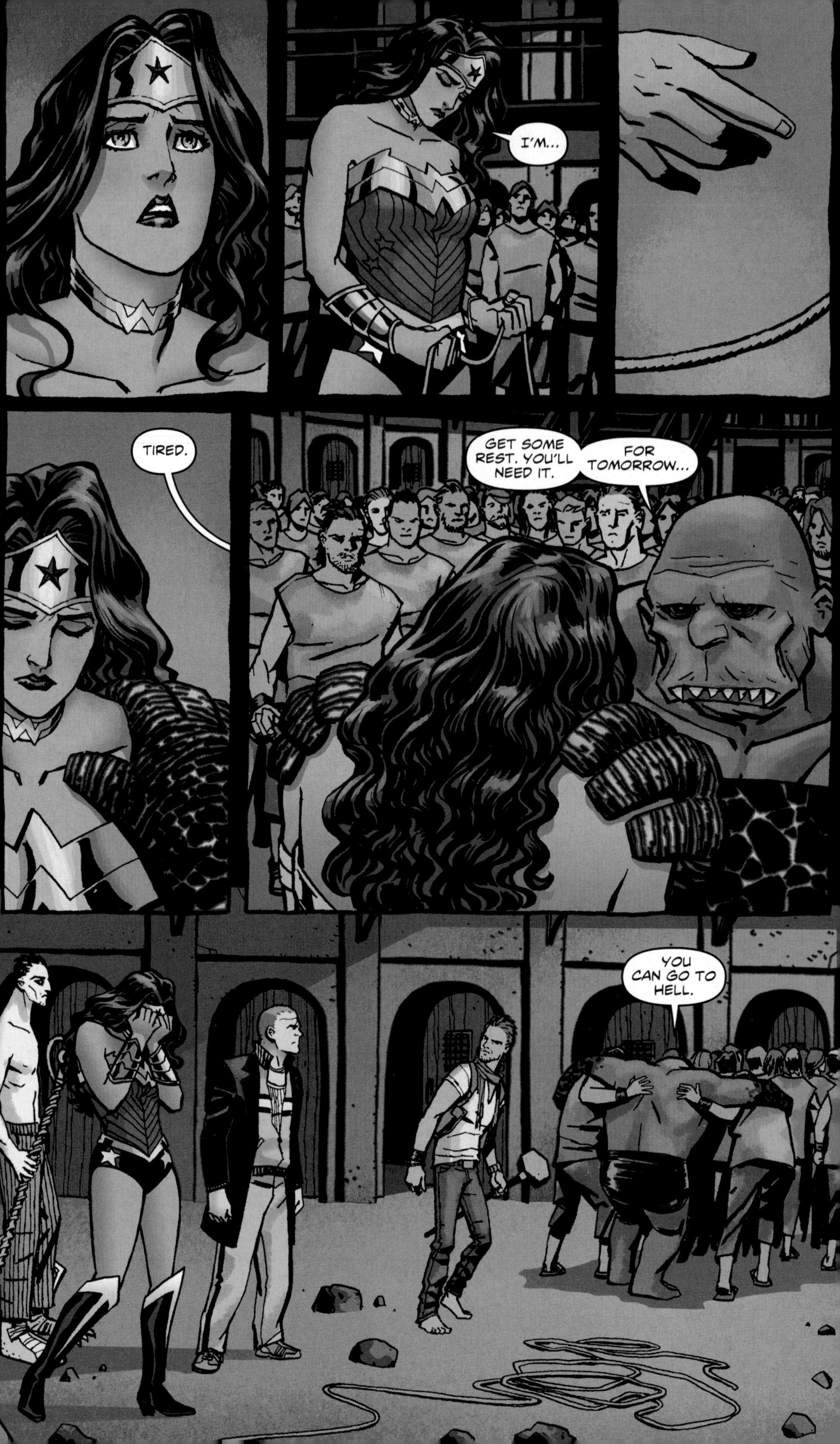
I'M...
TIRED.
GET SOME REST. YOU'LL NEED IT.
FOR TOMORROW...
YOU CAN GO TO HELL.

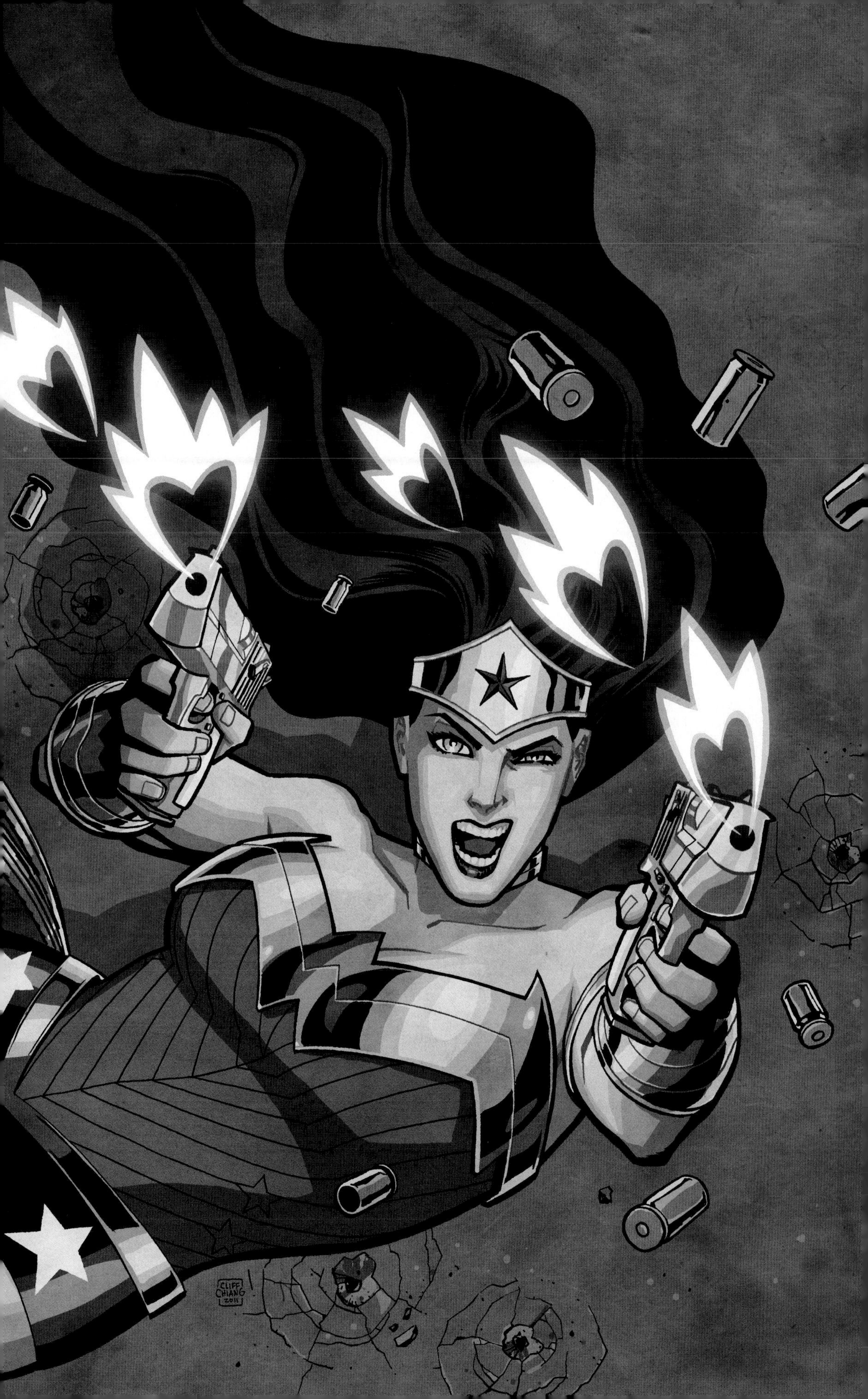
CLIFF CHIANG 2011

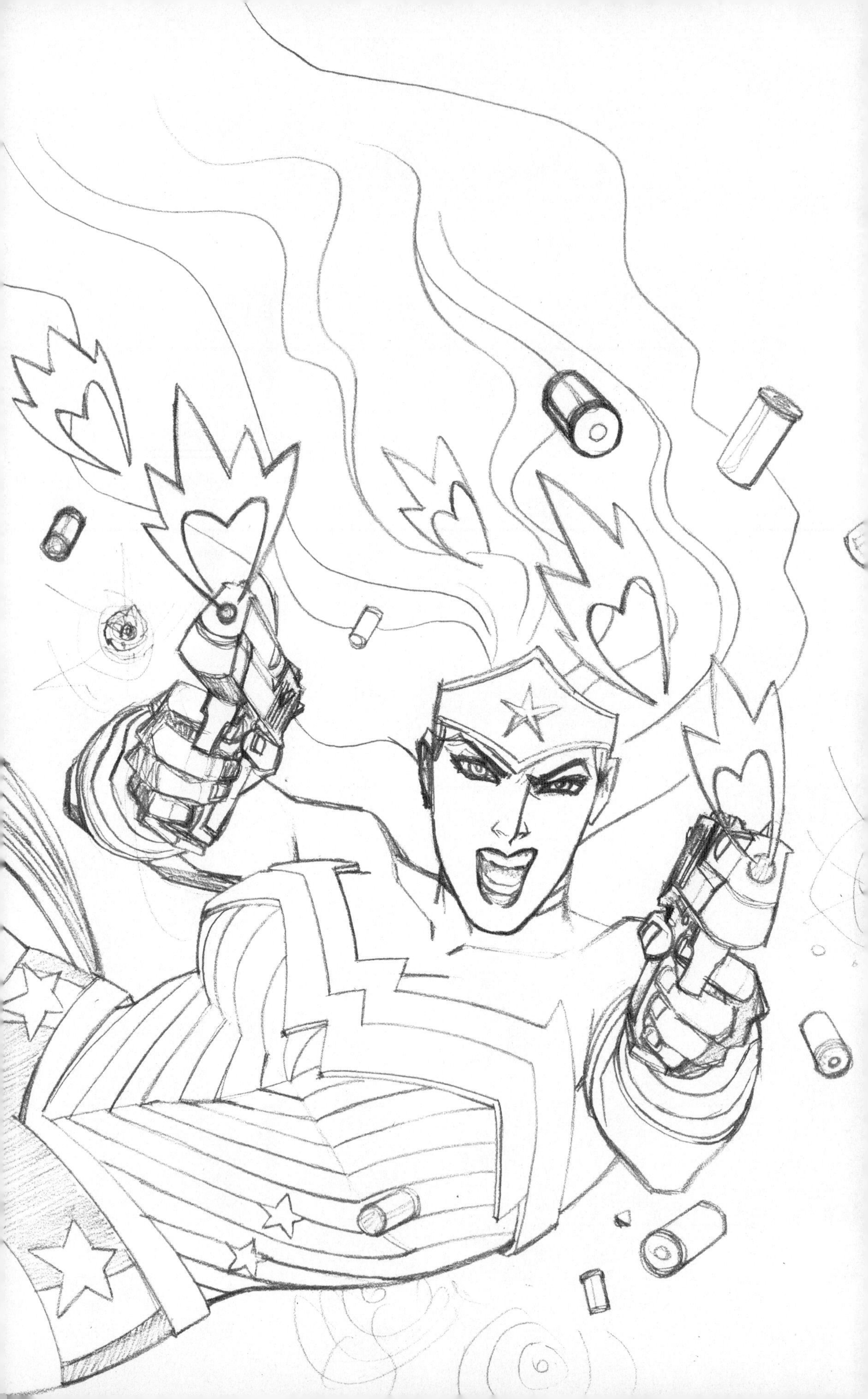

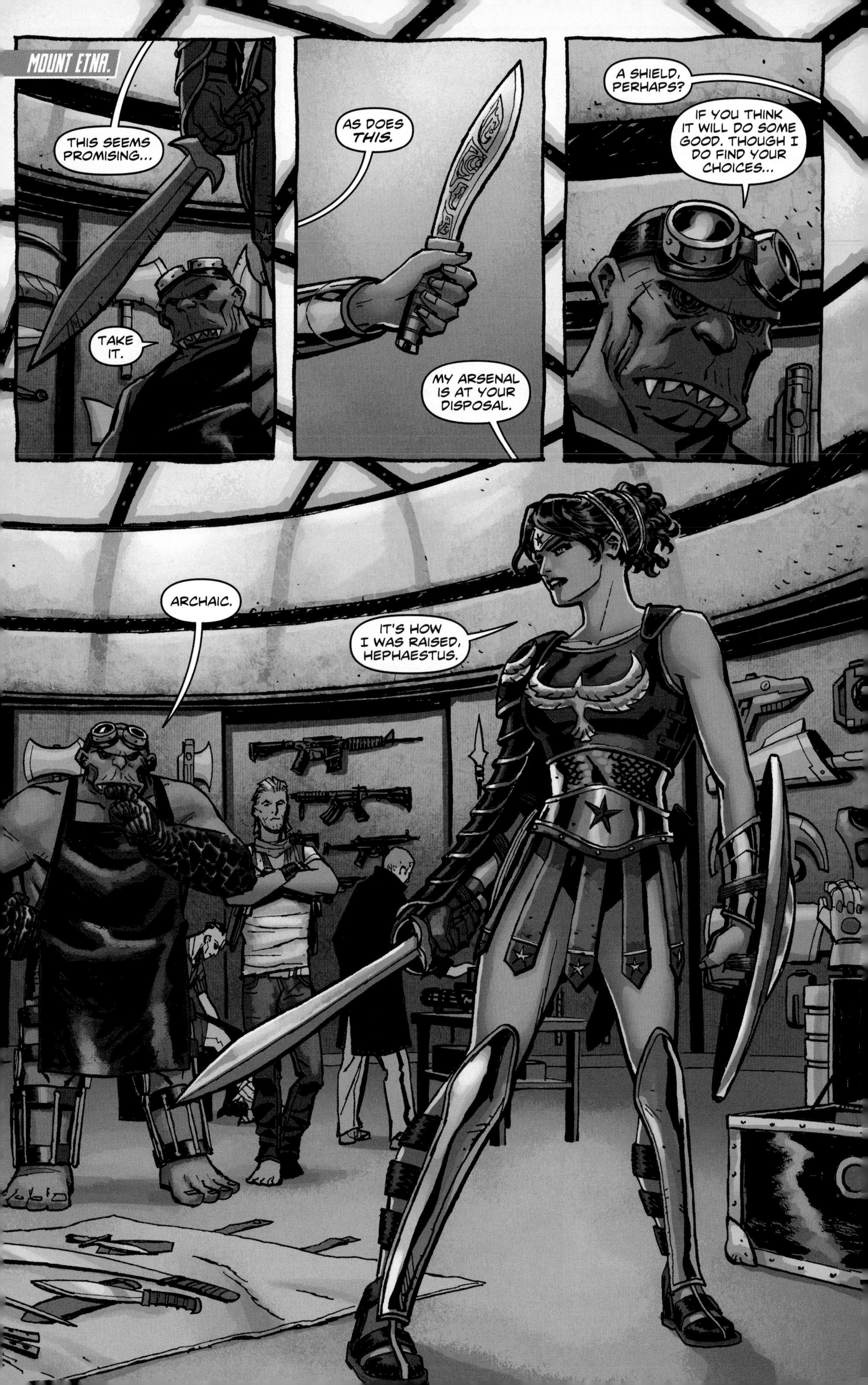
MOUNT ETNA.
THIS SEEMS PROMISING...
TAKE IT.
AS DOES THIS.
MY ARSENAL IS AT YOUR DISPOSAL.
A SHIELD, PERHAPS?
IF YOU THINK IT WILL DO SOME GOOD. THOUGH I DO FIND YOUR CHOICES...
ARCHAIC.
IT'S HOW I WAS RAISED, HEPHAESTUS.

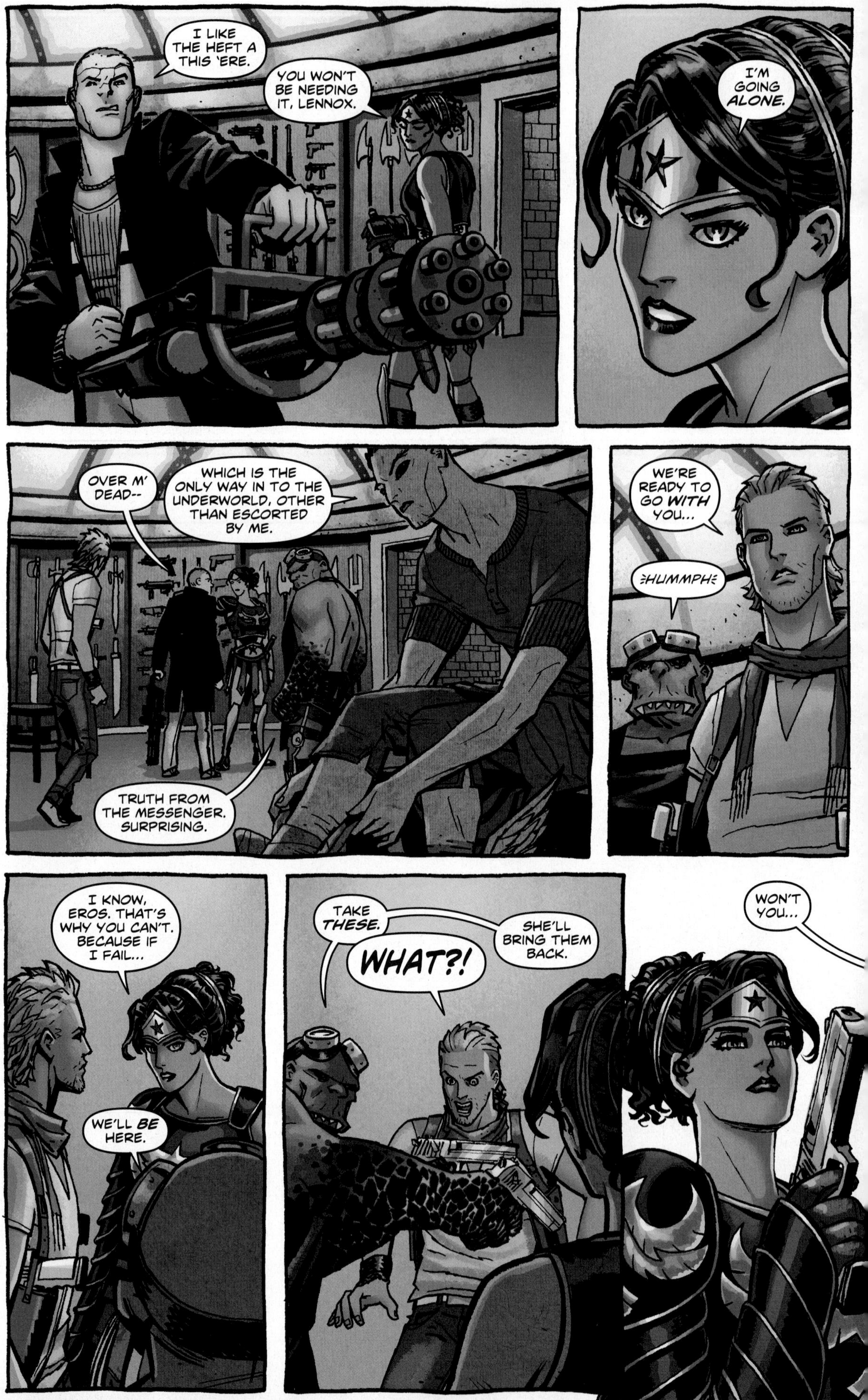
I LIKE THE HEFT A THIS 'ERE.
YOU WON'T BE NEEDING IT, LENNOX.
I'M GOING ALONE.
OVER M' DEAD--
WHICH IS THE ONLY WAY IN TO THE UNDERWORLD, OTHER THAN ESCORTED BY ME.
TRUTH FROM THE MESSENGER. SURPRISING.
WE'RE READY TO GO WITH YOU...
HUMMPH
I KNOW, EROS. THAT'S WHY YOU CAN'T. BECAUSE IF I FAIL...
WE'LL BE HERE.
TAKE THESE.
WHAT?!
SHE'LL BRING THEM BACK.
WON'T YOU...

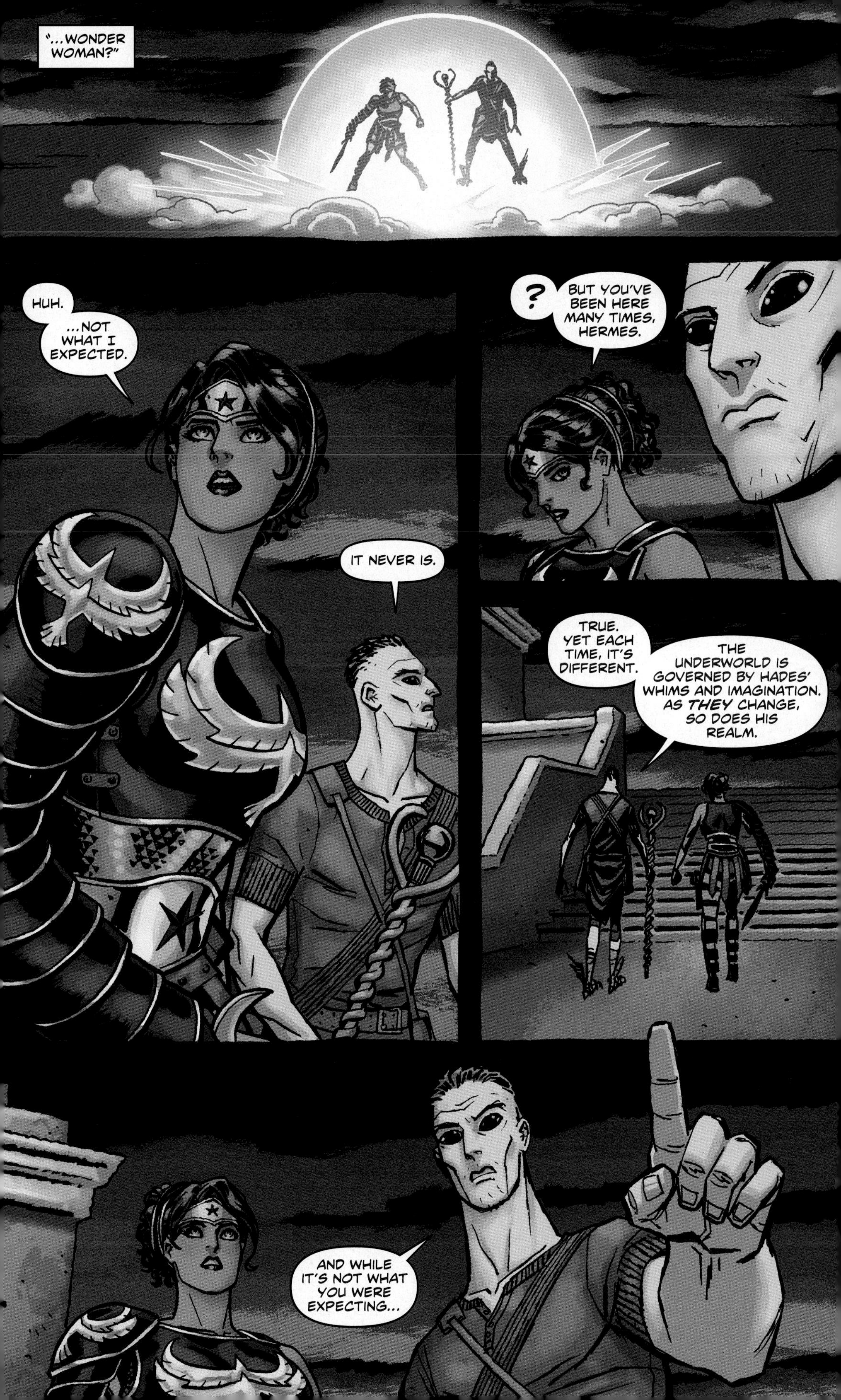
"...WONDER WOMAN?"
HUH. ...NOT WHAT I EXPECTED.
IT NEVER IS.
? BUT YOU'VE BEEN HERE MANY TIMES, HERMES.
TRUE. YET EACH TIME, IT'S DIFFERENT.
THE UNDERWORLD IS GOVERNED BY HADES' WHIMS AND IMAGINATION. AS *THEY* CHANGE, SO DOES HIS REALM.
AND WHILE IT'S NOT WHAT YOU WERE EXPECTING...

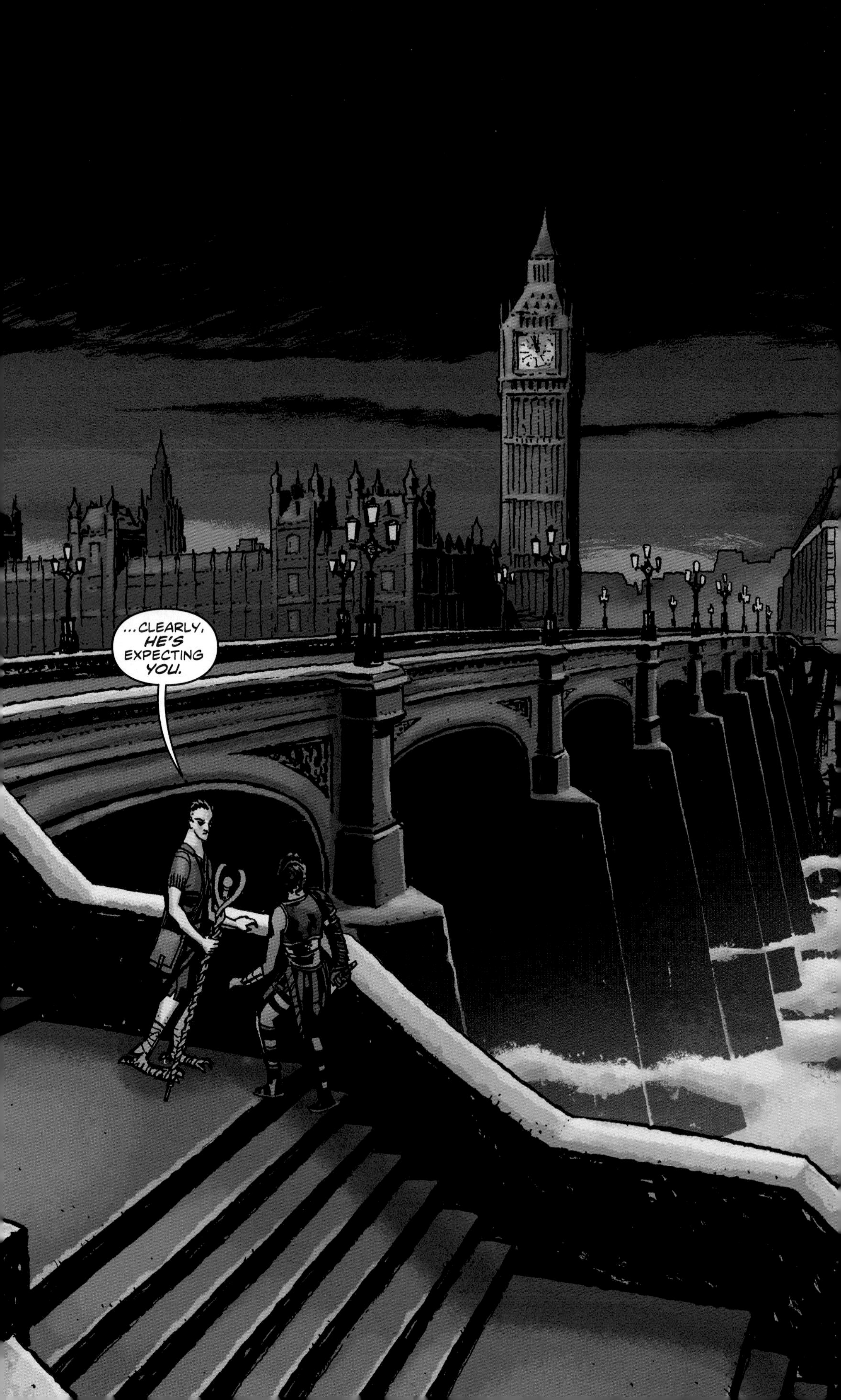
...CLEARLY, HE'S EXPECTING YOU.

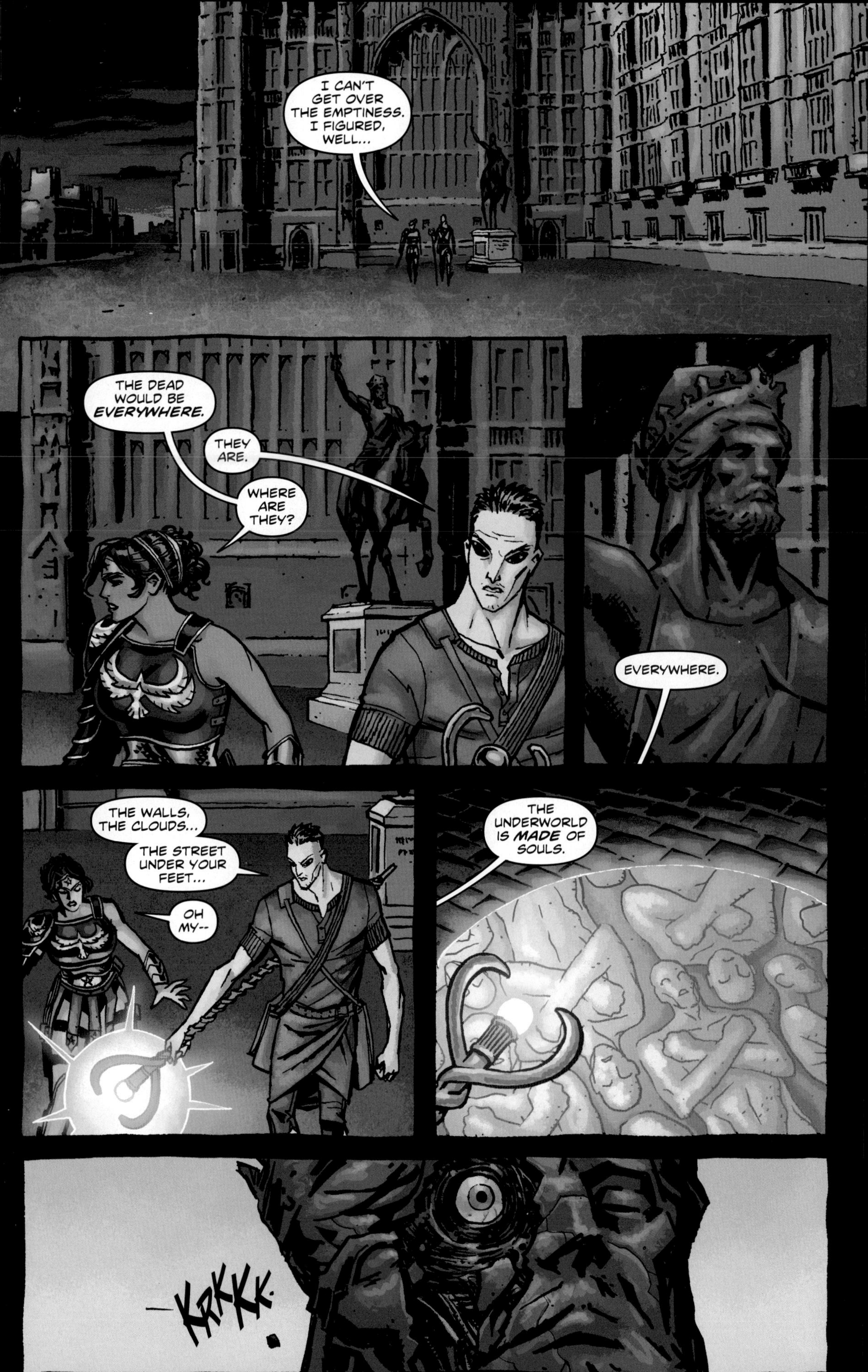
I CAN'T GET OVER THE EMPTINESS. I FIGURED, WELL...
THE DEAD WOULD BE *EVERYWHERE.*
THEY ARE.
WHERE ARE THEY?
EVERYWHERE.
THE WALLS, THE CLOUDS...
THE STREET UNDER YOUR FEET...
OH MY--
THE UNDERWORLD IS *MADE* OF SOULS.
KRKKK

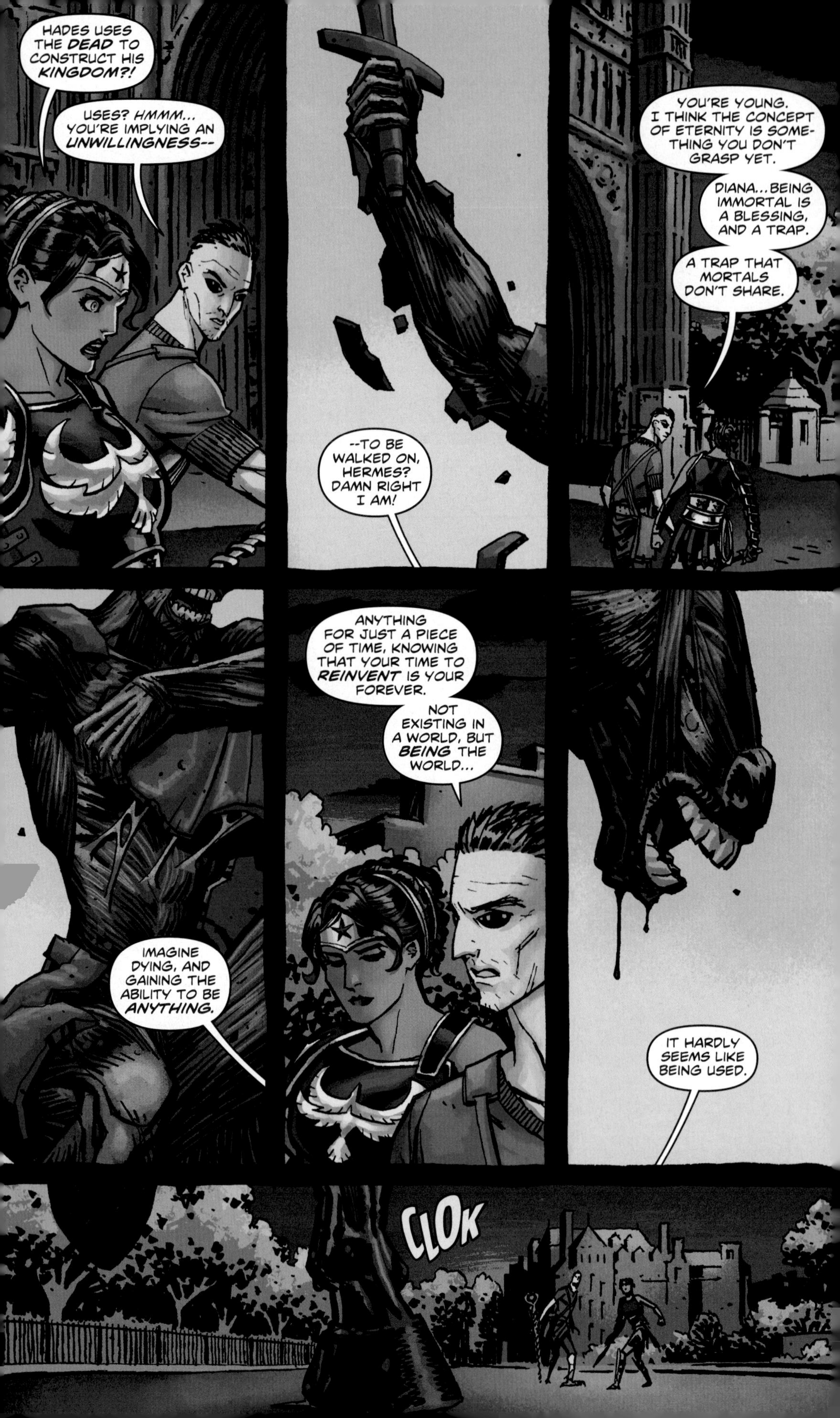
HADES USES THE DEAD TO CONSTRUCT HIS KINGDOM?!
USES? HMMM... YOU'RE IMPLYING AN UNWILLINGNESS--
--TO BE WALKED ON, HERMES? DAMN RIGHT I AM!
YOU'RE YOUNG. I THINK THE CONCEPT OF ETERNITY IS SOMETHING YOU DON'T GRASP YET.
DIANA... BEING IMMORTAL IS A BLESSING, AND A TRAP.
A TRAP THAT MORTALS DON'T SHARE.
IMAGINE DYING, AND GAINING THE ABILITY TO BE ANYTHING.
ANYTHING FOR JUST A PIECE OF TIME, KNOWING THAT YOUR TIME TO REINVENT IS YOUR FOREVER.
NOT EXISTING IN A WORLD, BUT BEING THE WORLD...
IT HARDLY SEEMS LIKE BEING USED.
CLOK

HRRRRRR

YOU CAN'T TELL ME *ANYONE* CHOSE TO BE THAT.

...FREE WILL IS A FUNNY THING.

EEEEEYYAAAA

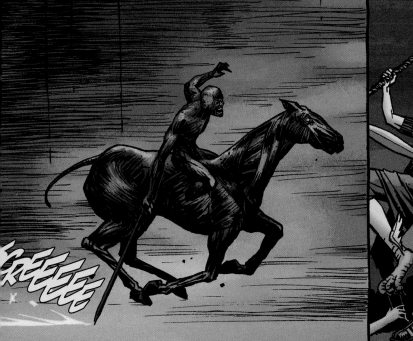

REEEEE

?

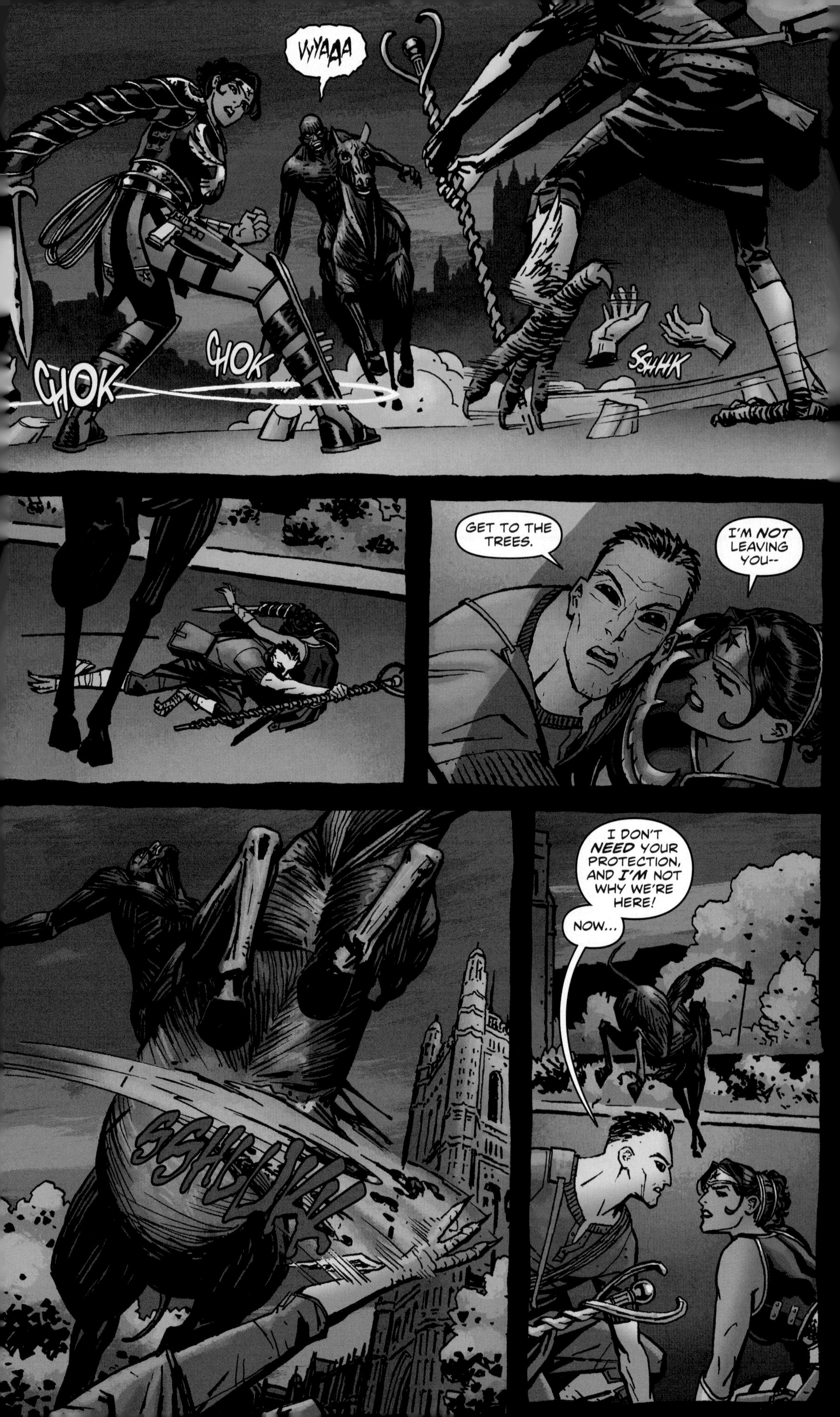
VYYAAA
CHOK
CHOK
SSHHK
GET TO THE TREES.
I'M NOT LEAVING YOU--
SSHUK
I DON'T NEED YOUR PROTECTION, AND I'M NOT WHY WE'RE HERE!
NOW...

...FIND ZOLA!

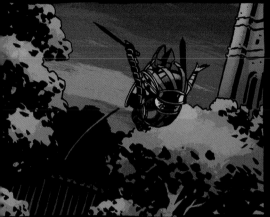

KKRAK

KKRAK

I KNEW YOU WOULD COME.

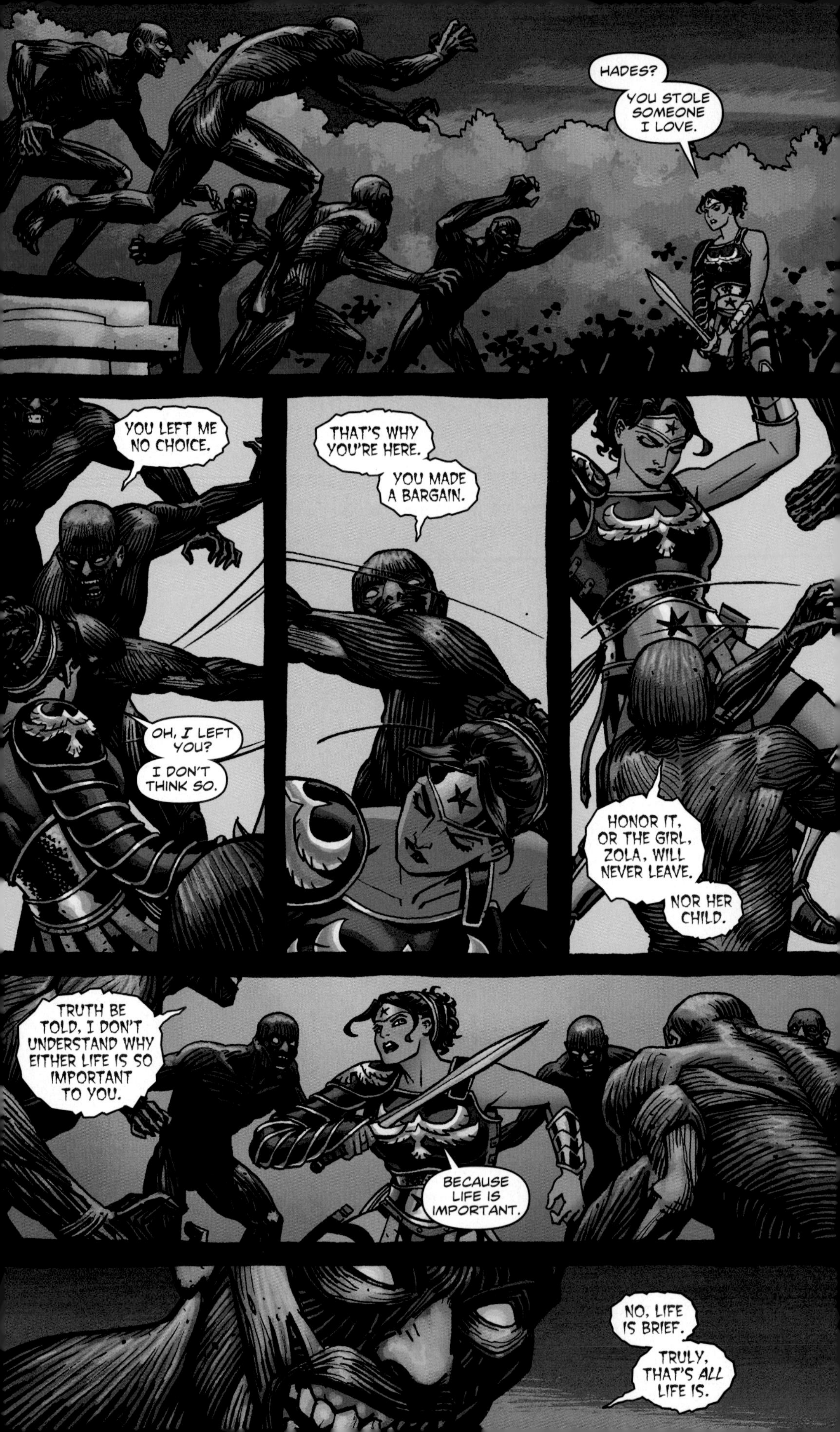
HADES?
YOU STOLE SOMEONE I LOVE.
YOU LEFT ME NO CHOICE.
OH, *I* LEFT YOU?
I DON'T THINK SO.
THAT'S WHY YOU'RE HERE.
YOU MADE A BARGAIN.
HONOR IT, OR THE GIRL, ZOLA, WILL NEVER LEAVE.
NOR HER CHILD.
TRUTH BE TOLD, I DON'T UNDERSTAND WHY EITHER LIFE IS SO IMPORTANT TO YOU.
BECAUSE LIFE IS IMPORTANT.
NO, LIFE IS BRIEF.
TRULY, THAT'S *ALL* LIFE IS.

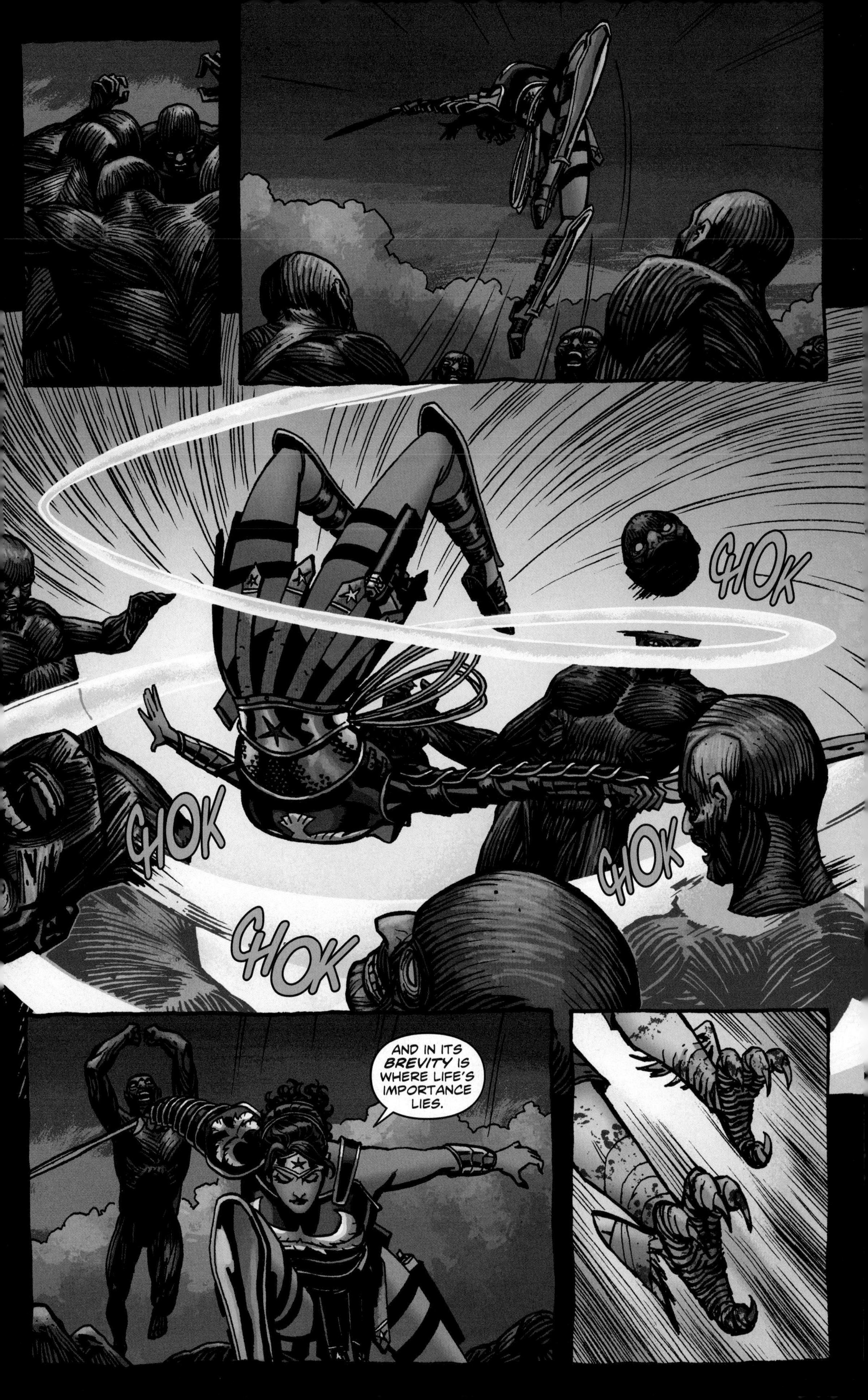
CHOK
CHOK
CHOK
CHOK
AND IN ITS *BREVITY* IS WHERE LIFE'S IMPORTANCE LIES.

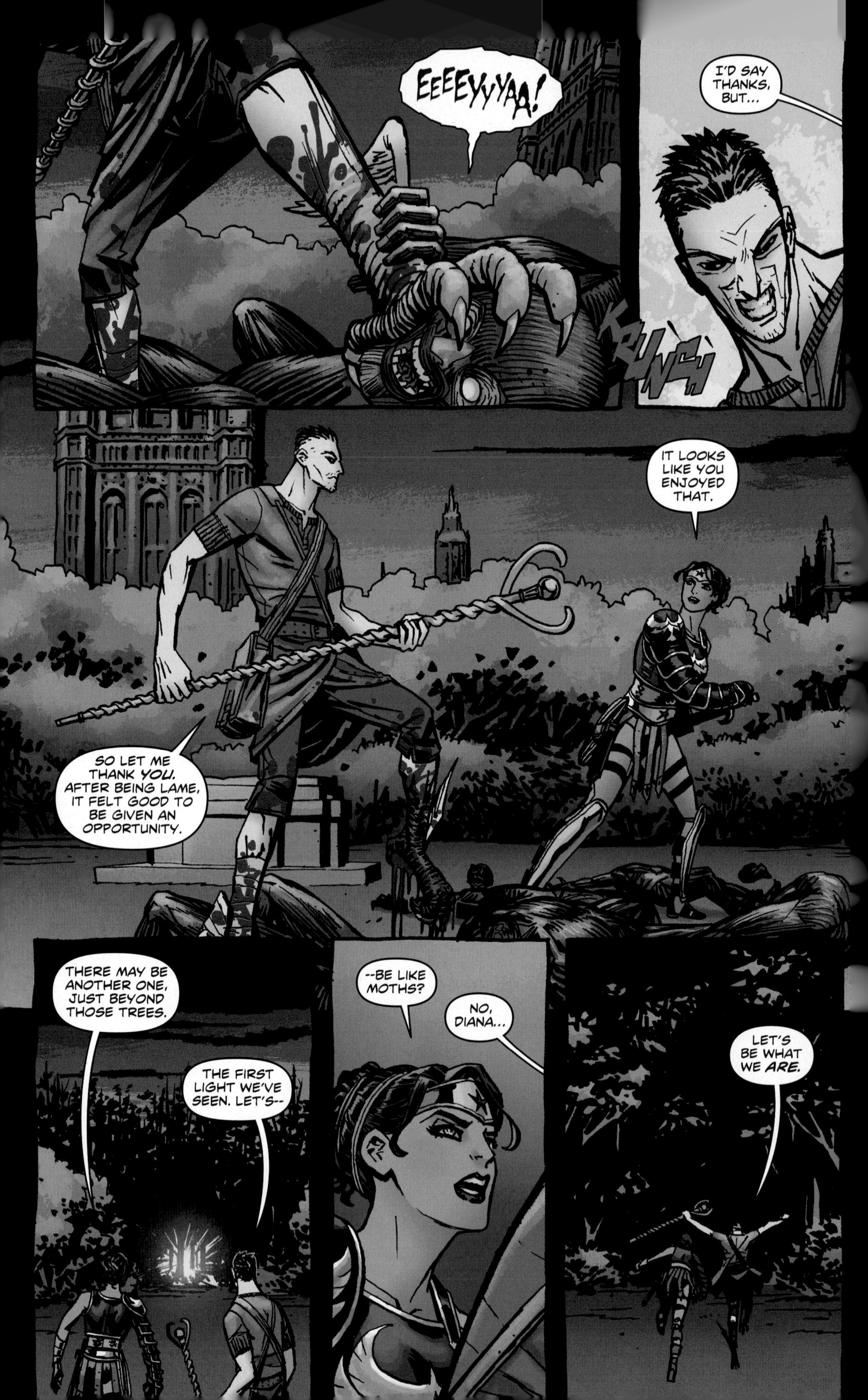
EEEEYYYAA!
I'D SAY THANKS, BUT...
KRUNCH
IT LOOKS LIKE YOU ENJOYED THAT.
SO LET ME THANK YOU. AFTER BEING LAME, IT FELT GOOD TO BE GIVEN AN OPPORTUNITY.
THERE MAY BE ANOTHER ONE, JUST BEYOND THOSE TREES.
THE FIRST LIGHT WE'VE SEEN. LET'S--
--BE LIKE MOTHS?
NO, DIANA...
LET'S BE WHAT WE ARE.

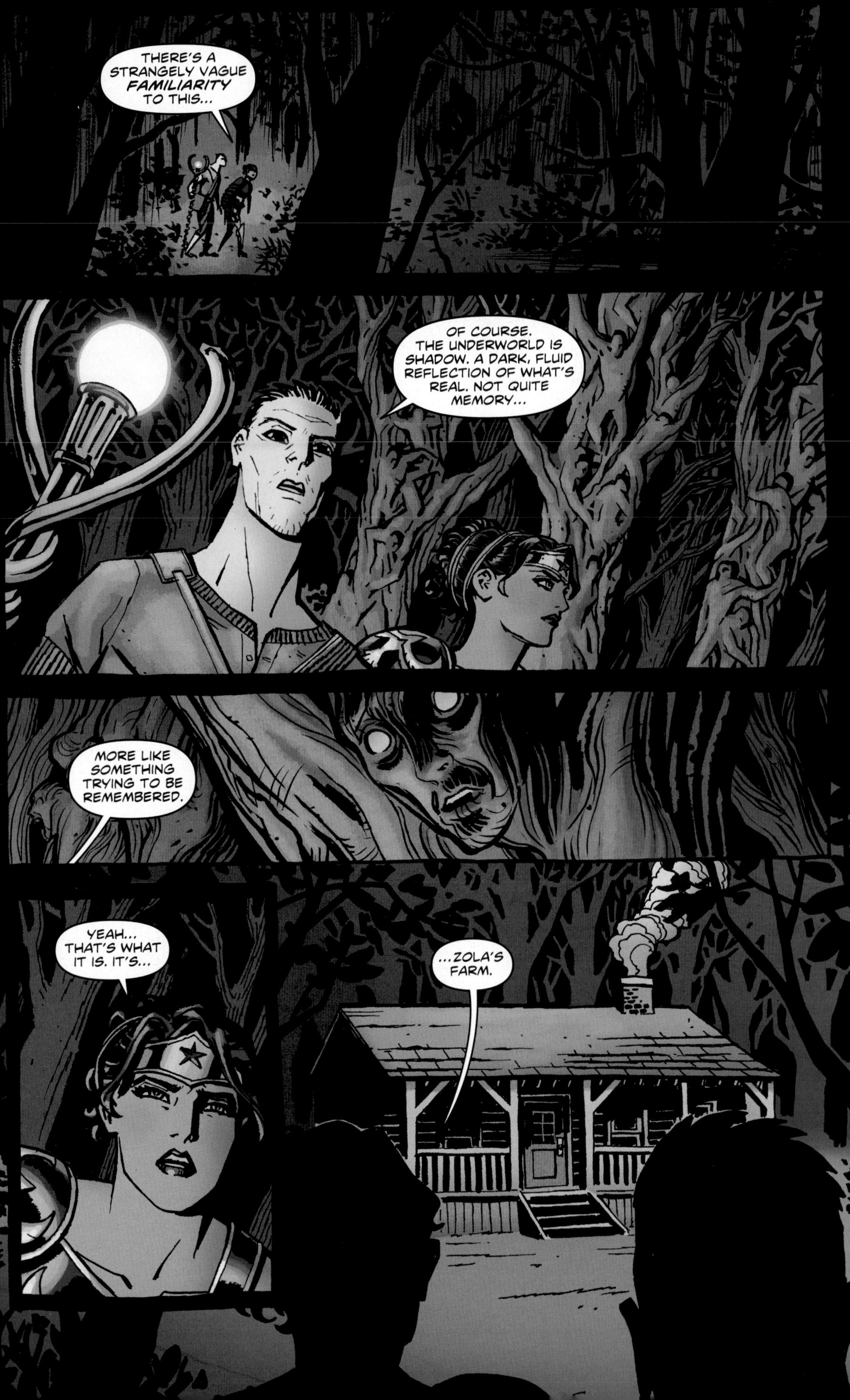
THERE'S A STRANGELY VAGUE *FAMILIARITY* TO THIS...
OF COURSE. THE UNDERWORLD IS SHADOW. A DARK, FLUID REFLECTION OF WHAT'S REAL. NOT QUITE MEMORY...
MORE LIKE SOMETHING TRYING TO BE REMEMBERED.
YEAH... THAT'S WHAT IT IS. IT'S...
...ZOLA'S FARM.

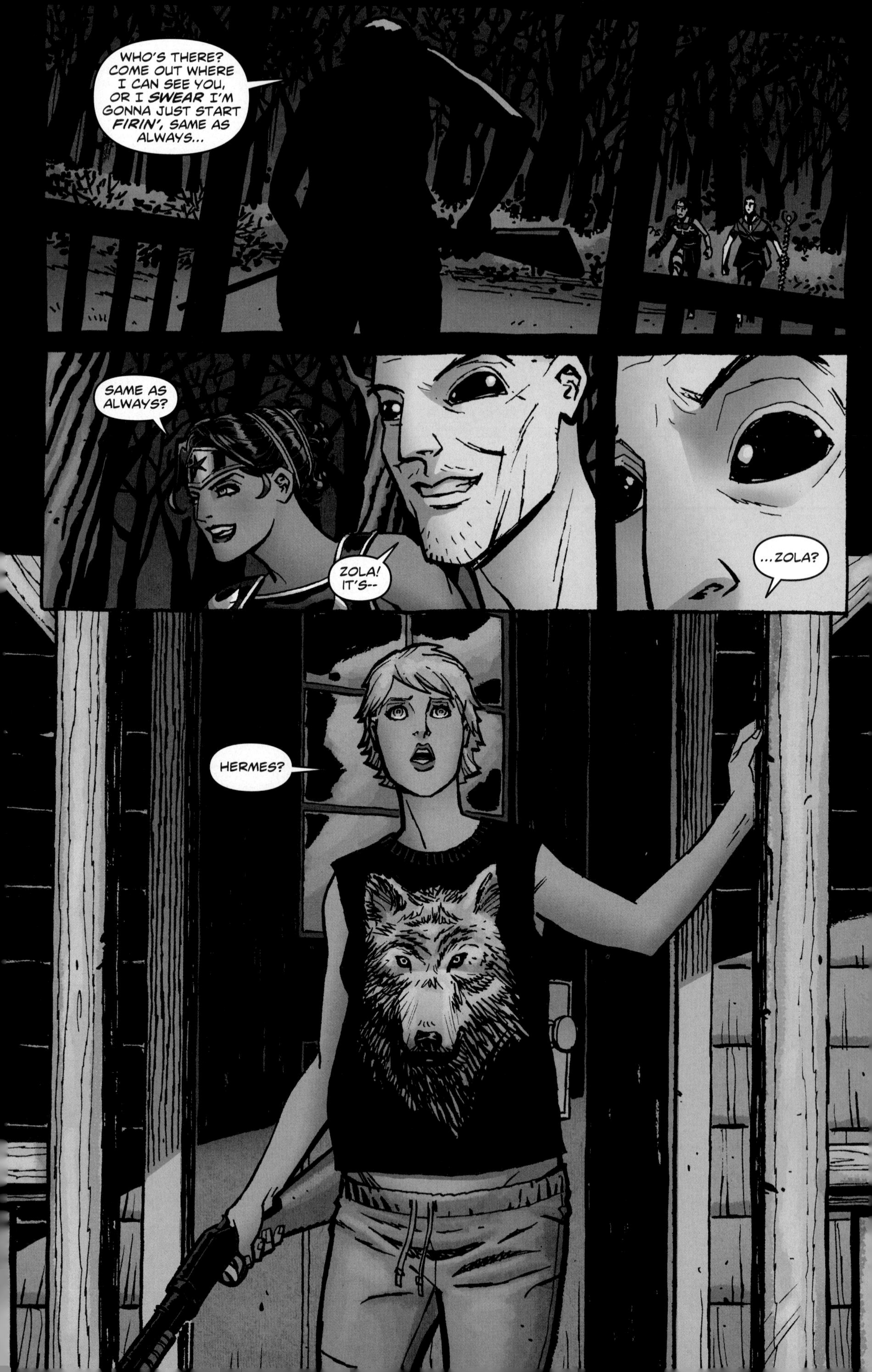
WHO'S THERE? COME OUT WHERE I CAN SEE YOU, OR I SWEAR I'M GONNA JUST START FIRIN', SAME AS ALWAYS...
SAME AS ALWAYS?
ZOLA! IT'S--
...ZOLA?
HERMES?

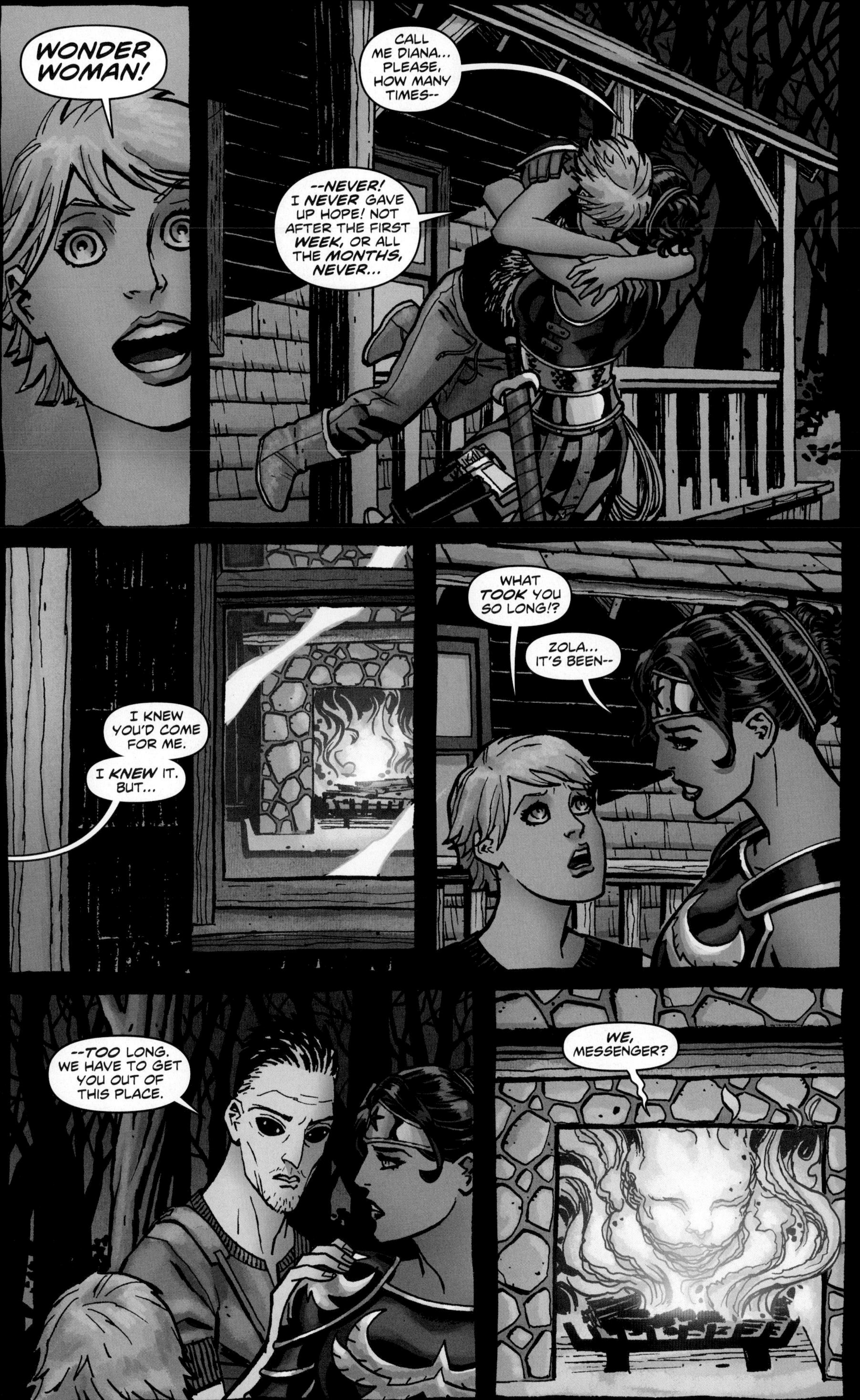
WONDER WOMAN!
CALL ME DIANA... PLEASE, HOW MANY TIMES--
--NEVER! I NEVER GAVE UP HOPE! NOT AFTER THE FIRST WEEK, OR ALL THE MONTHS, NEVER...
I KNEW YOU'D COME FOR ME.
I KNEW IT. BUT...
WHAT TOOK YOU SO LONG!?
ZOLA... IT'S BEEN--
--TOO LONG. WE HAVE TO GET YOU OUT OF THIS PLACE.
WE, MESSENGER?

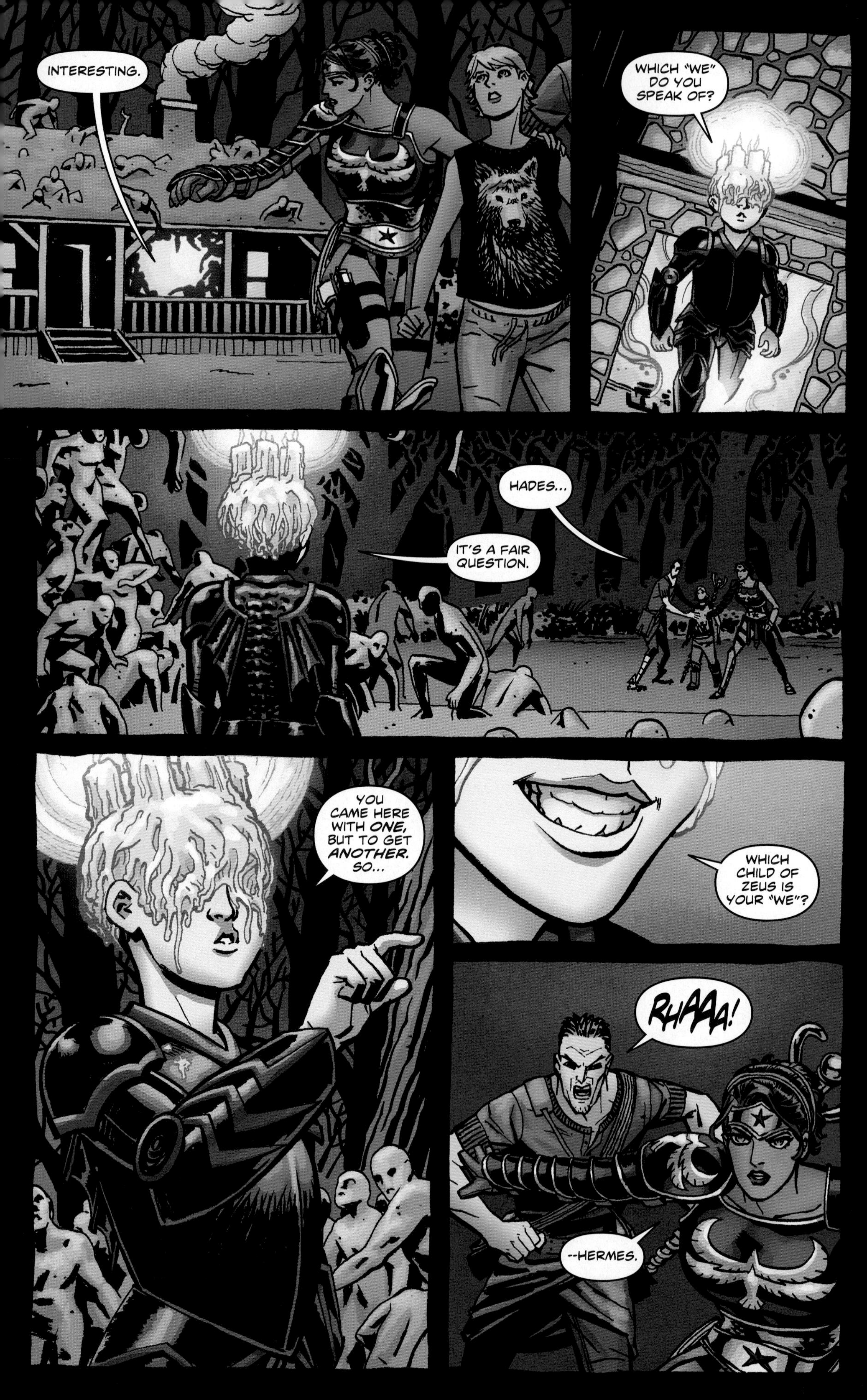
INTERESTING.
WHICH "WE" DO YOU SPEAK OF?
HADES...
IT'S A FAIR QUESTION.
YOU CAME HERE WITH *ONE*, BUT TO GET *ANOTHER*. SO...
WHICH CHILD OF ZEUS IS YOUR "WE"?
RHAAA!
--HERMES.

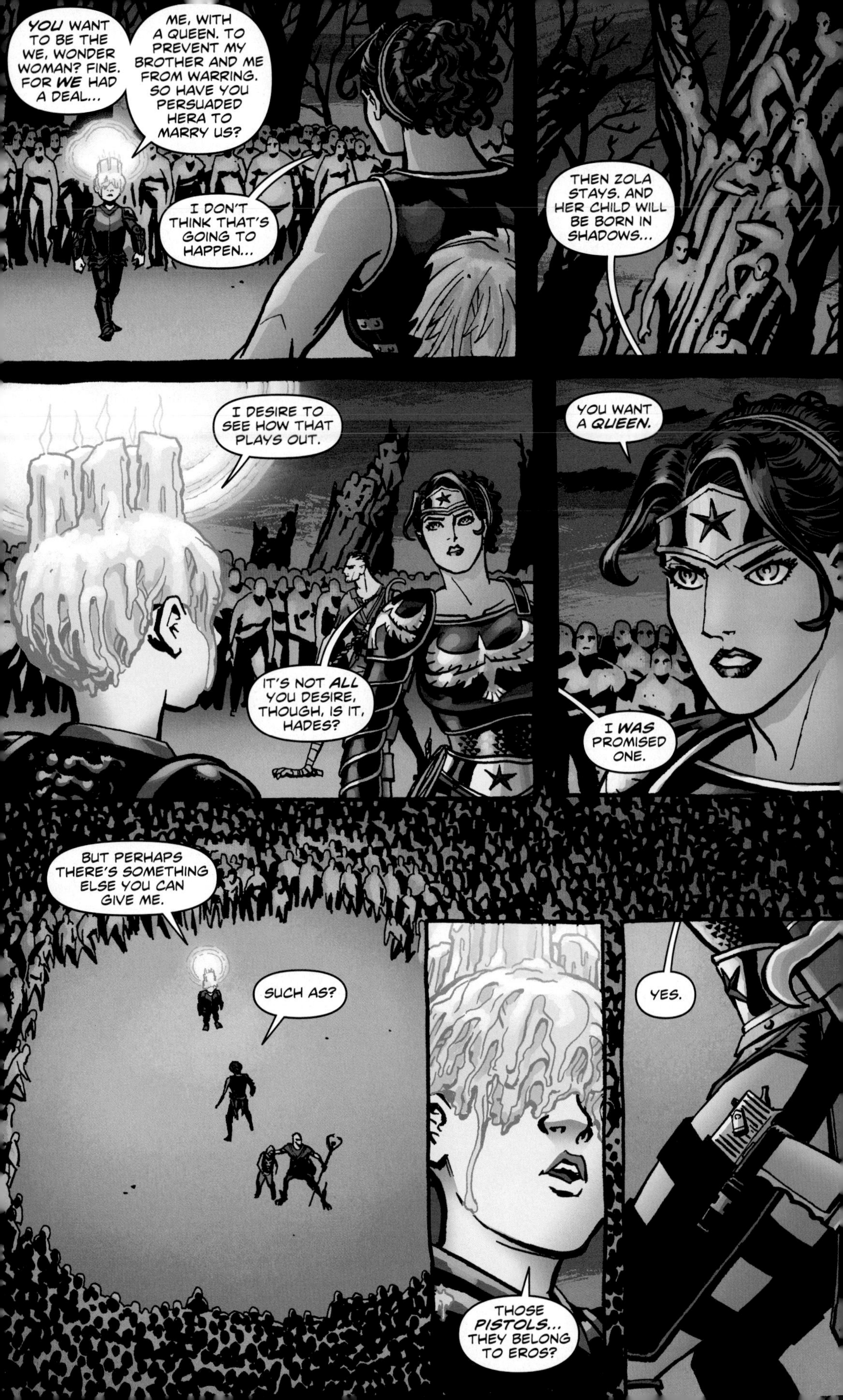
YOU WANT TO BE THE WE, WONDER WOMAN? FINE. FOR WE HAD A DEAL...
ME, WITH A QUEEN. TO PREVENT MY BROTHER AND ME FROM WARRING. SO HAVE YOU PERSUADED HERA TO MARRY US?
I DON'T THINK THAT'S GOING TO HAPPEN...
THEN ZOLA STAYS. AND HER CHILD WILL BE BORN IN SHADOWS...
I DESIRE TO SEE HOW THAT PLAYS OUT.
IT'S NOT ALL YOU DESIRE, THOUGH, IS IT, HADES?
YOU WANT A QUEEN.
I WAS PROMISED ONE.
BUT PERHAPS THERE'S SOMETHING ELSE YOU CAN GIVE ME.
SUCH AS?
THOSE PISTOLS... THEY BELONG TO EROS?
YES.

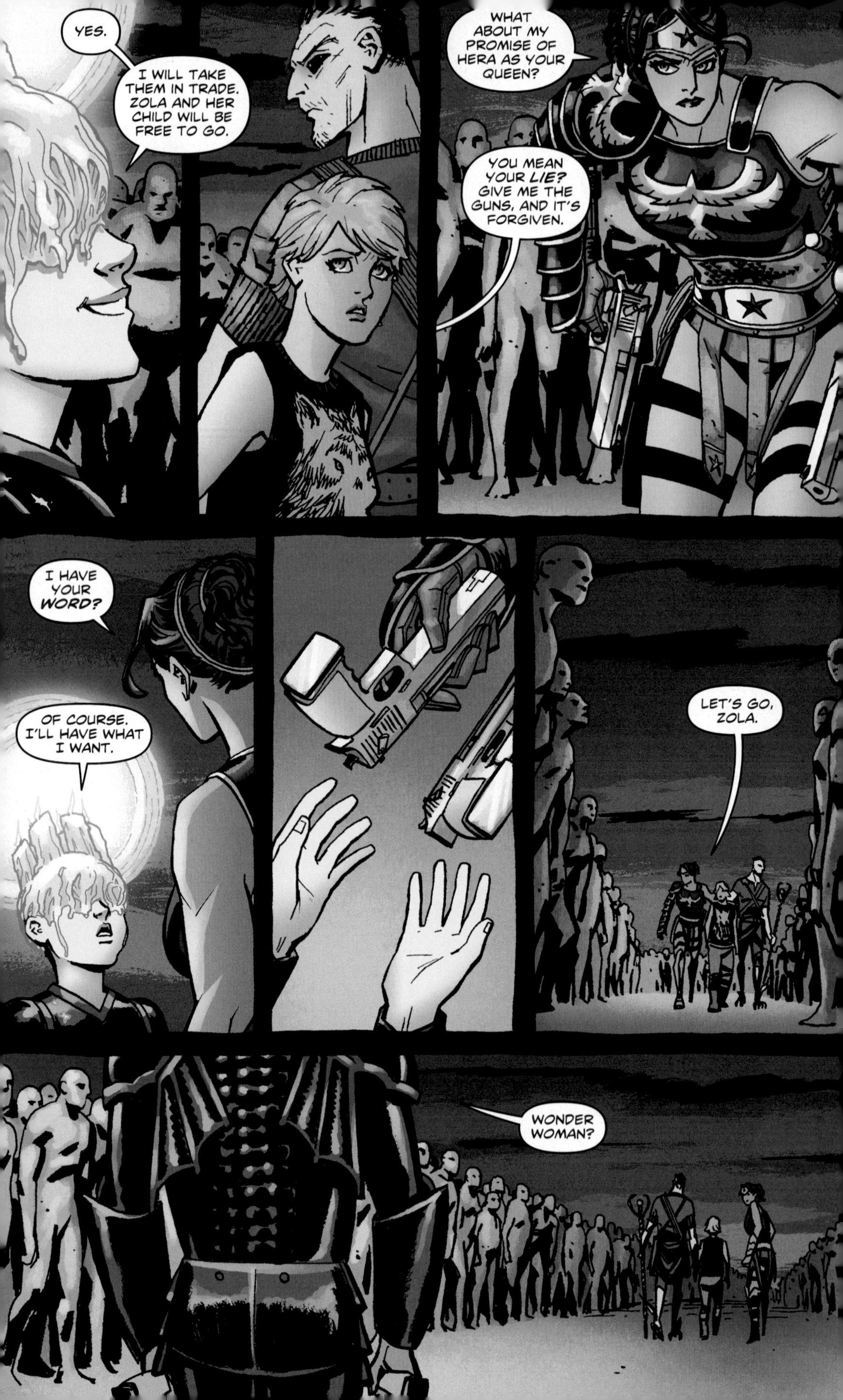
YES.
I WILL TAKE THEM IN TRADE. ZOLA AND HER CHILD WILL BE FREE TO GO.
WHAT ABOUT MY PROMISE OF HERA AS YOUR QUEEN?
YOU MEAN YOUR *LIE?* GIVE ME THE GUNS, AND IT'S FORGIVEN.
I HAVE YOUR *WORD?*
OF COURSE. I'LL HAVE WHAT I WANT.
LET'S GO, ZOLA.
WONDER WOMAN?

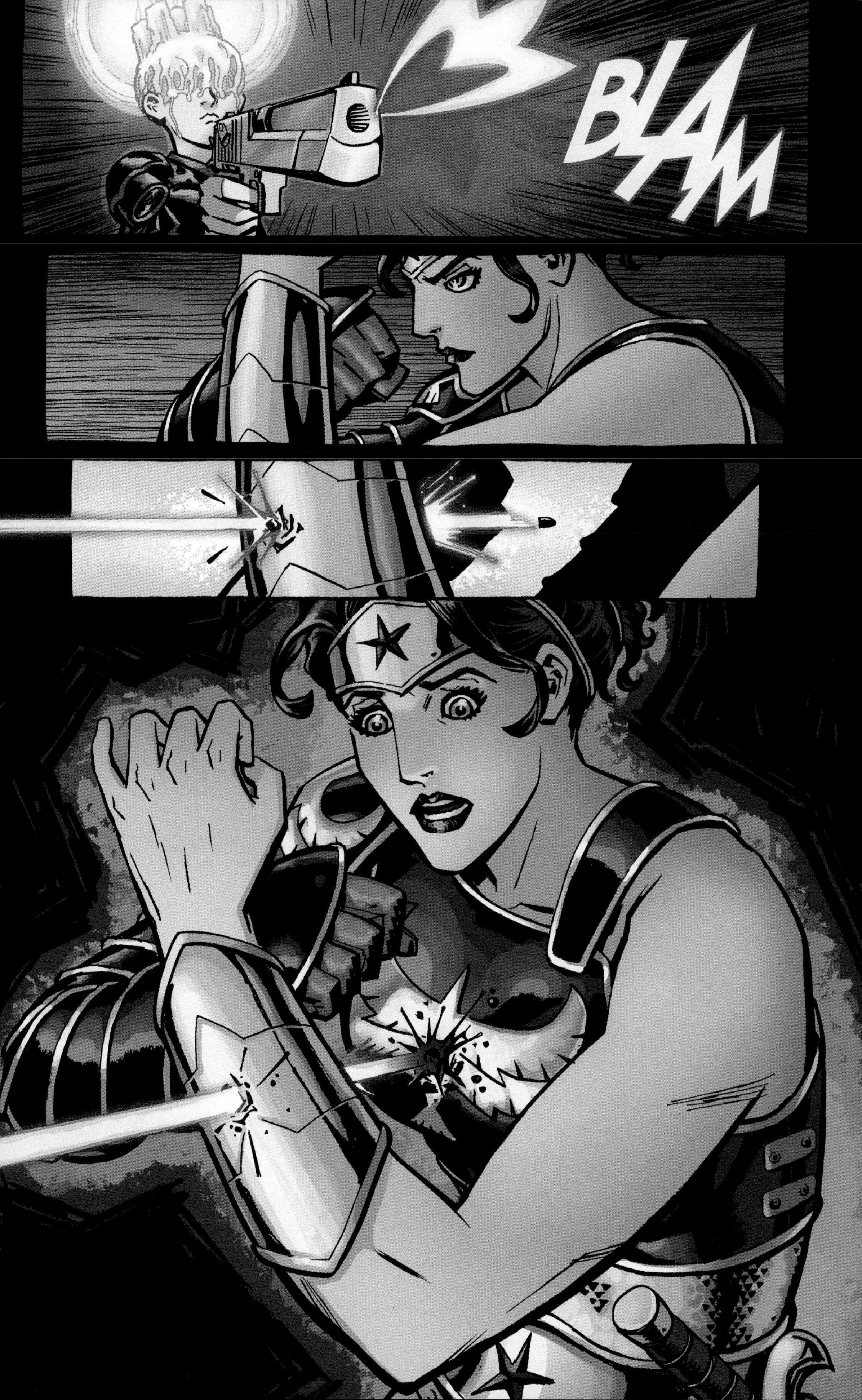
BLAM

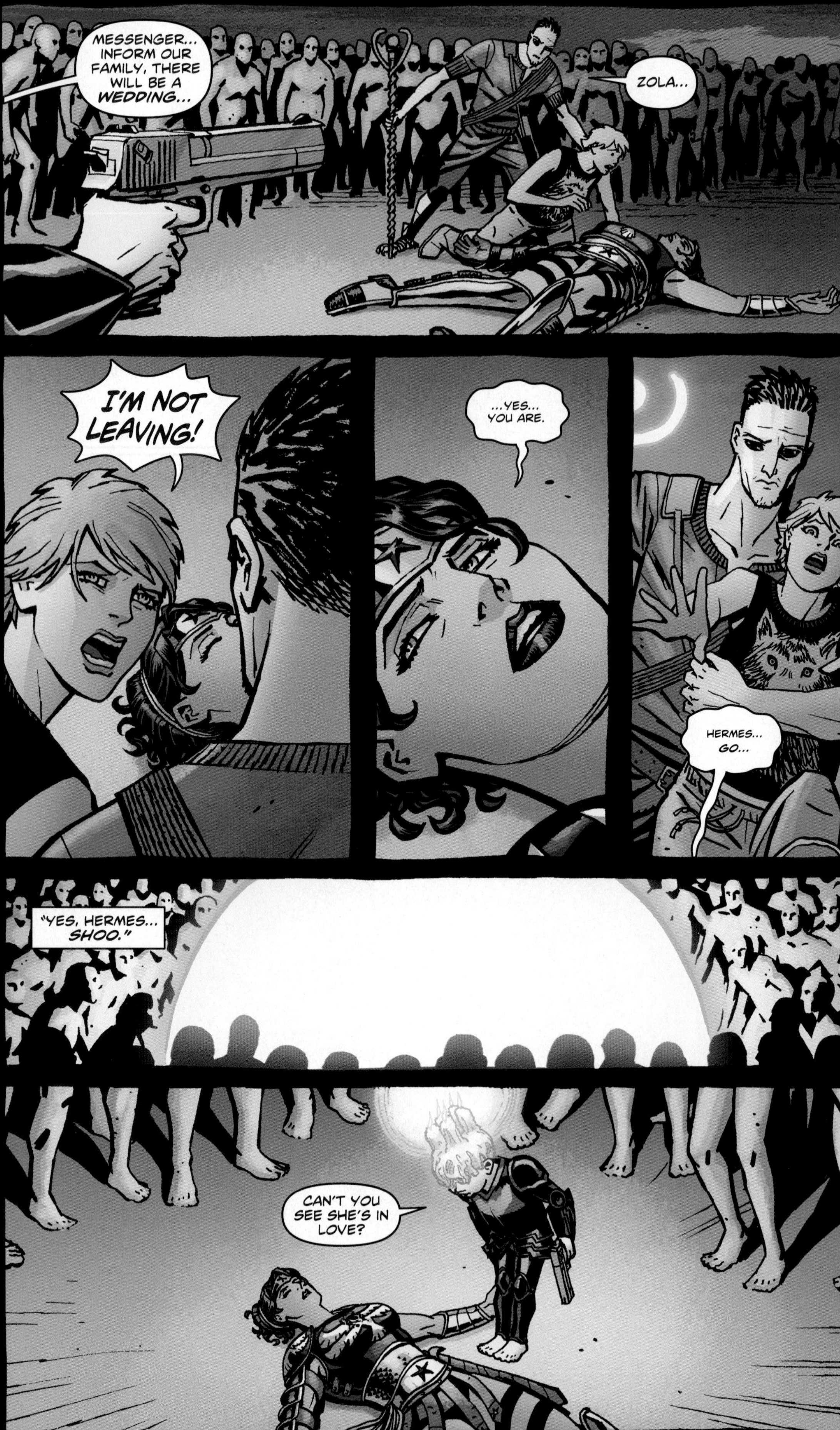
MESSENGER... INFORM OUR FAMILY, THERE WILL BE A WEDDING...
ZOLA...
I'M NOT LEAVING!
...YES... YOU ARE.
HERMES... GO...
"YES, HERMES... SHOO."
CAN'T YOU SEE SHE'S IN LOVE?

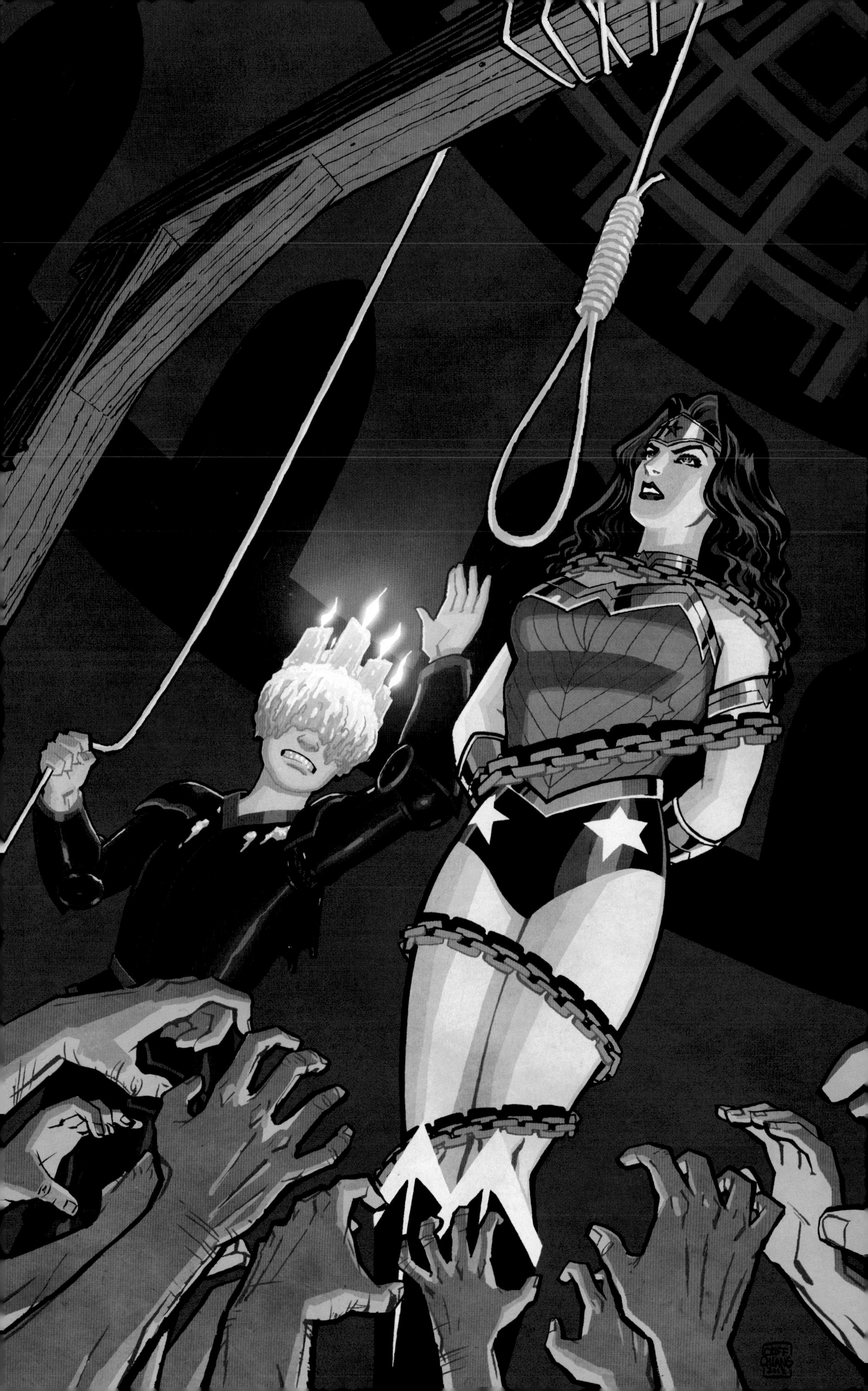
CLIFF CHIANG

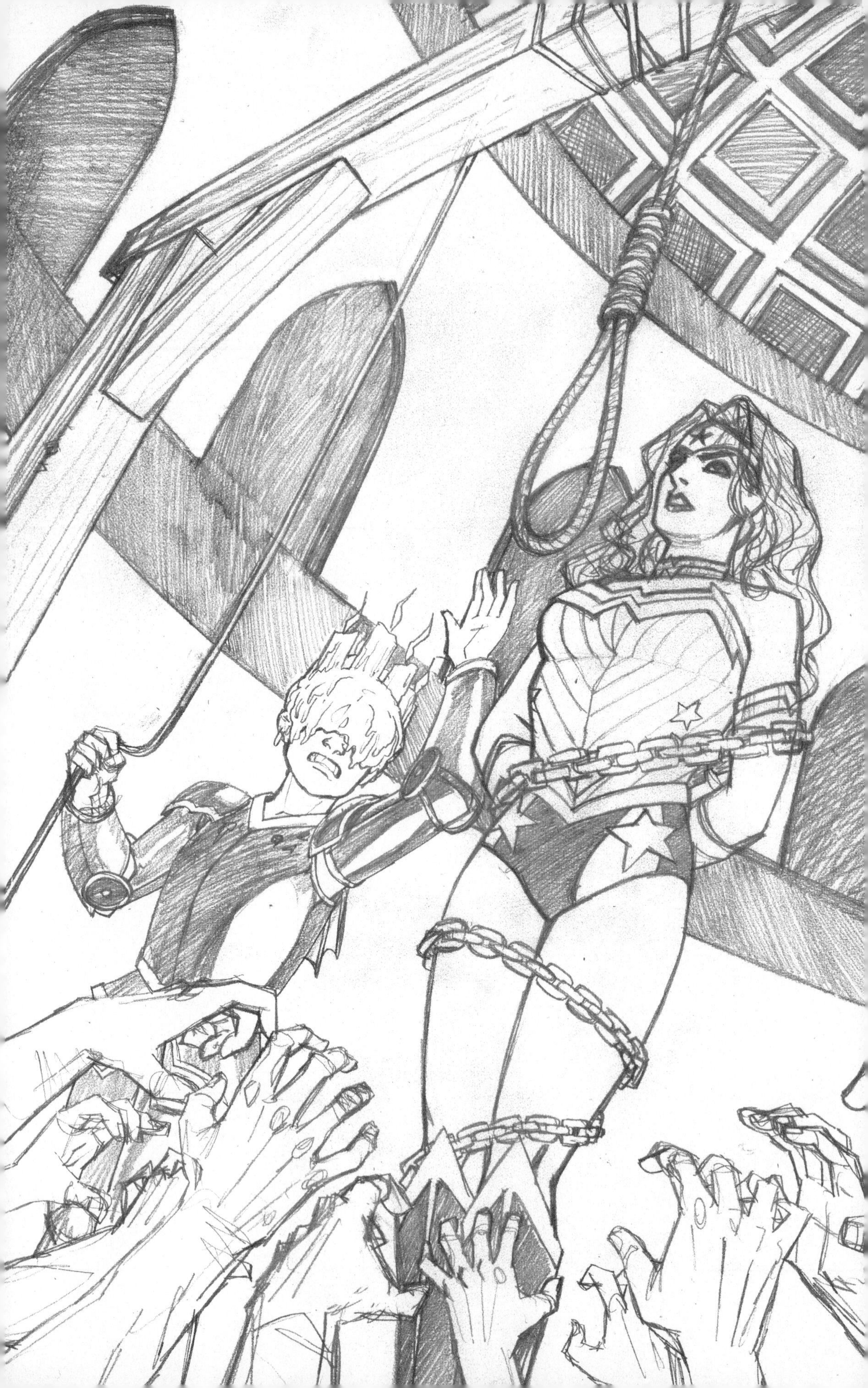

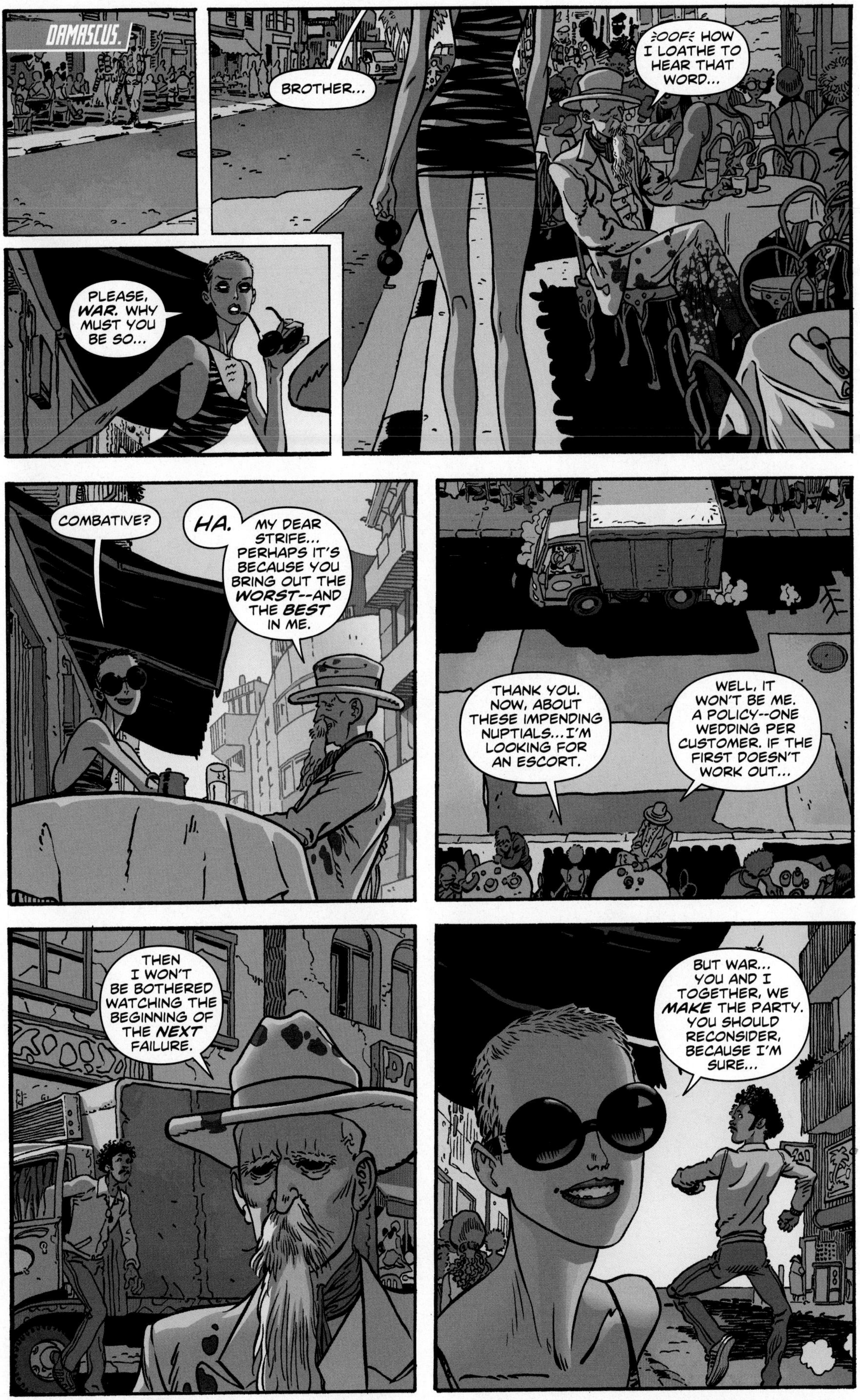
DAMASCUS.
BROTHER...
OOF. HOW I LOATHE TO HEAR THAT WORD...
PLEASE, WAR. WHY MUST YOU BE SO...
COMBATIVE?
HA.
MY DEAR STRIFE... PERHAPS IT'S BECAUSE YOU BRING OUT THE WORST--AND THE BEST IN ME.
THANK YOU. NOW, ABOUT THESE IMPENDING NUPTIALS... I'M LOOKING FOR AN ESCORT.
WELL, IT WON'T BE ME. A POLICY--ONE WEDDING PER CUSTOMER. IF THE FIRST DOESN'T WORK OUT...
THEN I WON'T BE BOTHERED WATCHING THE BEGINNING OF THE NEXT FAILURE.
BUT WAR... YOU AND I TOGETHER, WE MAKE THE PARTY. YOU SHOULD RECONSIDER, BECAUSE I'M SURE...

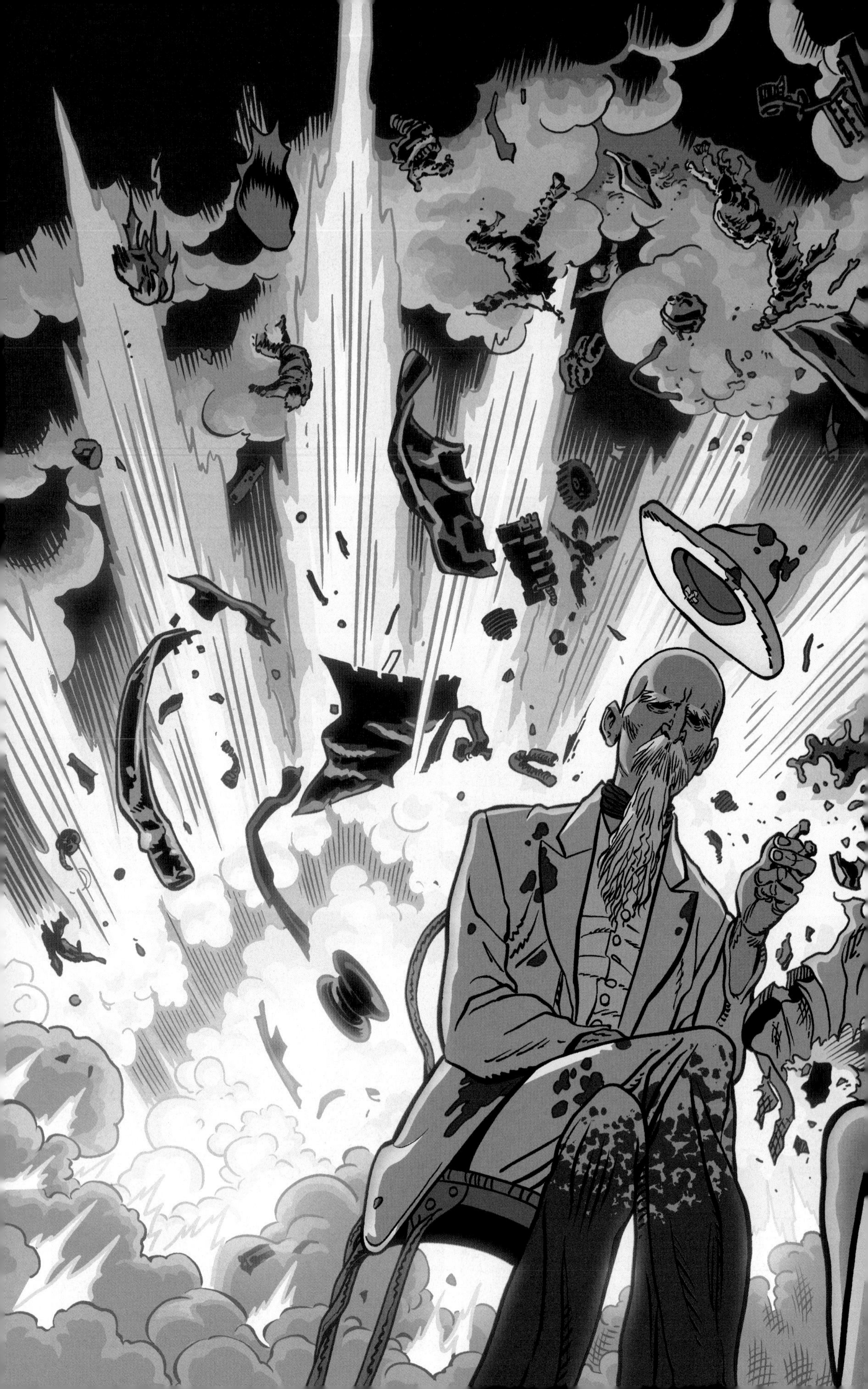

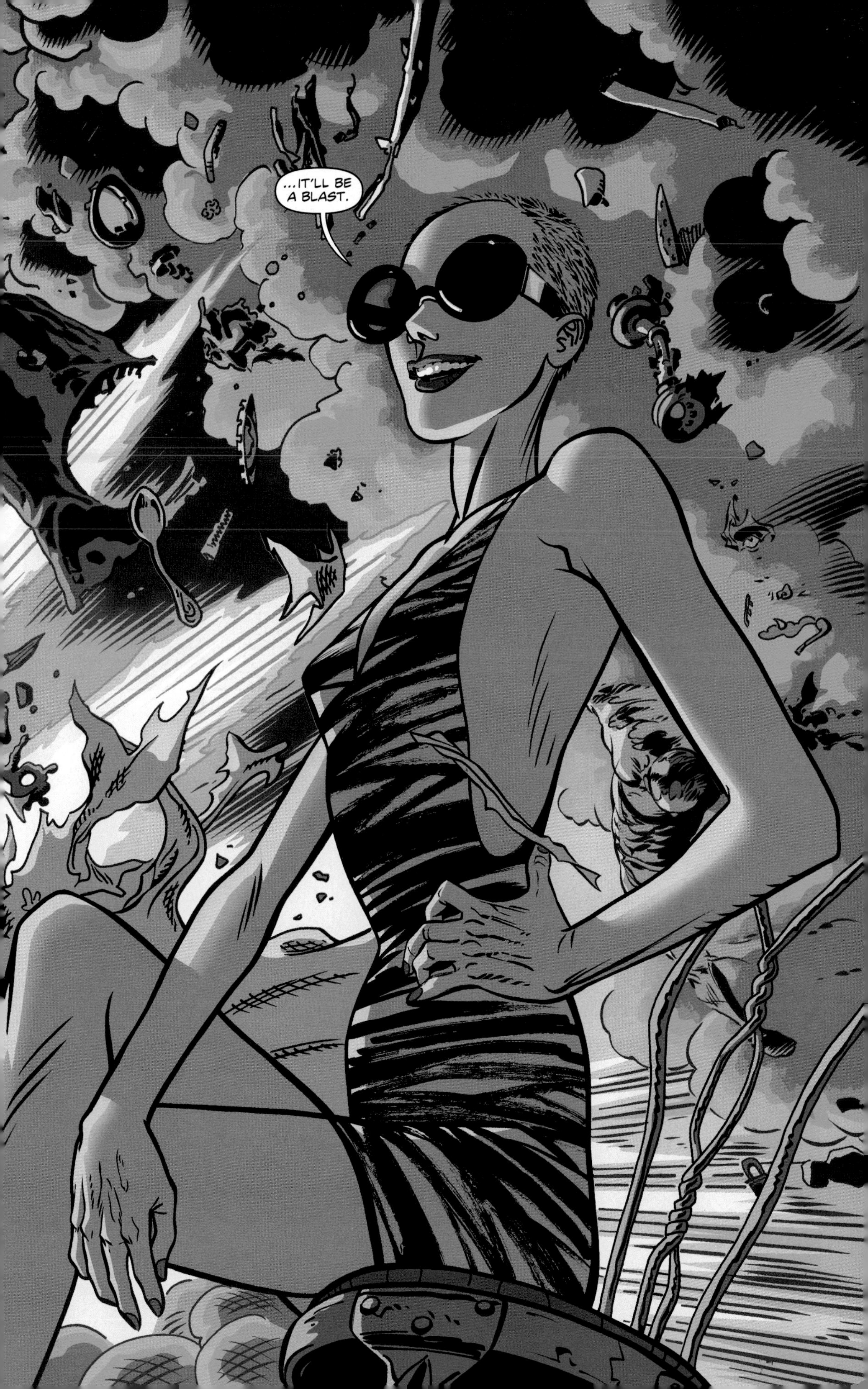
...IT'LL BE A BLAST.

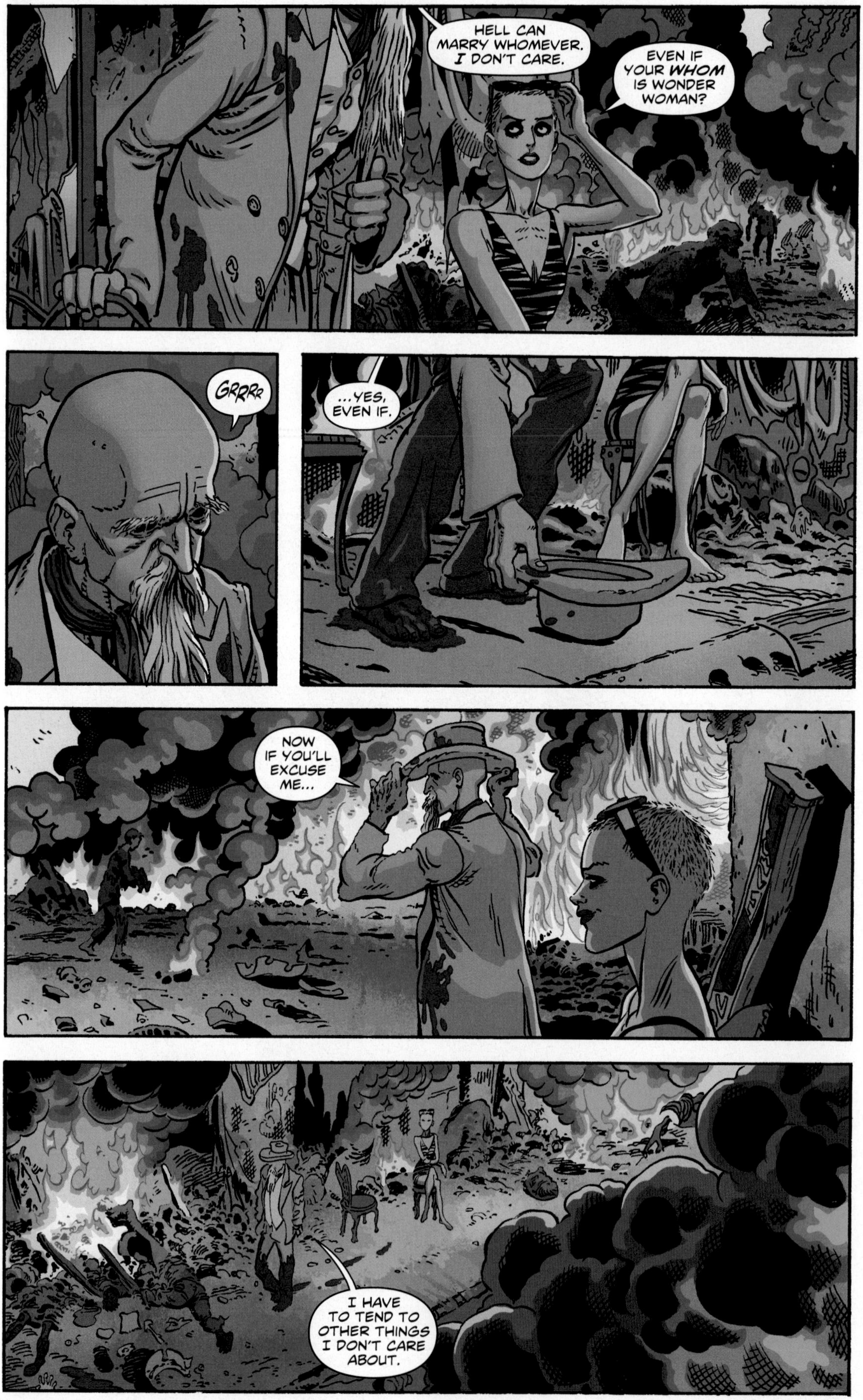
HELL CAN MARRY WHOMEVER. I DON'T CARE.
EVEN IF YOUR WHOM IS WONDER WOMAN?
GRRRR
...YES, EVEN IF.
NOW IF YOU'LL EXCUSE ME...
I HAVE TO TEND TO OTHER THINGS I DON'T CARE ABOUT.

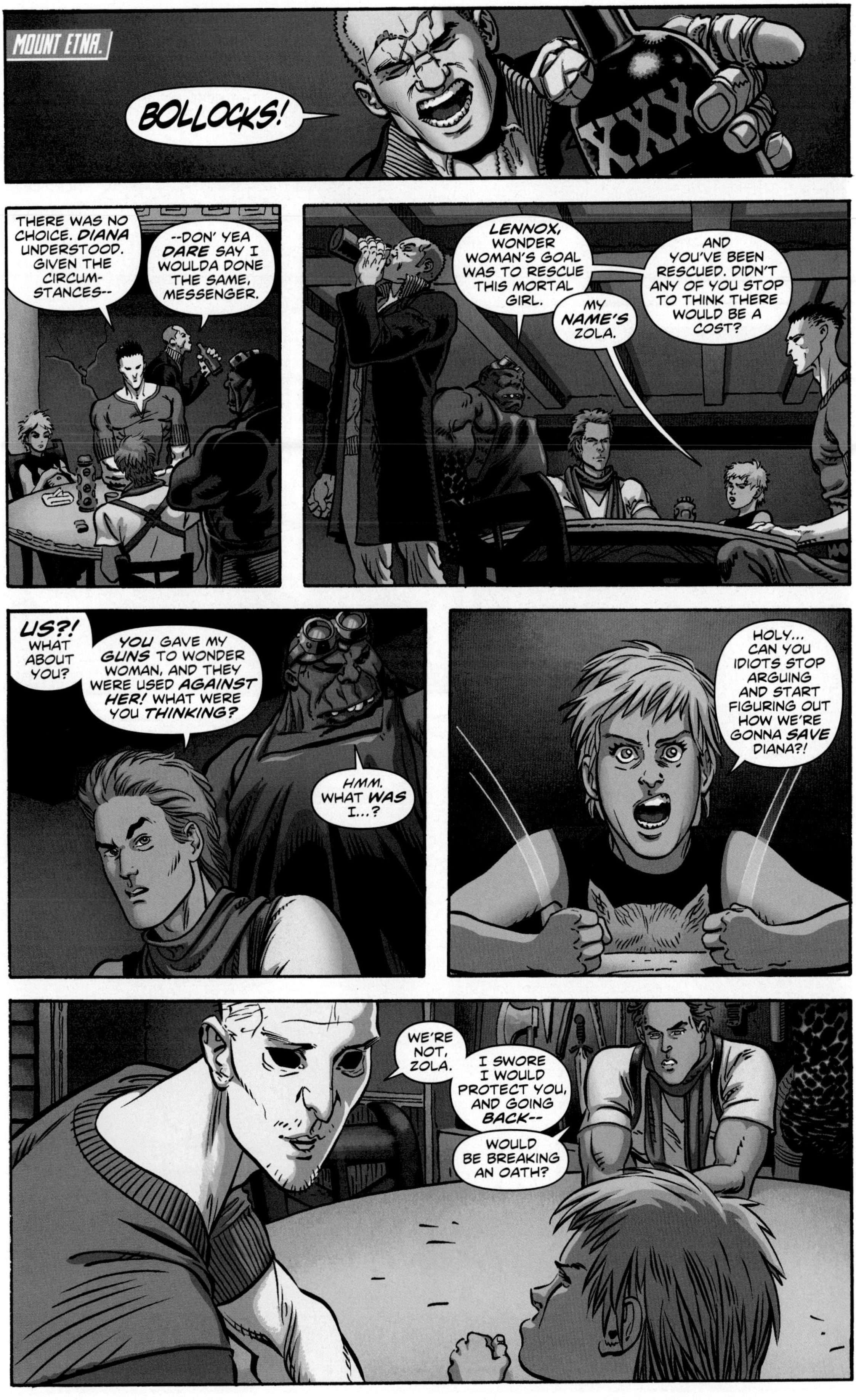
MOUNT ETNA.
BOLLOCKS!
THERE WAS NO CHOICE. DIANA UNDERSTOOD. GIVEN THE CIRCUM-STANCES--
--DON' YEA DARE SAY I WOULDA DONE THE SAME, MESSENGER.
LENNOX, WONDER WOMAN'S GOAL WAS TO RESCUE THIS MORTAL GIRL.
MY NAME'S ZOLA.
AND YOU'VE BEEN RESCUED. DIDN'T ANY OF YOU STOP TO THINK THERE WOULD BE A COST?
US?! WHAT ABOUT YOU?
YOU GAVE MY GUNS TO WONDER WOMAN, AND THEY WERE USED AGAINST HER! WHAT WERE YOU THINKING?
HMM. WHAT WAS I...?
HOLY... CAN YOU IDIOTS STOP ARGUING AND START FIGURING OUT HOW WE'RE GONNA SAVE DIANA?!
WE'RE NOT, ZOLA.
I SWORE I WOULD PROTECT YOU, AND GOING BACK--
WOULD BE BREAKING AN OATH?

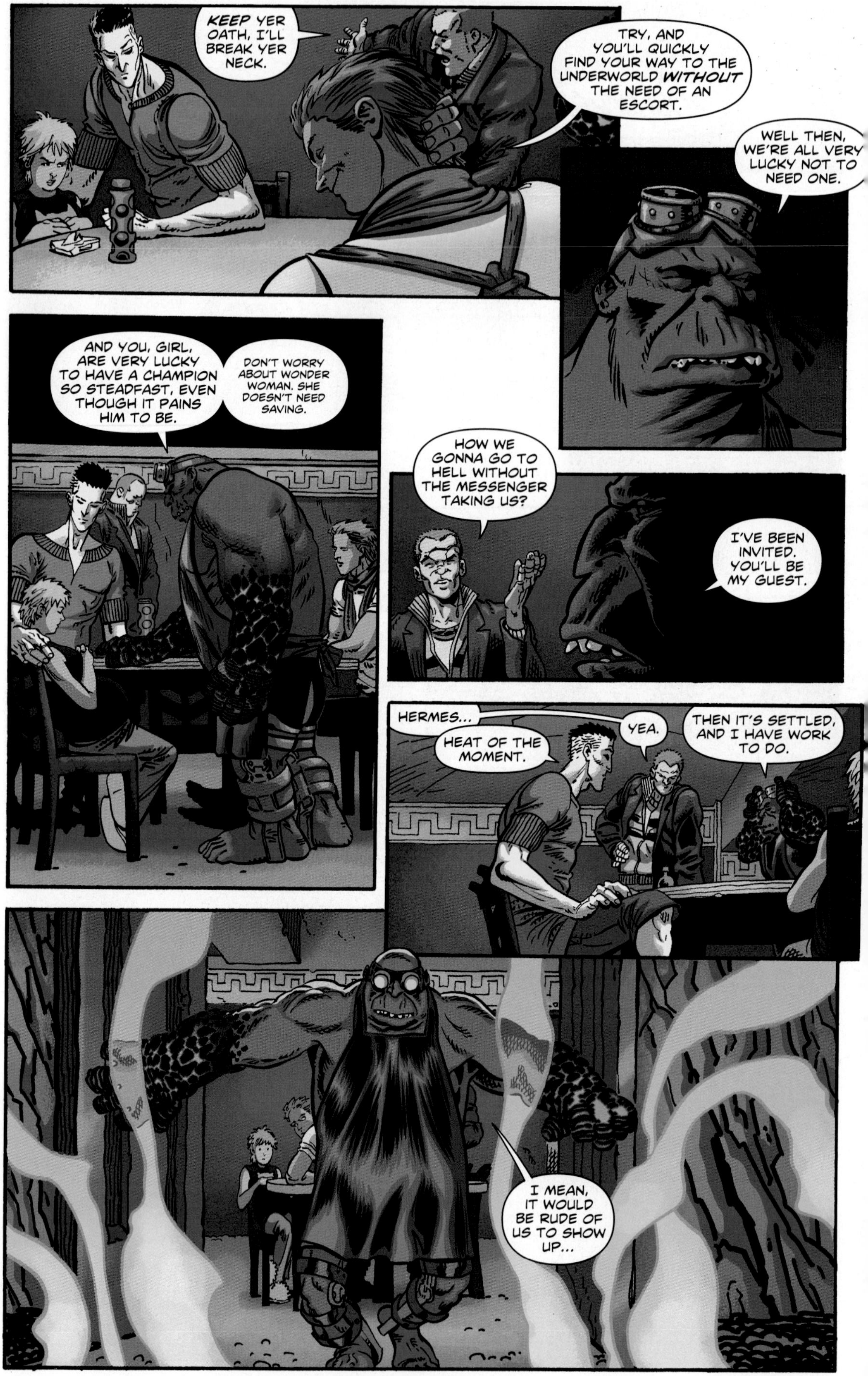
KEEP YER OATH, I'LL BREAK YER NECK.
TRY, AND YOU'LL QUICKLY FIND YOUR WAY TO THE UNDERWORLD WITHOUT THE NEED OF AN ESCORT.
WELL THEN, WE'RE ALL VERY LUCKY NOT TO NEED ONE.
AND YOU, GIRL, ARE VERY LUCKY TO HAVE A CHAMPION SO STEADFAST, EVEN THOUGH IT PAINS HIM TO BE.
DON'T WORRY ABOUT WONDER WOMAN. SHE DOESN'T NEED SAVING.
HOW WE GONNA GO TO HELL WITHOUT THE MESSENGER TAKING US?
I'VE BEEN INVITED. YOU'LL BE MY GUEST.
HERMES...
HEAT OF THE MOMENT.
YEA.
THEN IT'S SETTLED, AND I HAVE WORK TO DO.
I MEAN, IT WOULD BE RUDE OF US TO SHOW UP...

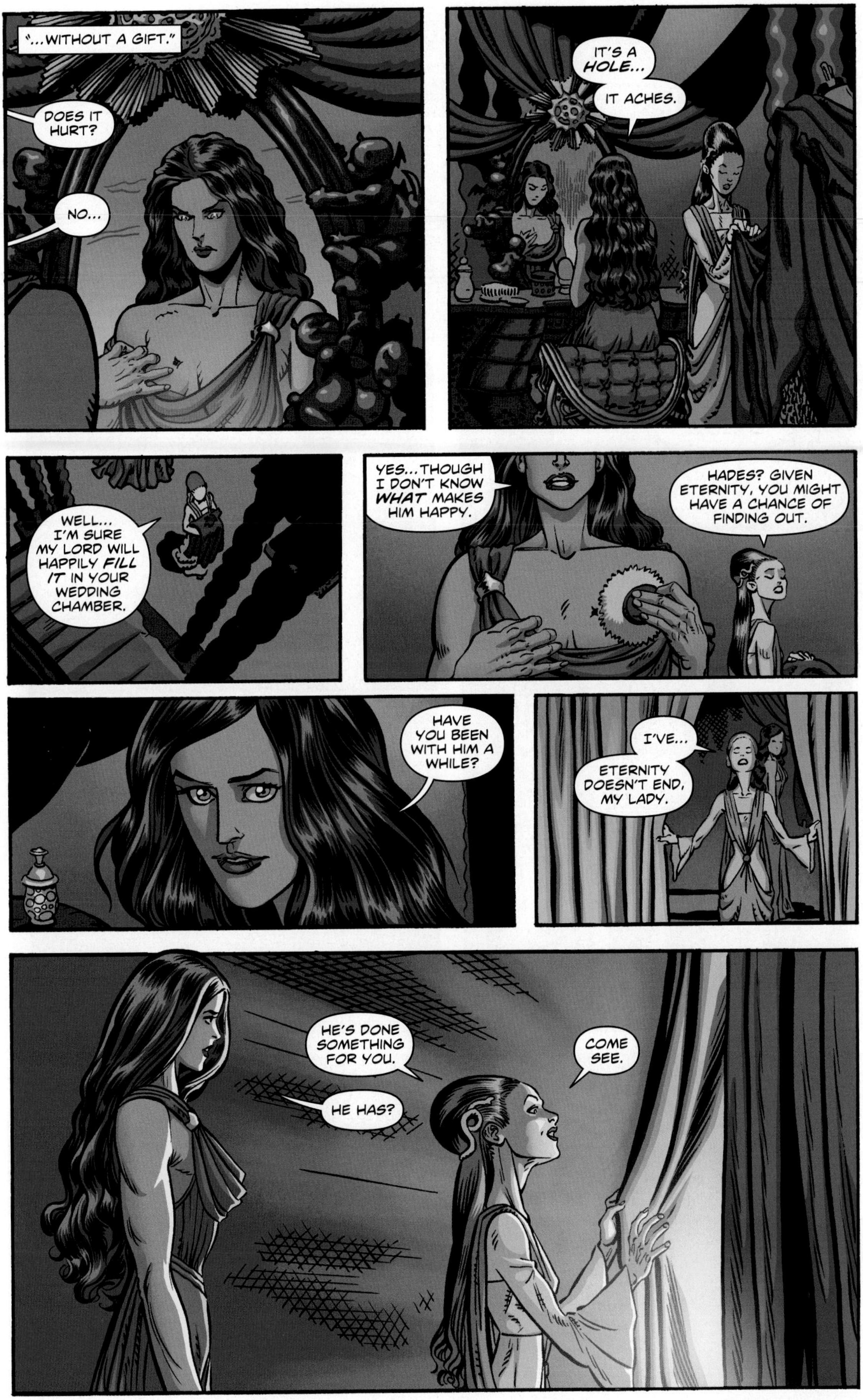
"...WITHOUT A GIFT."
DOES IT HURT?
NO...
IT'S A *HOLE*...
IT ACHES.
WELL... I'M SURE MY LORD WILL HAPPILY *FILL IT* IN YOUR WEDDING CHAMBER.
YES...THOUGH I DON'T KNOW *WHAT* MAKES HIM HAPPY.
HADES? GIVEN ETERNITY, YOU MIGHT HAVE A CHANCE OF FINDING OUT.
HAVE YOU BEEN WITH HIM A WHILE?
I'VE...
ETERNITY DOESN'T END, MY LADY.
HE'S DONE SOMETHING FOR YOU.
HE HAS?
COME SEE.

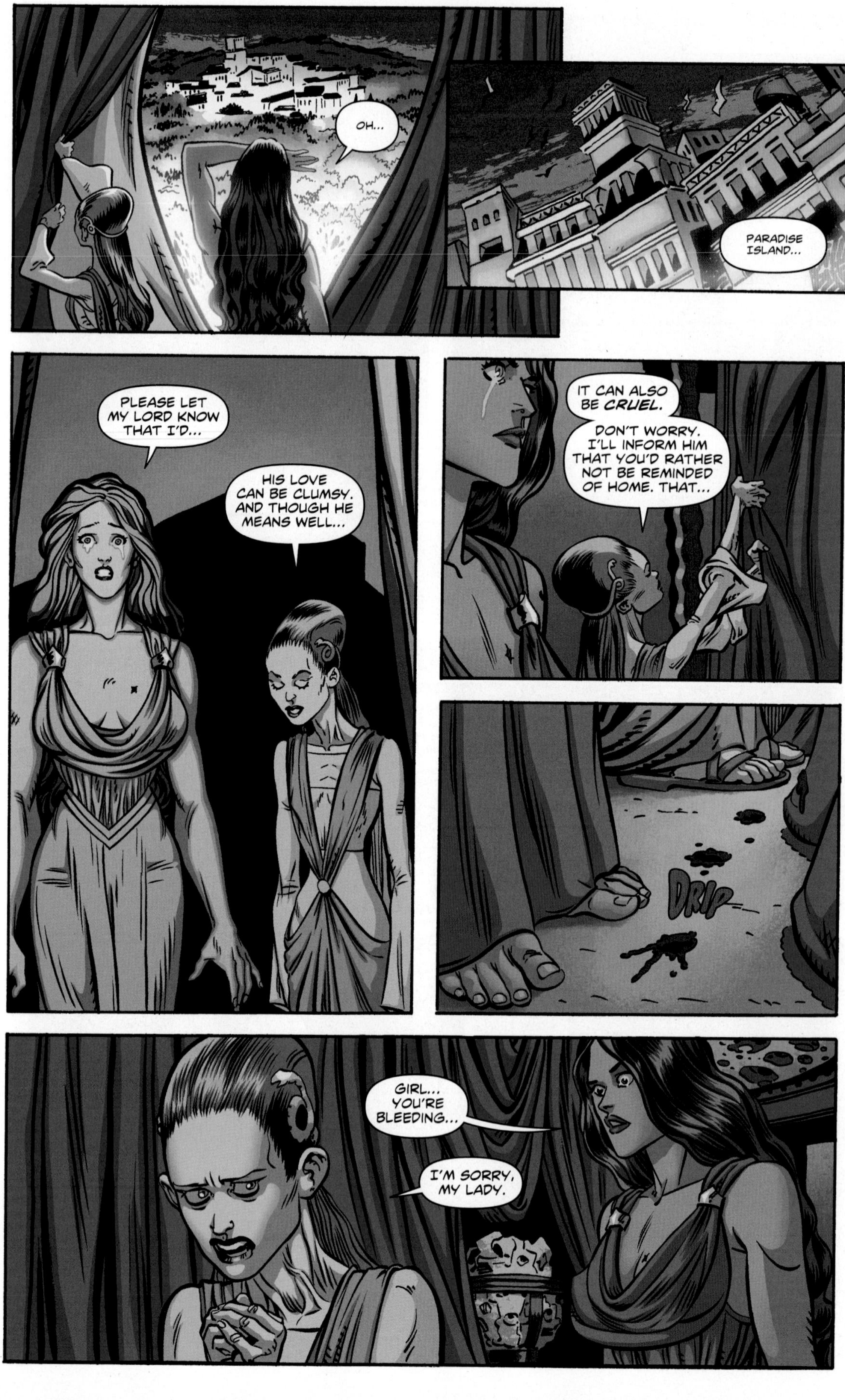
OH...
PARADISE ISLAND...
PLEASE LET MY LORD KNOW THAT I'D...
HIS LOVE CAN BE CLUMSY. AND THOUGH HE MEANS WELL...
IT CAN ALSO BE ***CRUEL.***
DON'T WORRY. I'LL INFORM HIM THAT YOU'D RATHER NOT BE REMINDED OF HOME. THAT...
DRIP
GIRL... YOU'RE BLEEDING...
I'M SORRY, MY LADY.

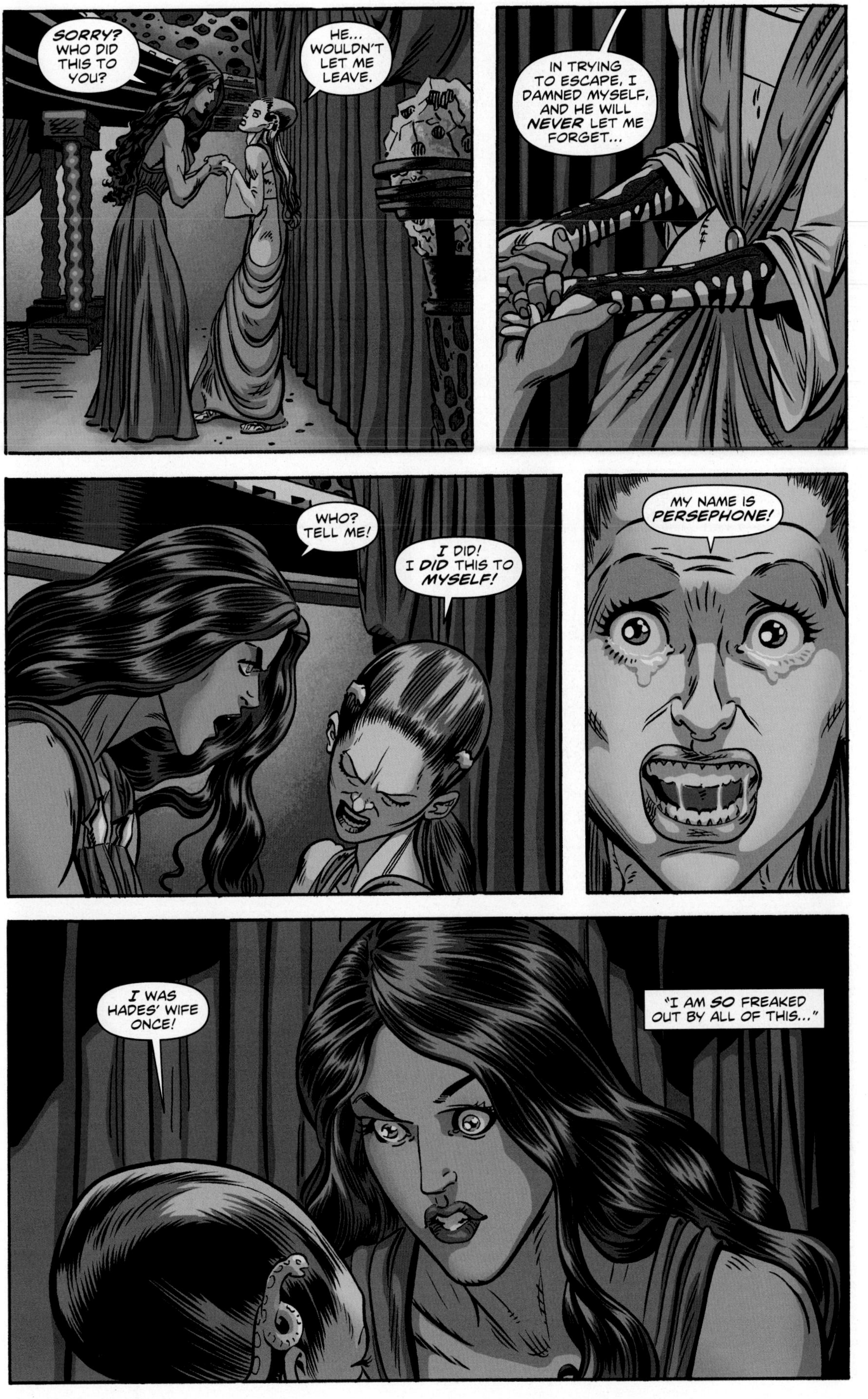
SORRY? WHO DID THIS TO YOU?
HE... WOULDN'T LET ME LEAVE.
IN TRYING TO ESCAPE, I DAMNED MYSELF, AND HE WILL NEVER LET ME FORGET...
WHO? TELL ME!
I DID! I DID THIS TO MYSELF!
MY NAME IS PERSEPHONE!
I WAS HADES' WIFE ONCE!
"I AM SO FREAKED OUT BY ALL OF THIS..."

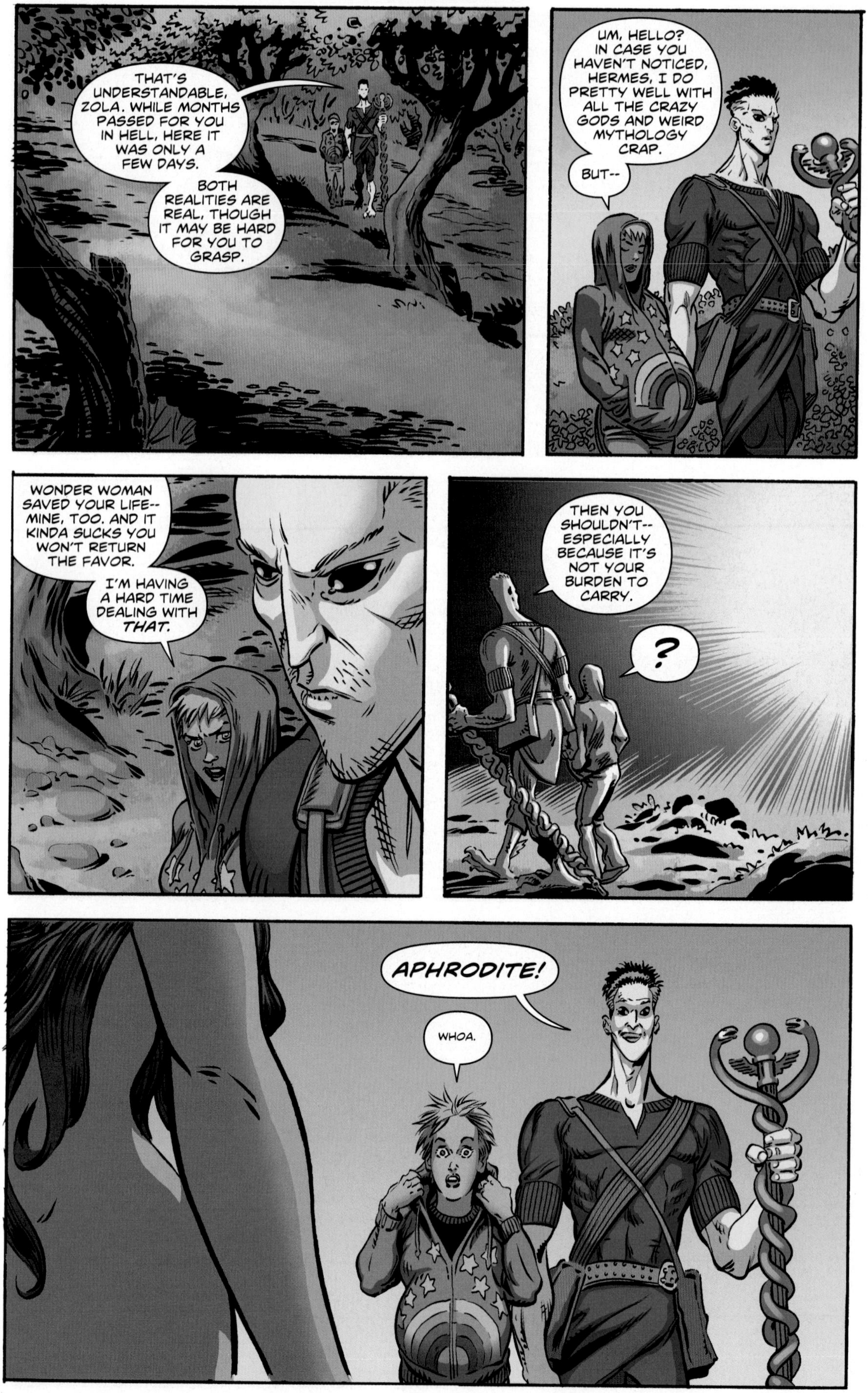
THAT'S UNDERSTANDABLE, ZOLA. WHILE MONTHS PASSED FOR YOU IN HELL, HERE IT WAS ONLY A FEW DAYS.
BOTH REALITIES ARE REAL, THOUGH IT MAY BE HARD FOR YOU TO GRASP.
UM, HELLO? IN CASE YOU HAVEN'T NOTICED, HERMES, I DO PRETTY WELL WITH ALL THE CRAZY GODS AND WEIRD MYTHOLOGY CRAP.
BUT--
WONDER WOMAN SAVED YOUR LIFE-- MINE, TOO. AND IT KINDA SUCKS YOU WON'T RETURN THE FAVOR.
I'M HAVING A HARD TIME DEALING WITH *THAT.*
THEN YOU SHOULDN'T-- ESPECIALLY BECAUSE IT'S NOT YOUR BURDEN TO CARRY.
?
APHRODITE!
WHOA.

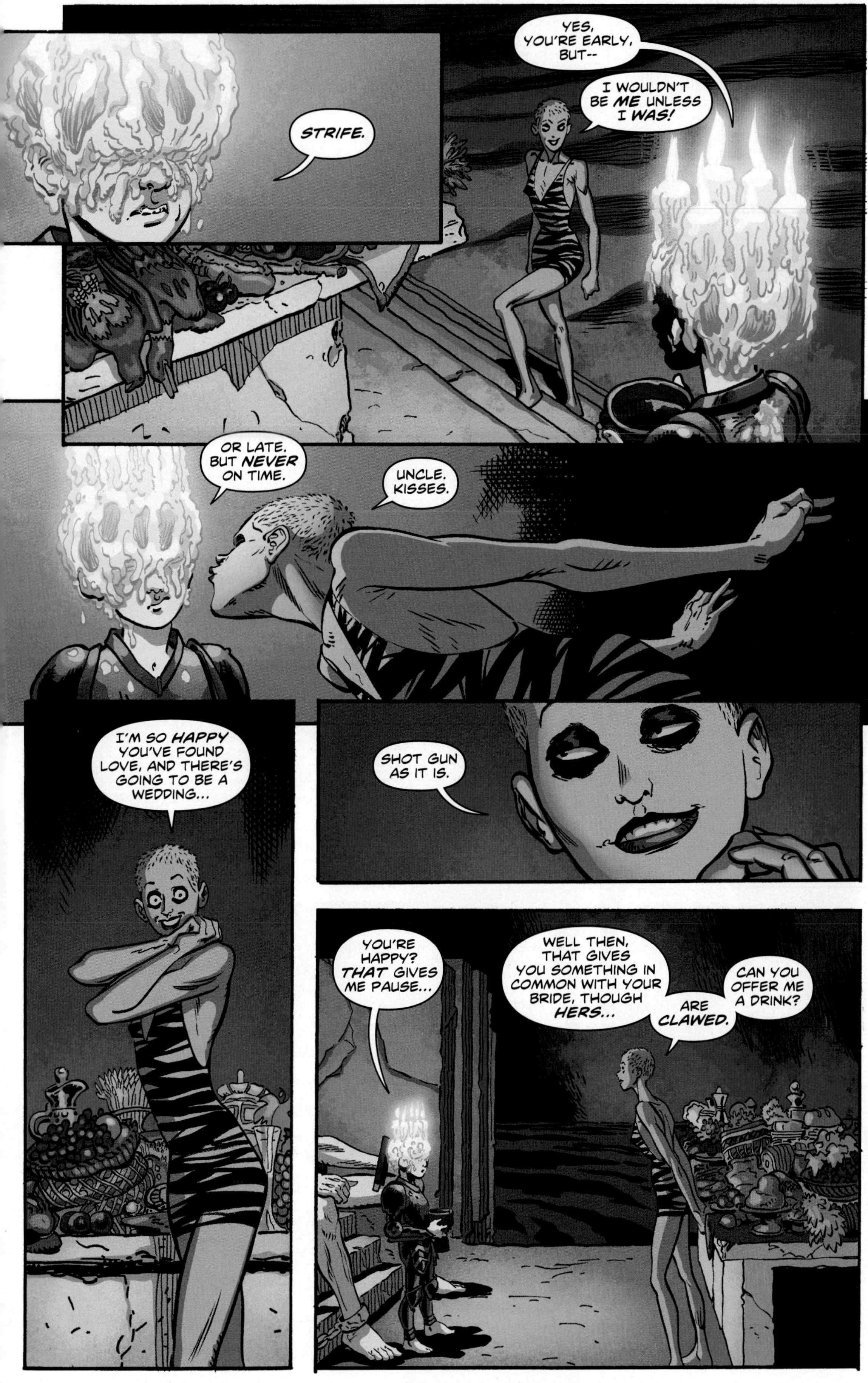
STRIFE.
YES, YOU'RE EARLY, BUT--
I WOULDN'T BE ME UNLESS I WAS!
OR LATE. BUT NEVER ON TIME.
UNCLE. KISSES.
I'M SO HAPPY YOU'VE FOUND LOVE, AND THERE'S GOING TO BE A WEDDING...
SHOT GUN AS IT IS.
YOU'RE HAPPY? THAT GIVES ME PAUSE...
WELL THEN, THAT GIVES YOU SOMETHING IN COMMON WITH YOUR BRIDE, THOUGH HERS...
ARE CLAWED.
CAN YOU OFFER ME A DRINK?

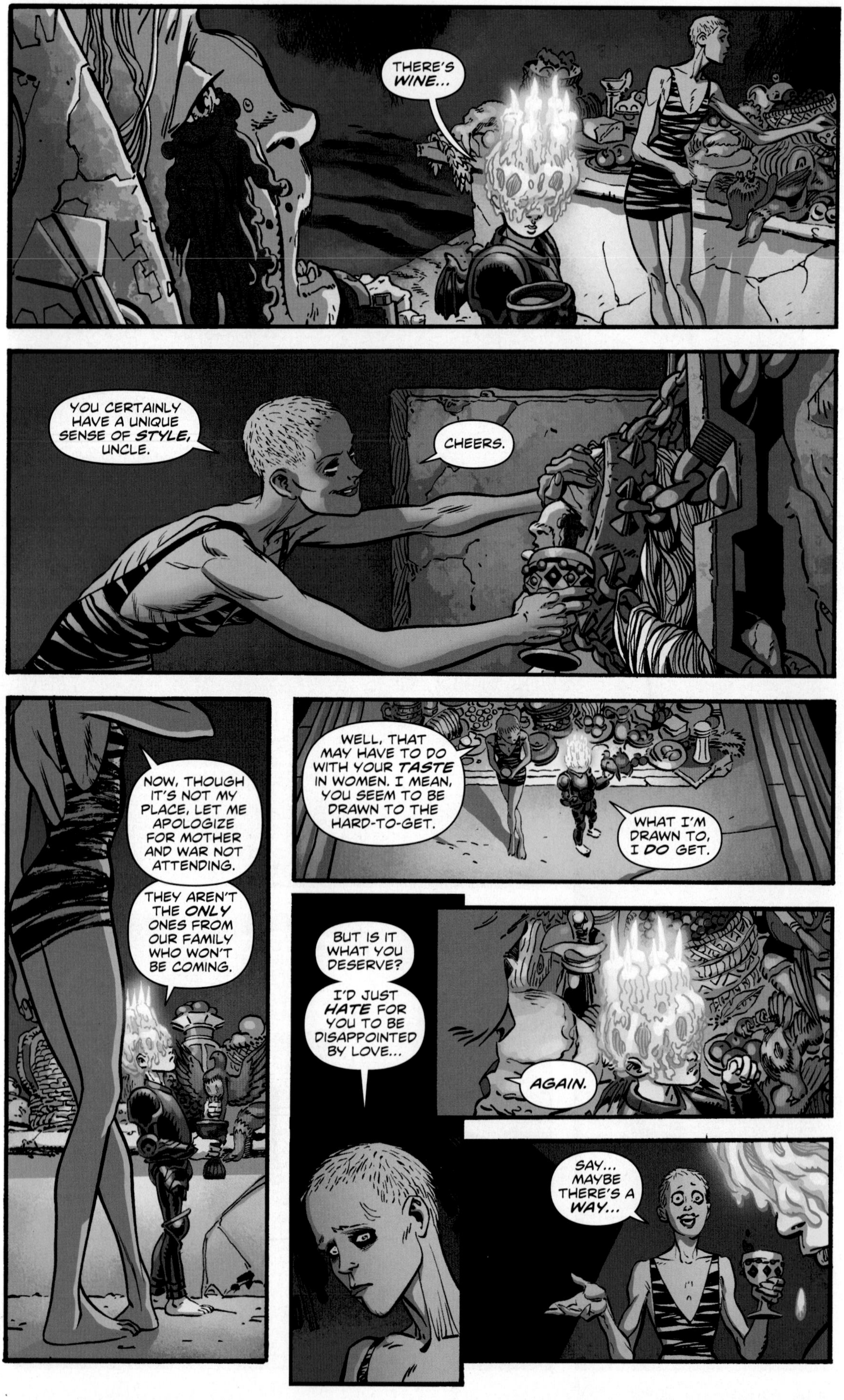
THERE'S *WINE...*
YOU CERTAINLY HAVE A UNIQUE SENSE OF *STYLE,* UNCLE.
CHEERS.
NOW, THOUGH IT'S NOT MY PLACE, LET ME APOLOGIZE FOR MOTHER AND WAR NOT ATTENDING.
THEY AREN'T THE *ONLY* ONES FROM OUR FAMILY WHO WON'T BE COMING.
WELL, THAT MAY HAVE TO DO WITH YOUR *TASTE* IN WOMEN. I MEAN, YOU SEEM TO BE DRAWN TO THE HARD-TO-GET.
WHAT I'M DRAWN TO, I *DO* GET.
BUT IS IT WHAT YOU DESERVE?
I'D JUST *HATE* FOR YOU TO BE DISAPPOINTED BY LOVE...
AGAIN.
SAY... MAYBE THERE'S A *WAY...*

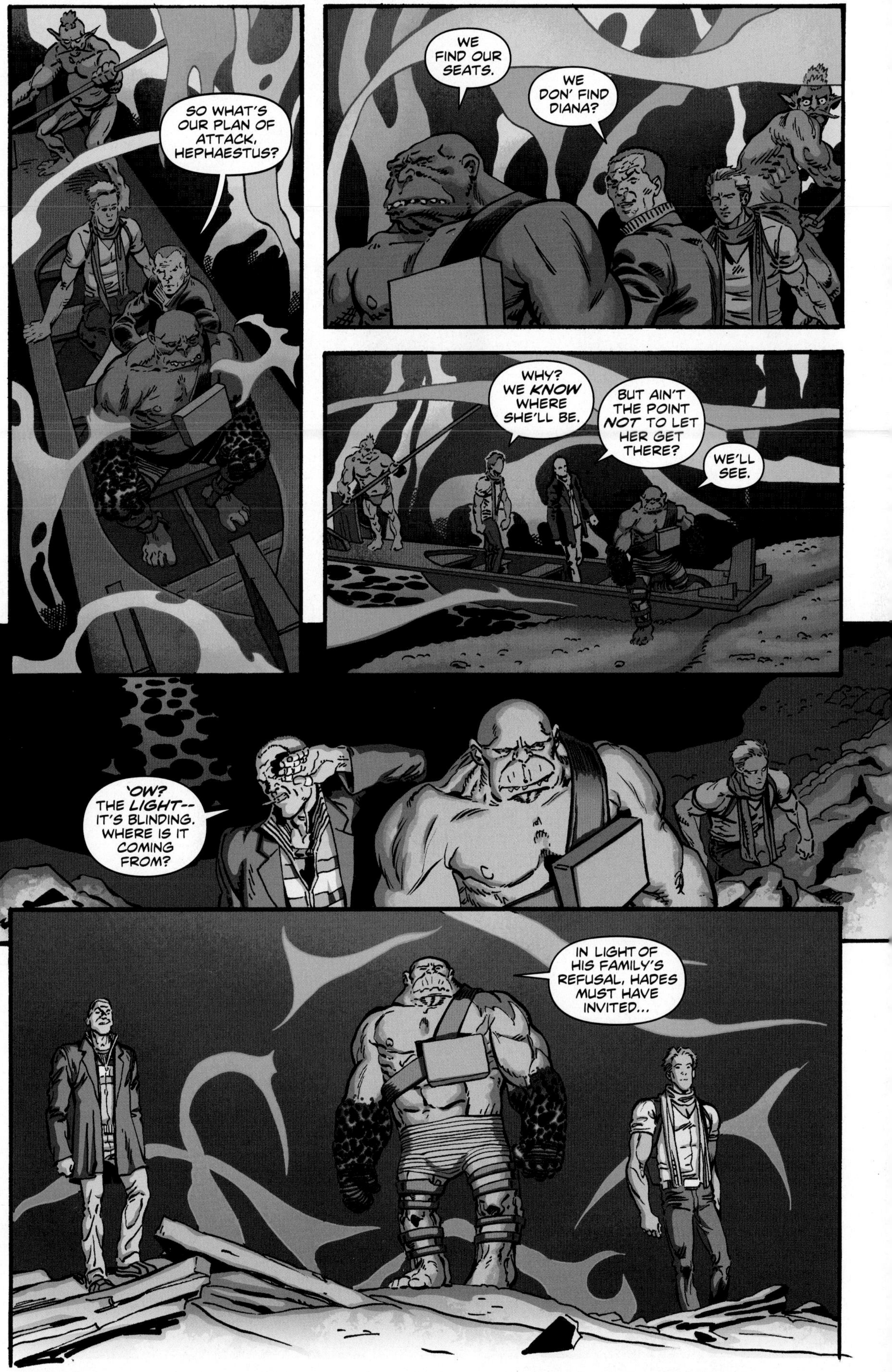
SO WHAT'S OUR PLAN OF ATTACK, HEPHAESTUS?
WE FIND OUR SEATS.
WE DON' FIND DIANA?
WHY? WE *KNOW* WHERE SHE'LL BE.
BUT AIN'T THE POINT *NOT* TO LET HER GET THERE?
WE'LL SEE.
'OW? THE *LIGHT*-- IT'S BLINDING. WHERE IS IT COMING FROM?
IN LIGHT OF HIS FAMILY'S REFUSAL, HADES MUST HAVE INVITED...

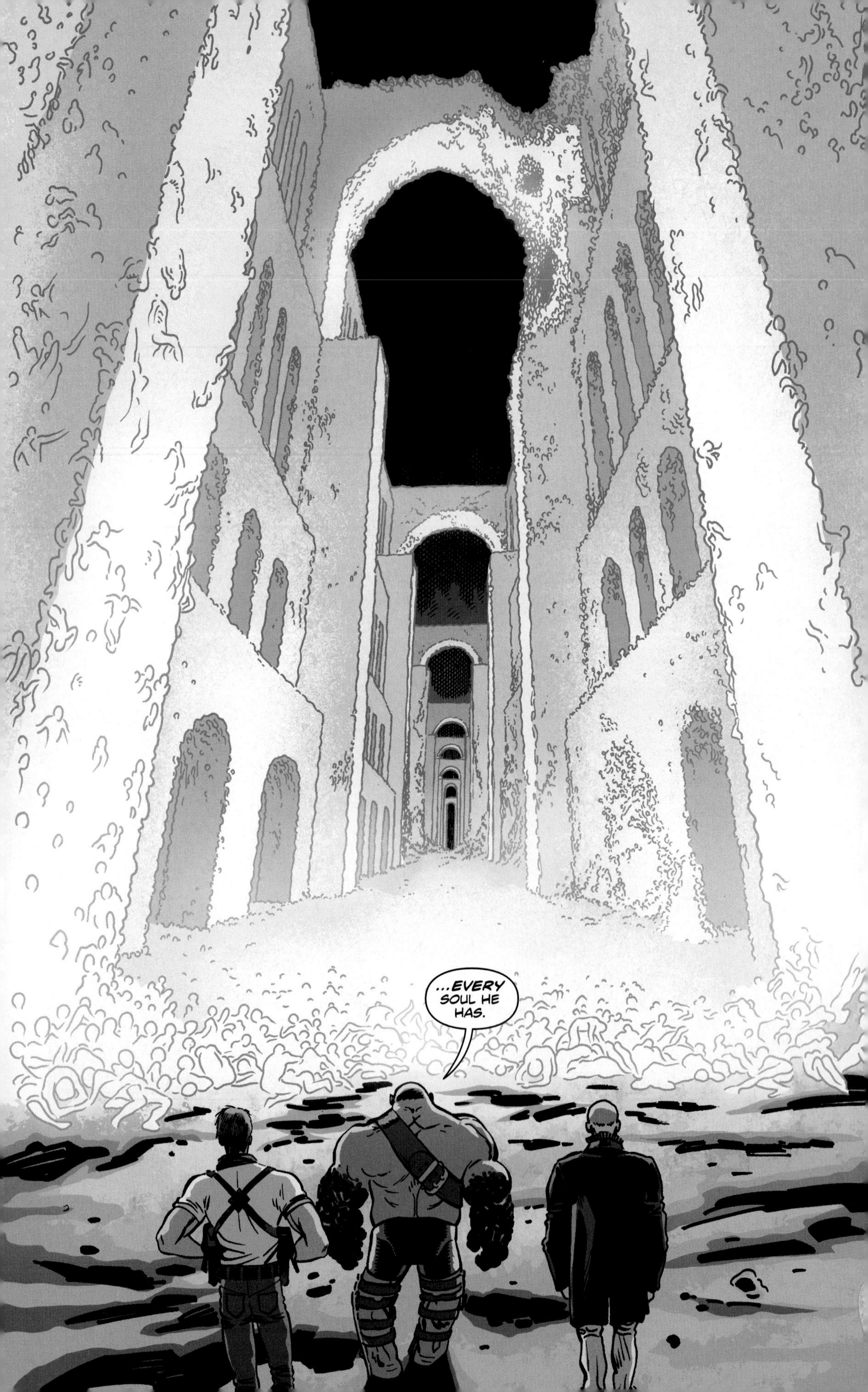
...EVERY SOUL HE HAS.

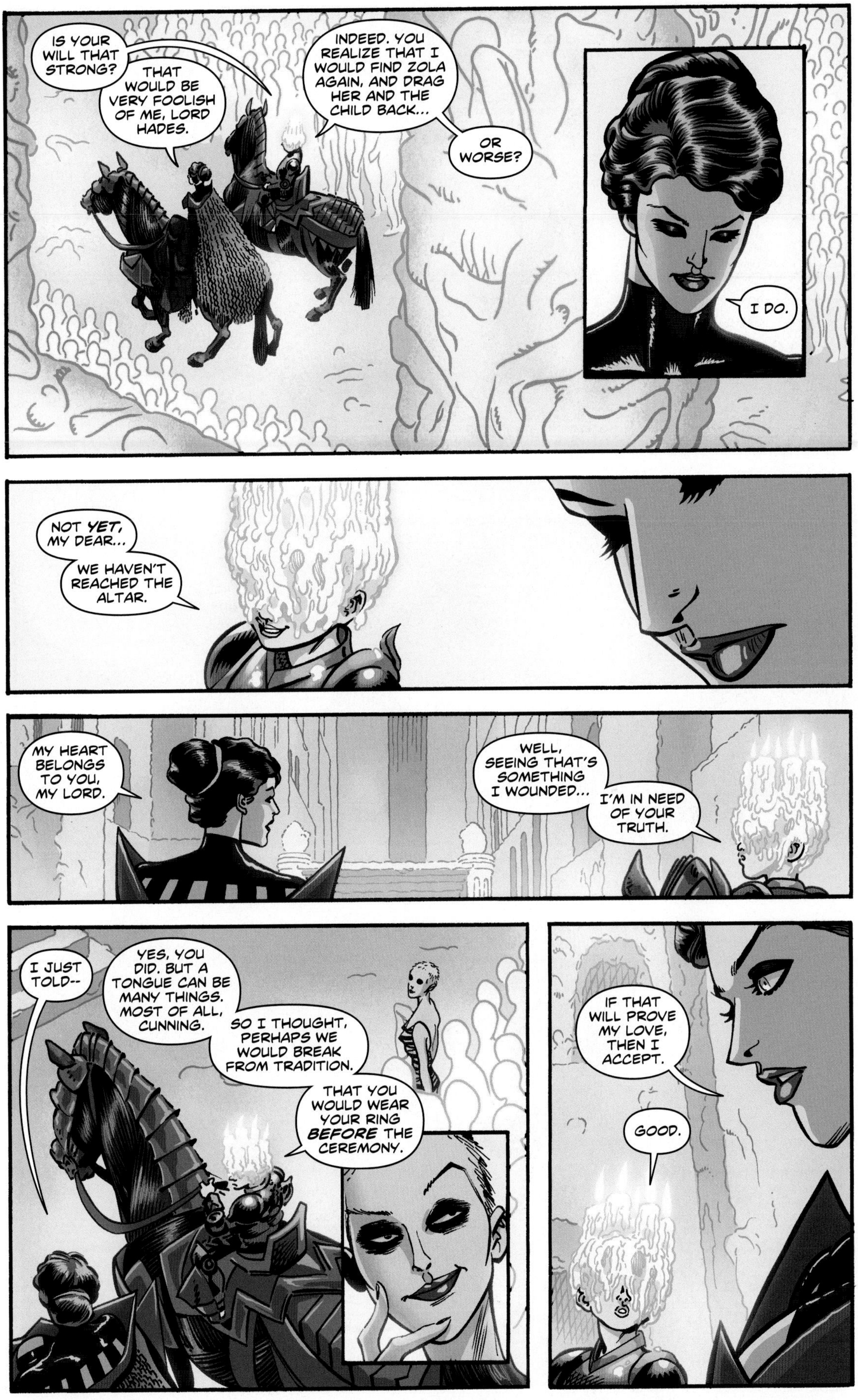
IS YOUR WILL THAT STRONG?
THAT WOULD BE VERY FOOLISH OF ME, LORD HADES.
INDEED. YOU REALIZE THAT I WOULD FIND ZOLA AGAIN, AND DRAG HER AND THE CHILD BACK...
OR WORSE?
I DO.
NOT YET, MY DEAR...
WE HAVEN'T REACHED THE ALTAR.
MY HEART BELONGS TO YOU, MY LORD.
WELL, SEEING THAT'S SOMETHING I WOUNDED...
I'M IN NEED OF YOUR TRUTH.
I JUST TOLD--
YES, YOU DID. BUT A TONGUE CAN BE MANY THINGS. MOST OF ALL, CUNNING.
SO I THOUGHT, PERHAPS WE WOULD BREAK FROM TRADITION.
THAT YOU WOULD WEAR YOUR RING BEFORE THE CEREMONY.
IF THAT WILL PROVE MY LOVE, THEN I ACCEPT.
GOOD.

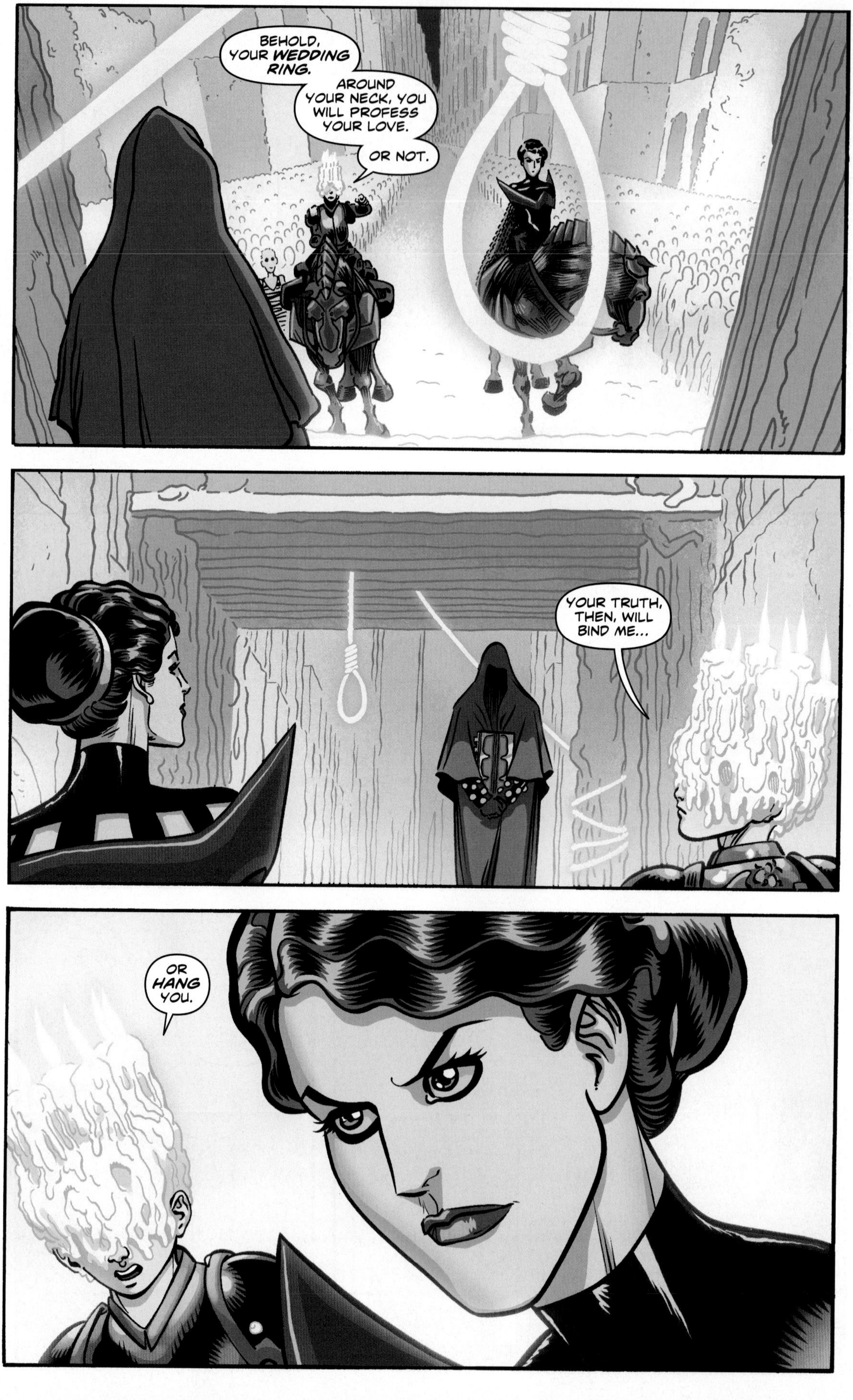
BEHOLD, YOUR WEDDING RING.
AROUND YOUR NECK, YOU WILL PROFESS YOUR LOVE.
OR NOT.
YOUR TRUTH, THEN, WILL BIND ME...
OR HANG YOU.

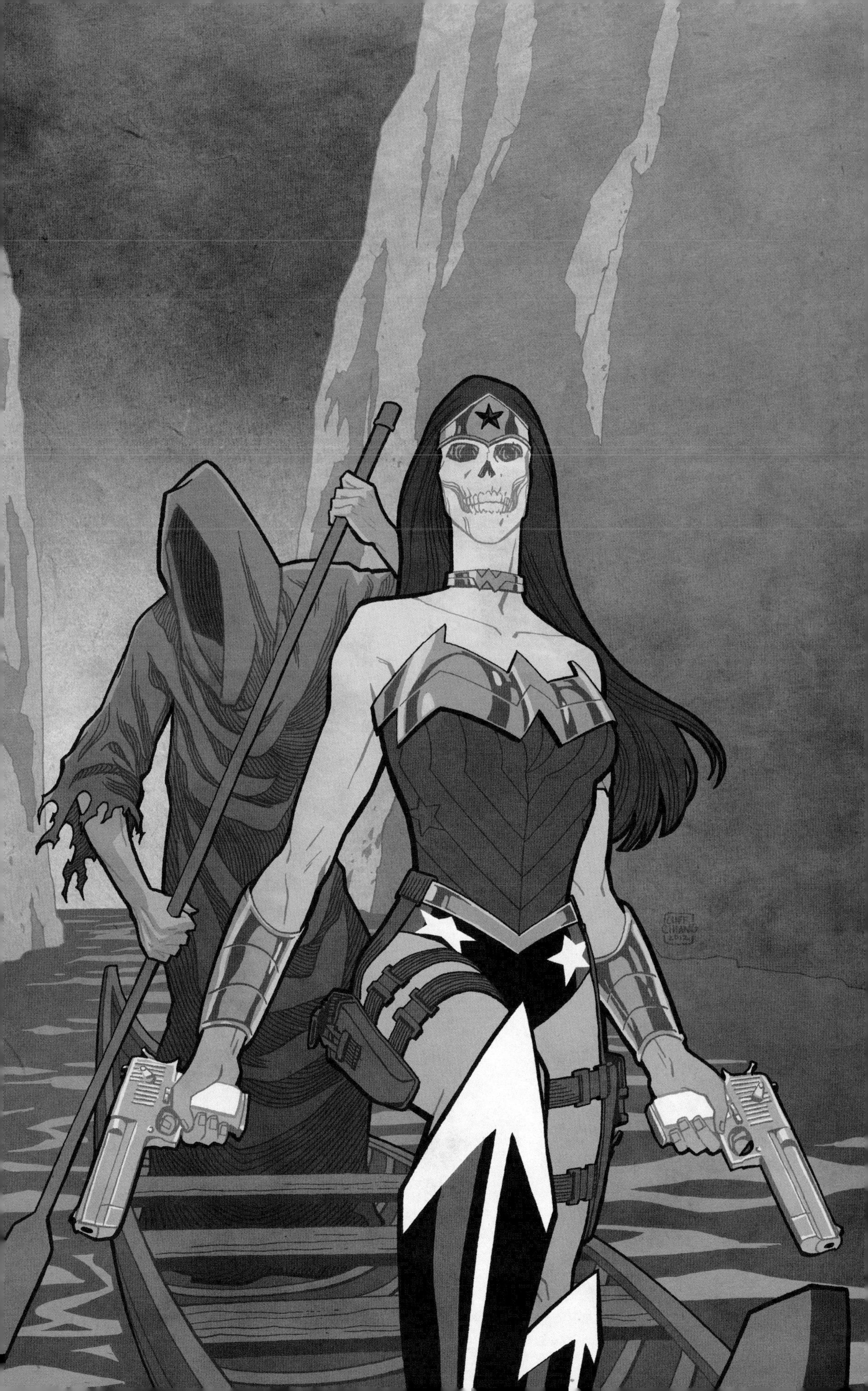

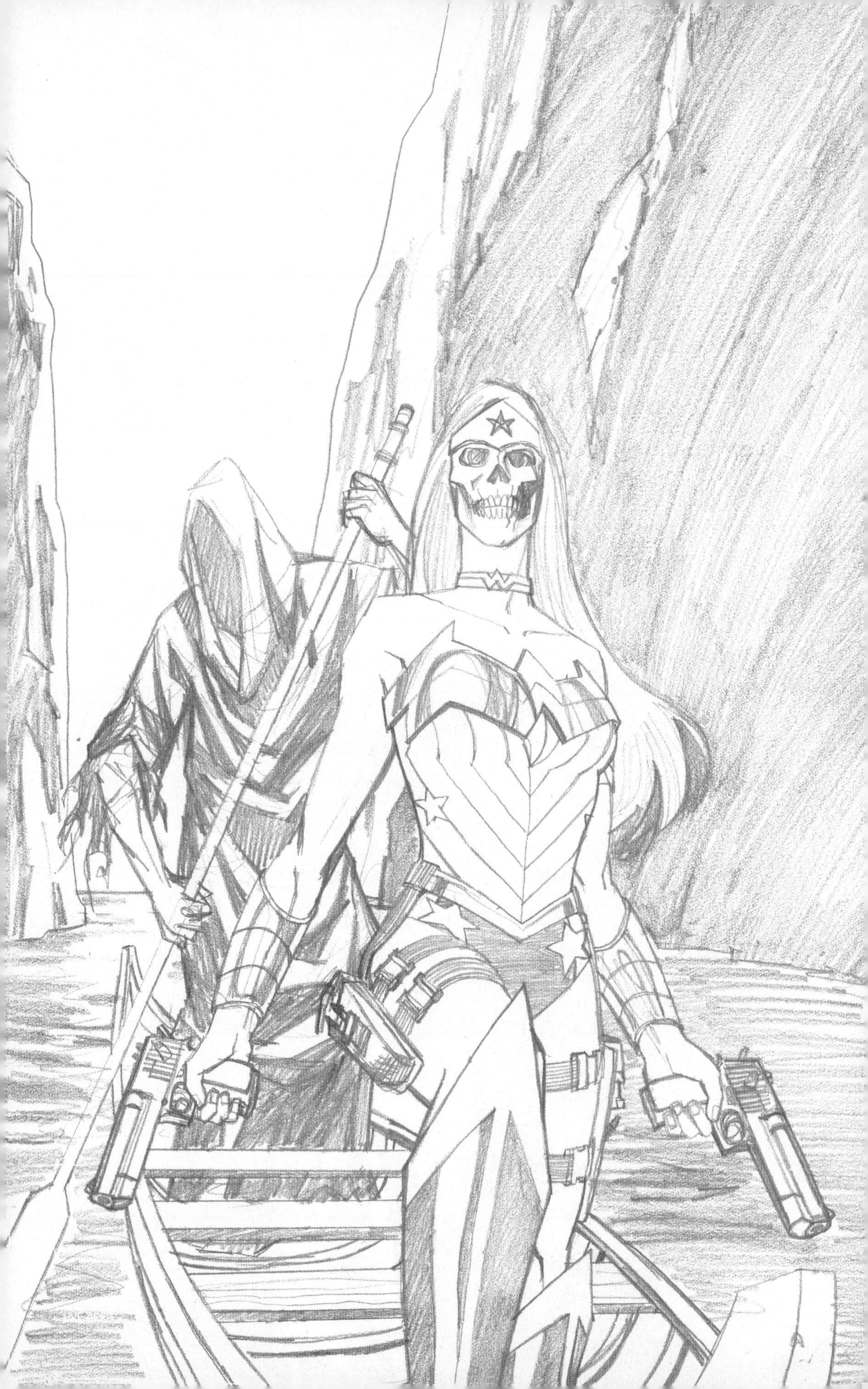

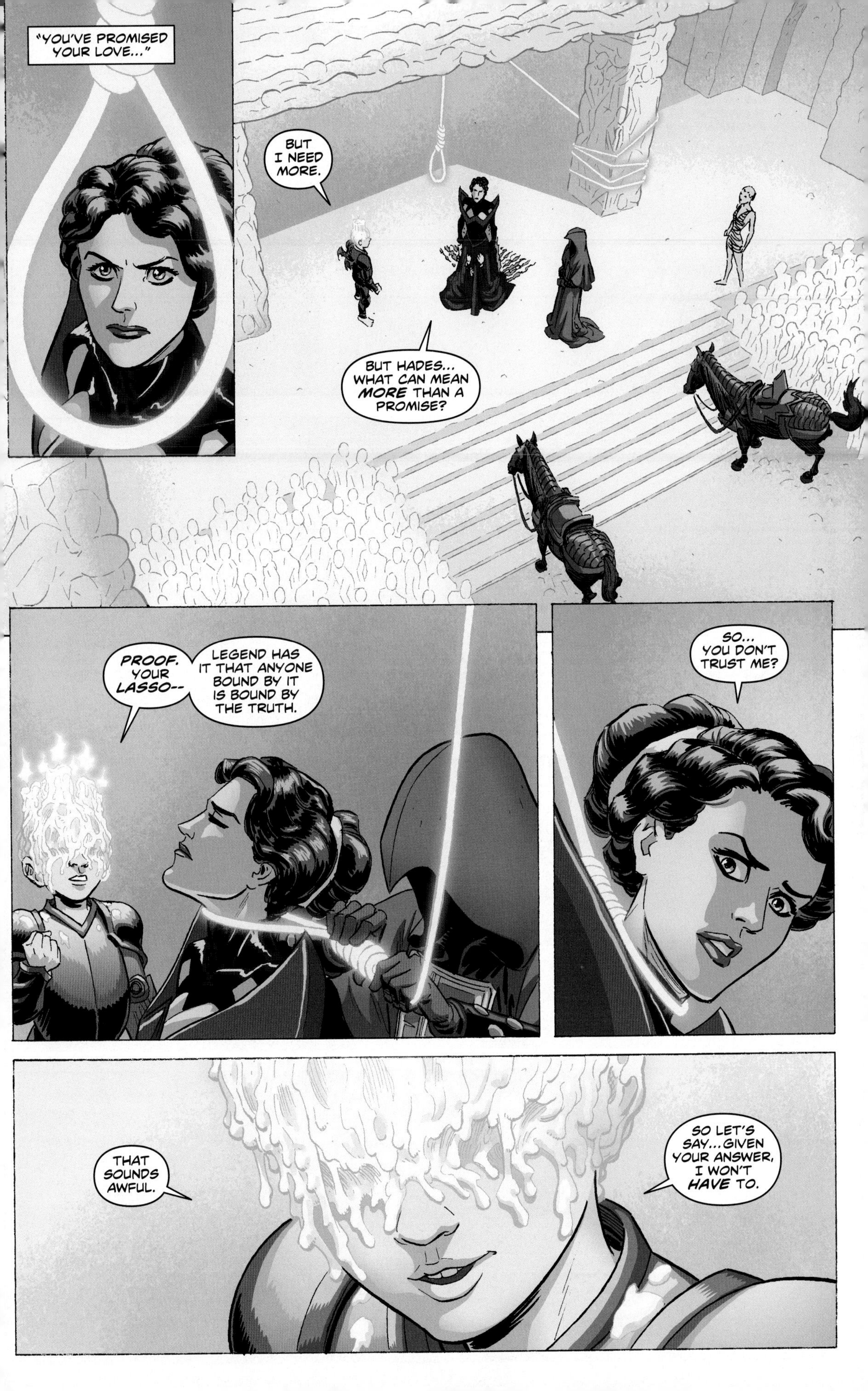
"YOU'VE PROMISED YOUR LOVE..."
BUT I NEED MORE.
BUT HADES... WHAT CAN MEAN MORE THAN A PROMISE?
PROOF. YOUR LASSO--
LEGEND HAS IT THAT ANYONE BOUND BY IT IS BOUND BY THE TRUTH.
SO... YOU DON'T TRUST ME?
THAT SOUNDS AWFUL.
SO LET'S SAY...GIVEN YOUR ANSWER, I WON'T HAVE TO.

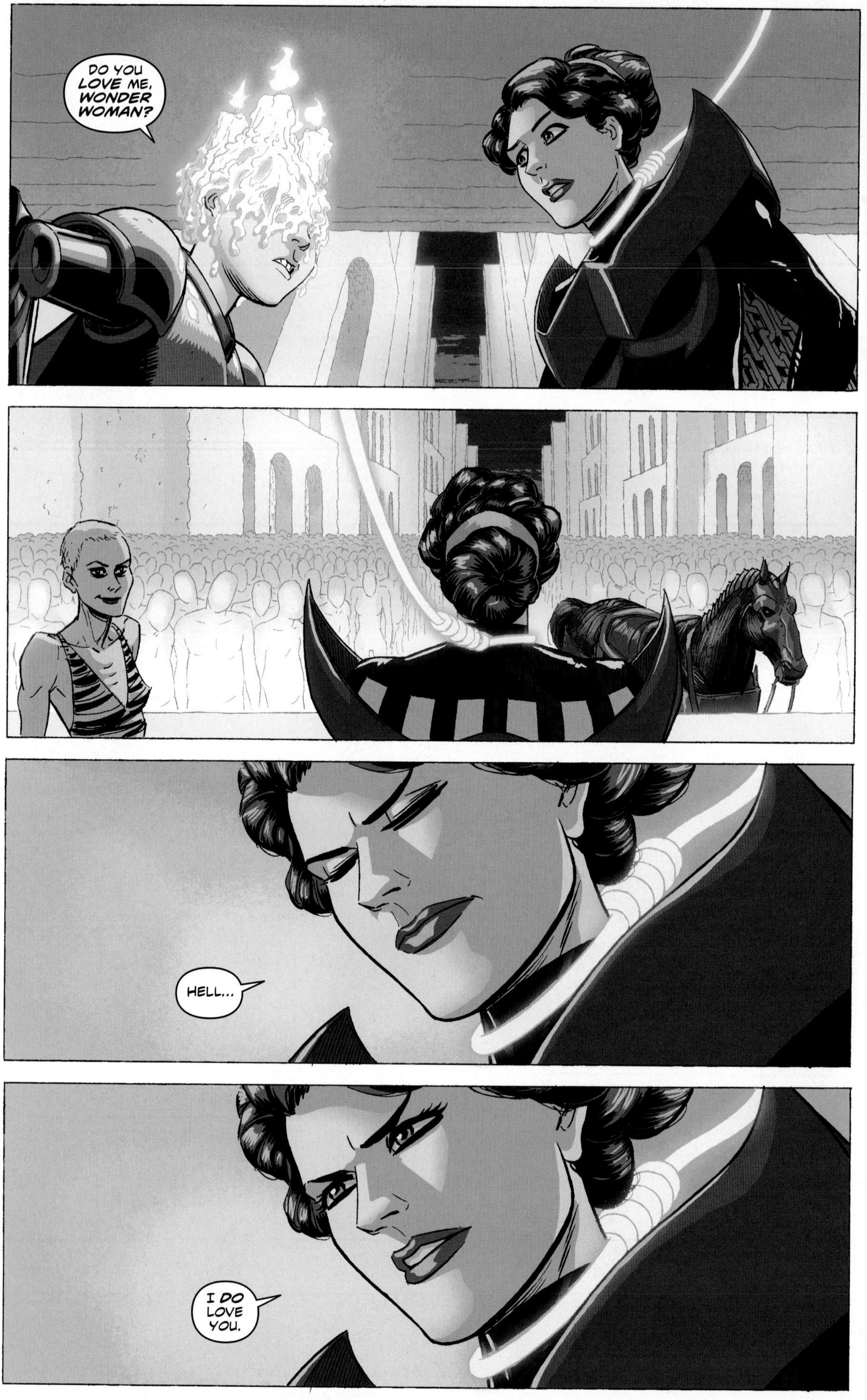
DO YOU LOVE ME, WONDER WOMAN?
HELL...
I DO LOVE YOU.

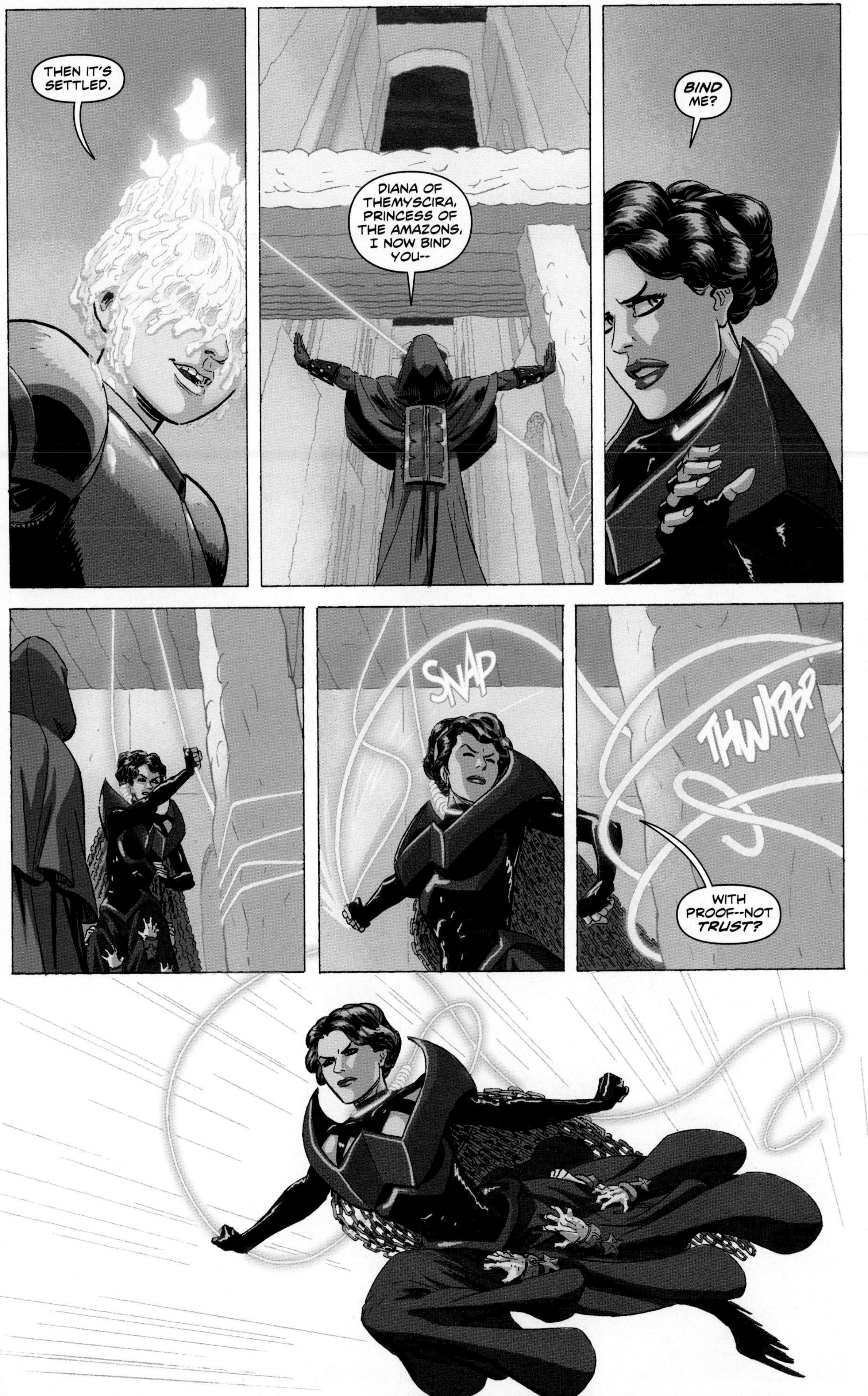
THEN IT'S SETTLED.
DIANA OF THEMYSCIRA, PRINCESS OF THE AMAZONS, I NOW BIND YOU--
BIND ME?
SNAP
THWIPP
WITH PROOF--NOT TRUST?

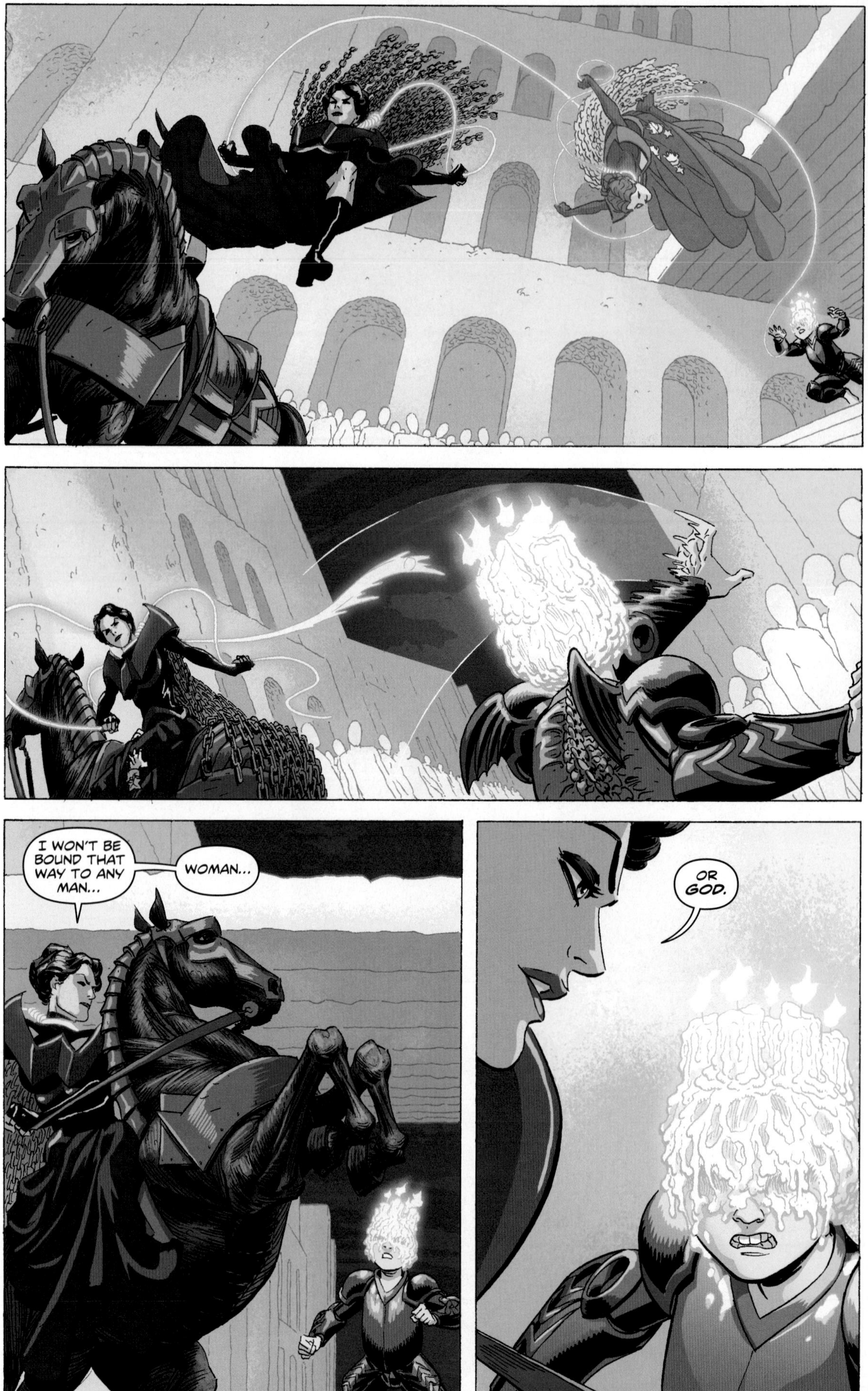
I WON'T BE BOUND THAT WAY TO ANY MAN...
WOMAN...
OR GOD.

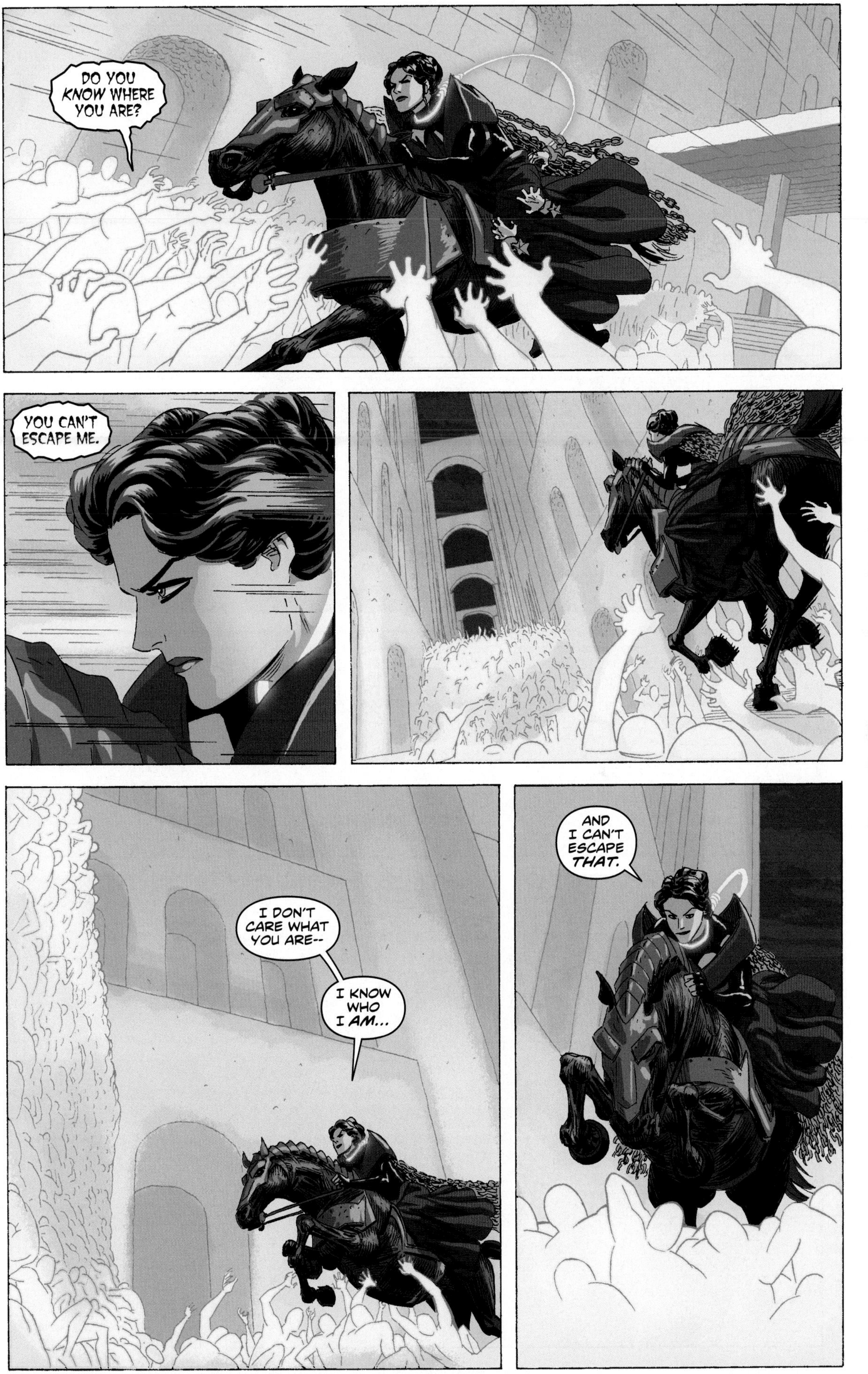
DO YOU KNOW WHERE YOU ARE?
YOU CAN'T ESCAPE ME.
I DON'T CARE WHAT YOU ARE--
I KNOW WHO I *AM*...
AND I CAN'T ESCAPE *THAT*.

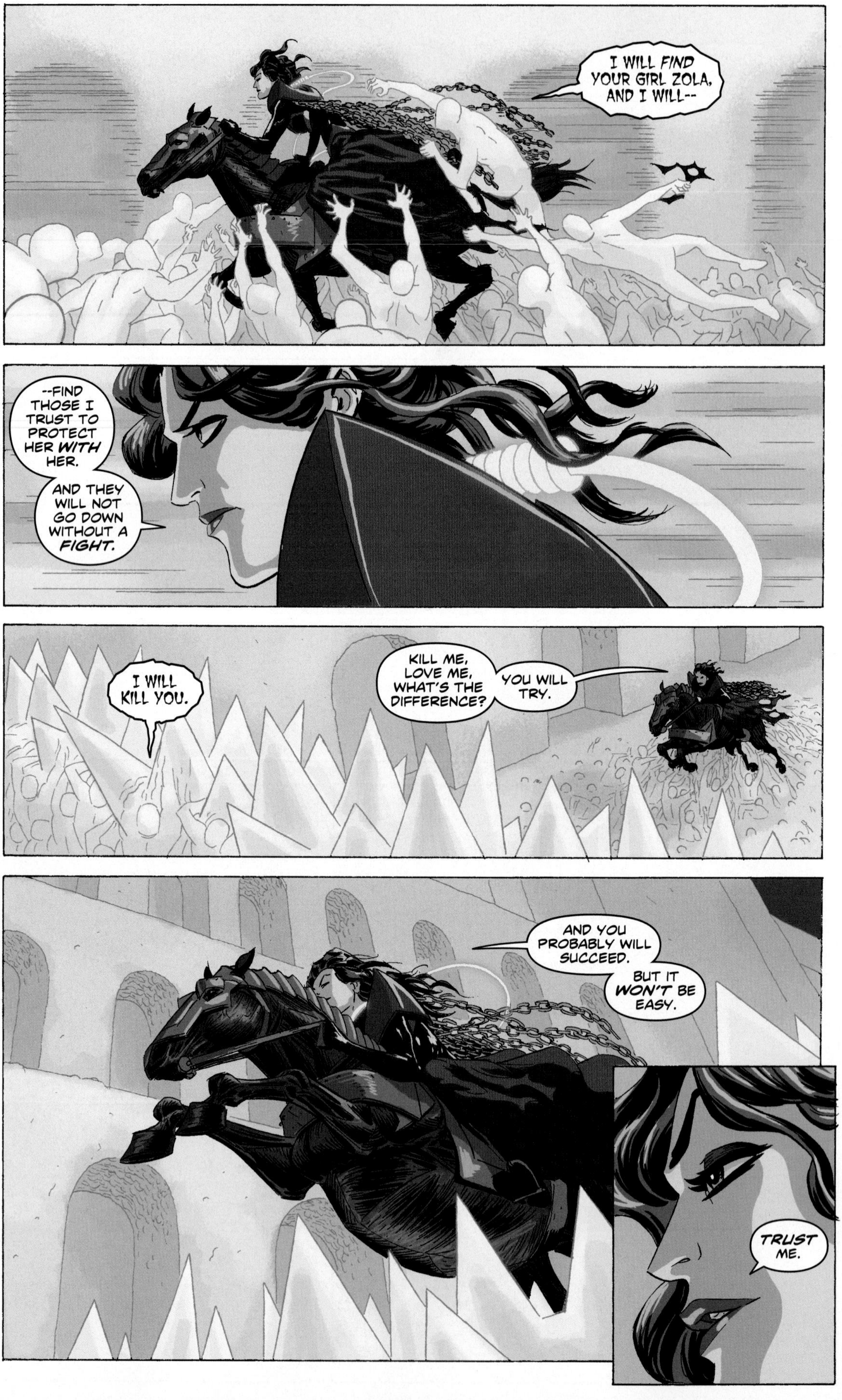
I WILL FIND YOUR GIRL ZOLA, AND I WILL--
--FIND THOSE I TRUST TO PROTECT HER WITH HER.
AND THEY WILL NOT GO DOWN WITHOUT A FIGHT.
KILL ME, LOVE ME, WHAT'S THE DIFFERENCE?
YOU WILL TRY.
I WILL KILL YOU.
AND YOU PROBABLY WILL SUCCEED.
BUT IT WON'T BE EASY.
TRUST ME.

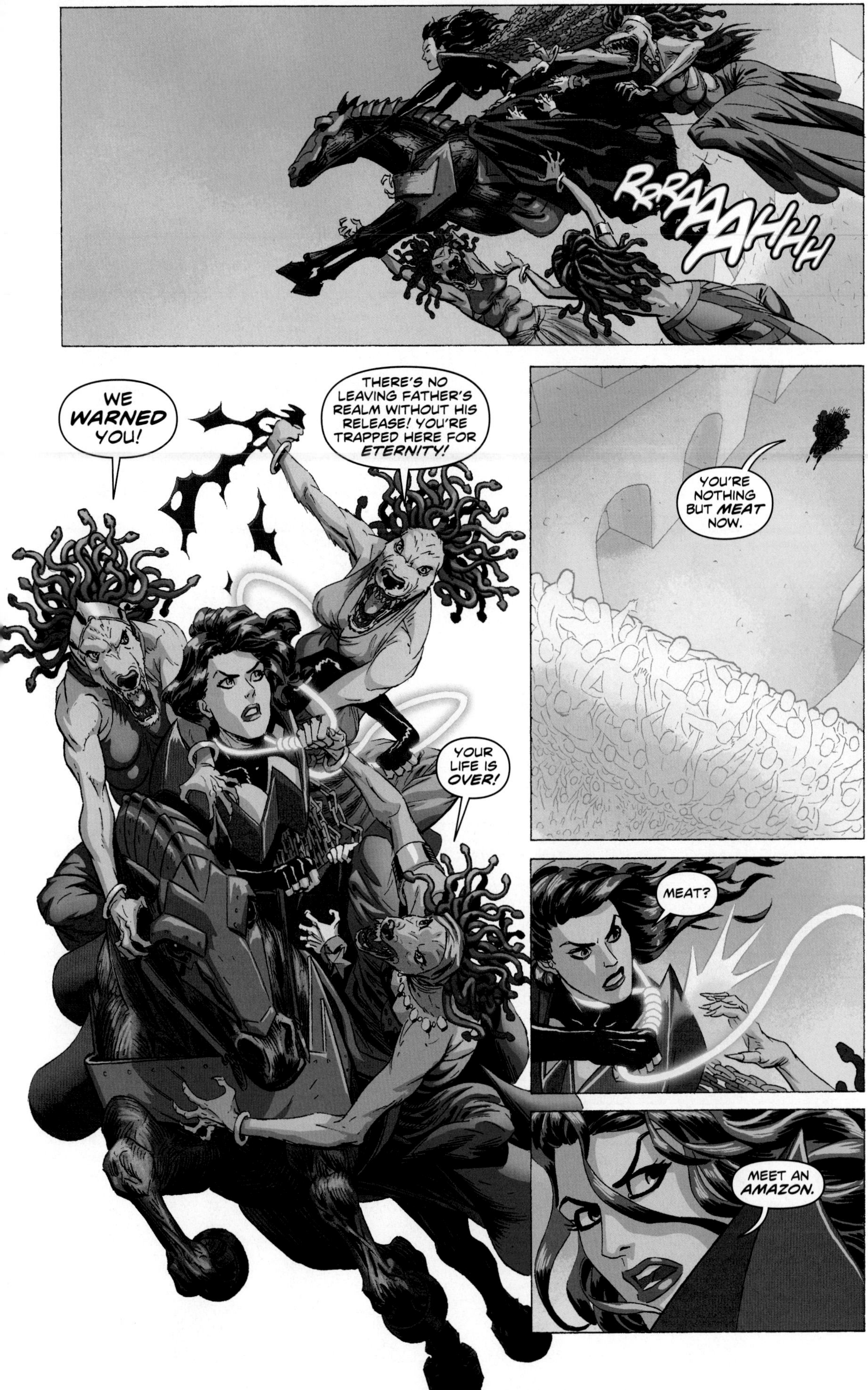
RRRAAAHHHH
WE WARNED YOU!
THERE'S NO LEAVING FATHER'S REALM WITHOUT HIS RELEASE! YOU'RE TRAPPED HERE FOR ETERNITY!
YOUR LIFE IS OVER!
YOU'RE NOTHING BUT MEAT NOW.
MEAT?
MEET AN AMAZON.

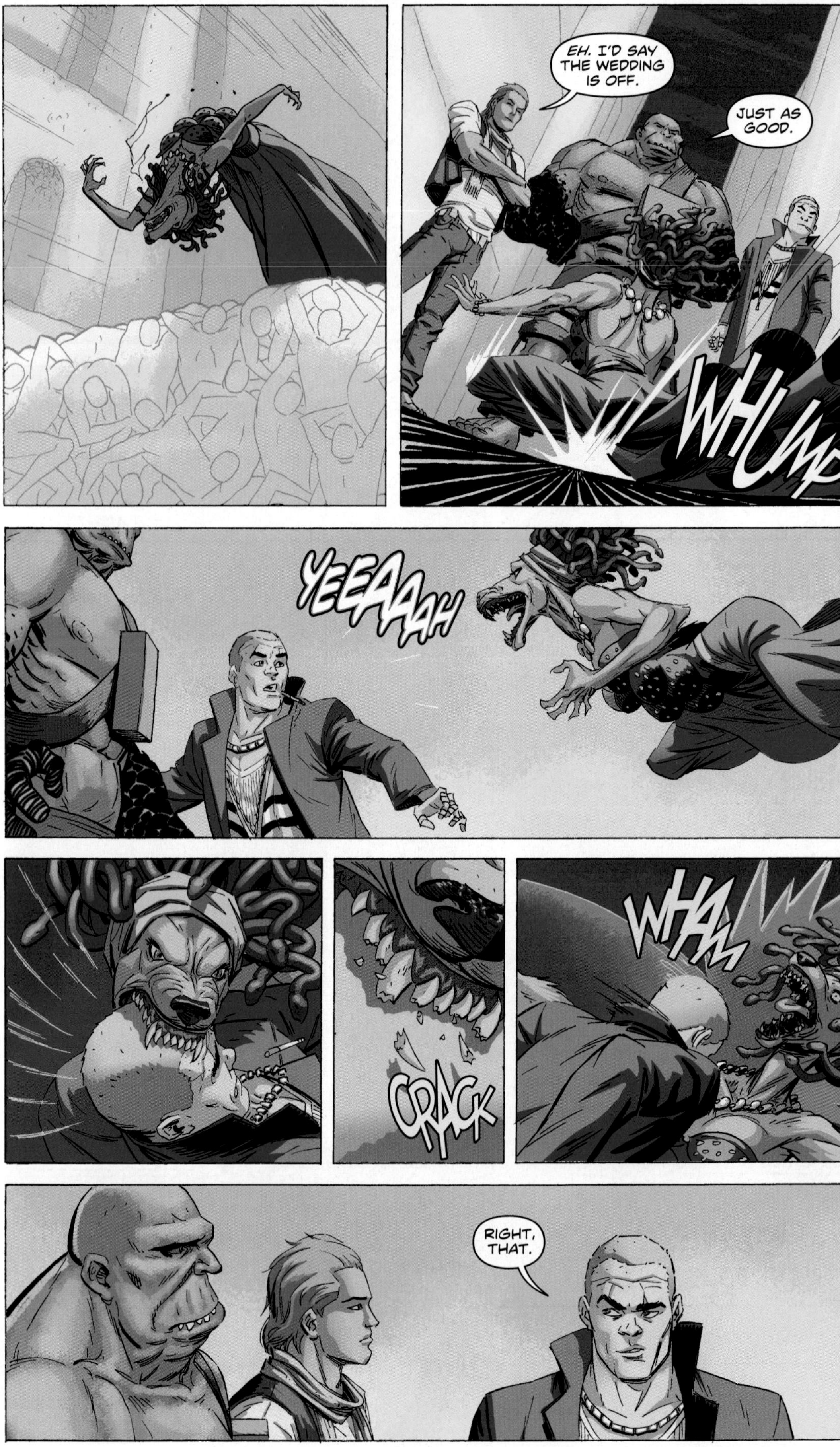
EH. I'D SAY THE WEDDING IS OFF.
JUST AS GOOD.
WHUMP
YEEAAAAH
CRACK
WHAM
RIGHT, THAT.

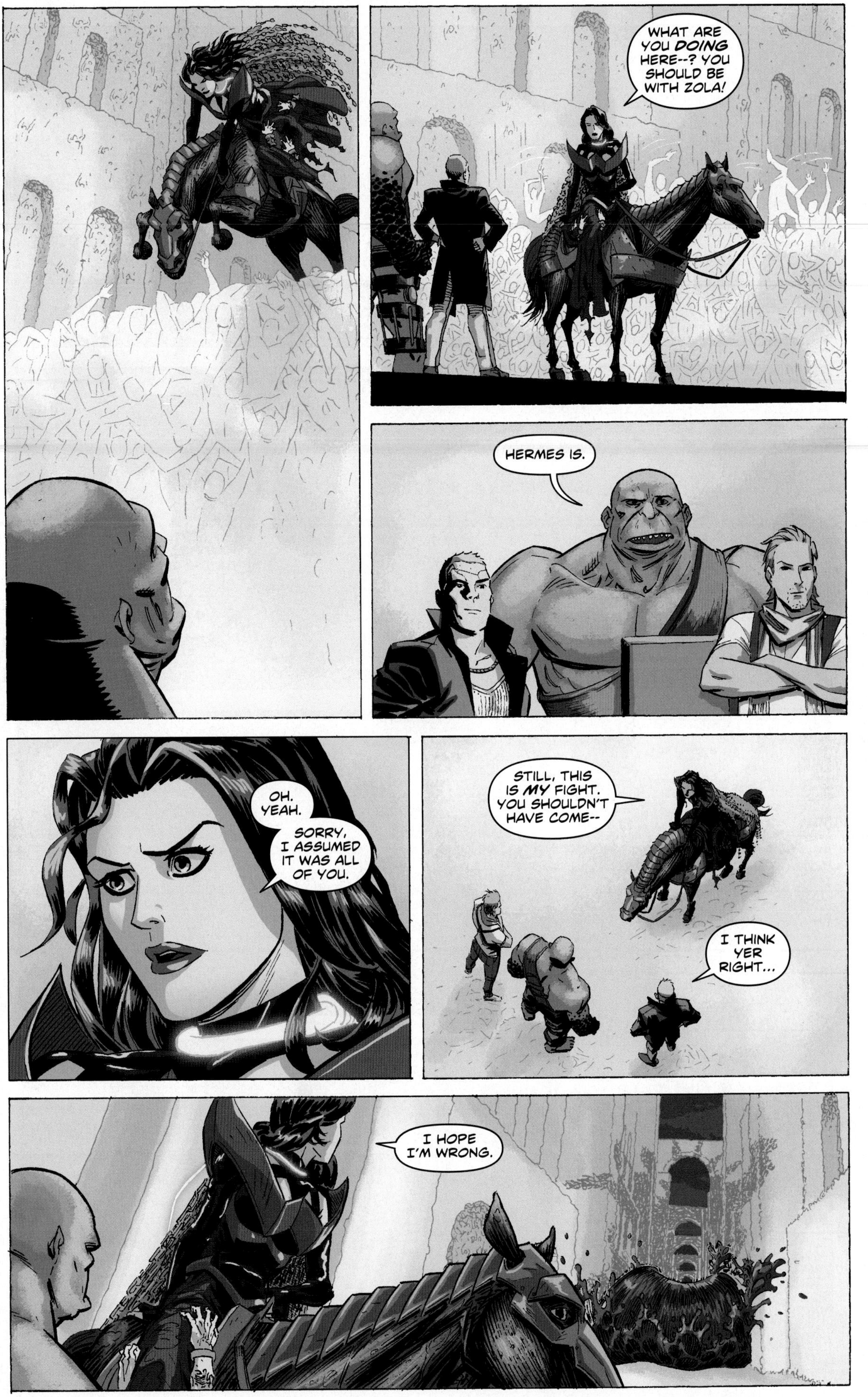
WHAT ARE YOU DOING HERE--? YOU SHOULD BE WITH ZOLA!
HERMES IS.
OH. YEAH.
SORRY, I ASSUMED IT WAS ALL OF YOU.
STILL, THIS IS MY FIGHT. YOU SHOULDN'T HAVE COME--
I THINK YER RIGHT...
I HOPE I'M WRONG.

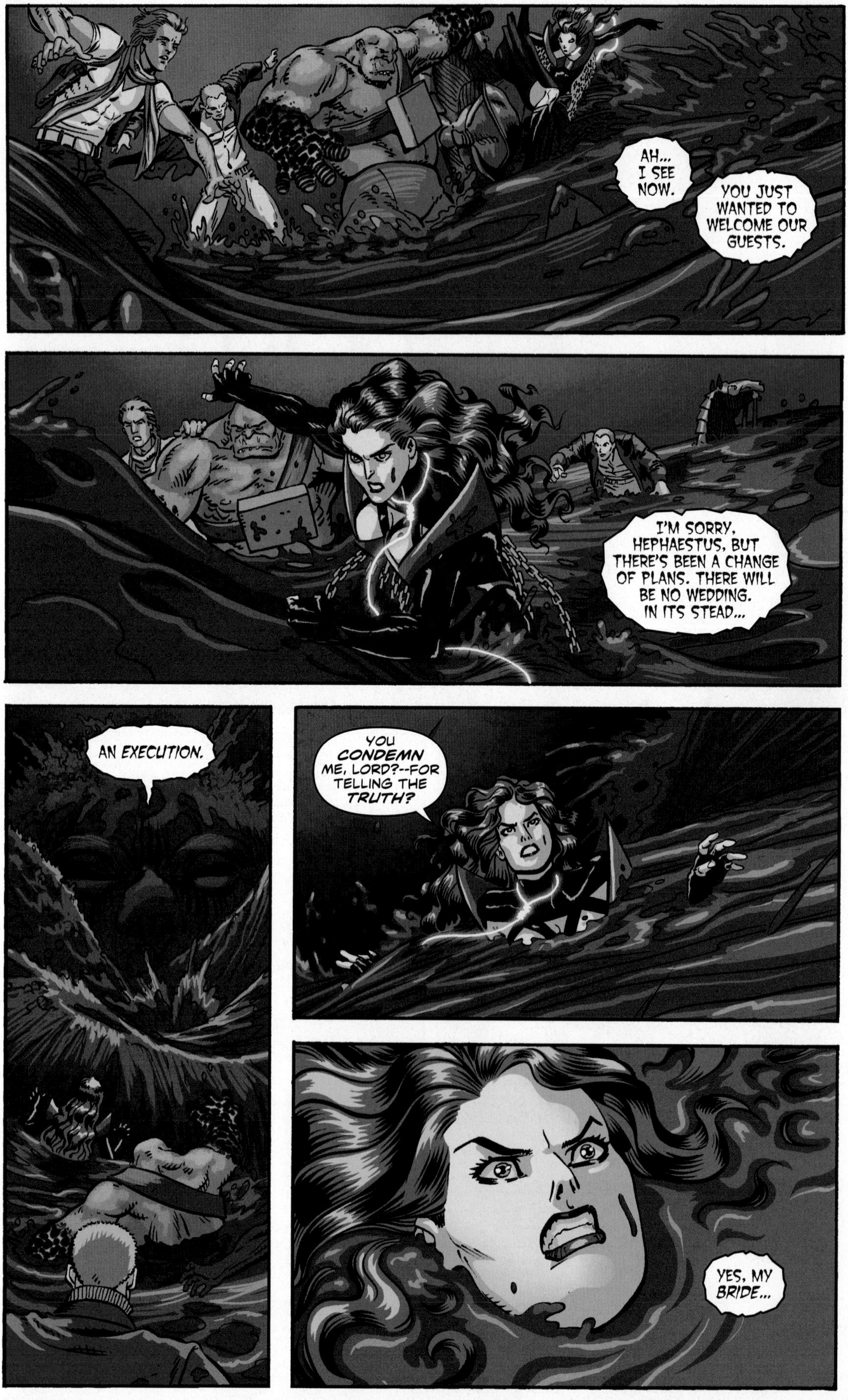
AH... I SEE NOW.
YOU JUST WANTED TO WELCOME OUR GUESTS.
I'M SORRY, HEPHAESTUS, BUT THERE'S BEEN A CHANGE OF PLANS. THERE WILL BE NO WEDDING. IN ITS STEAD...
AN EXECUTION.
YOU CONDEMN ME, LORD?--FOR TELLING THE TRUTH?
YES, MY BRIDE...

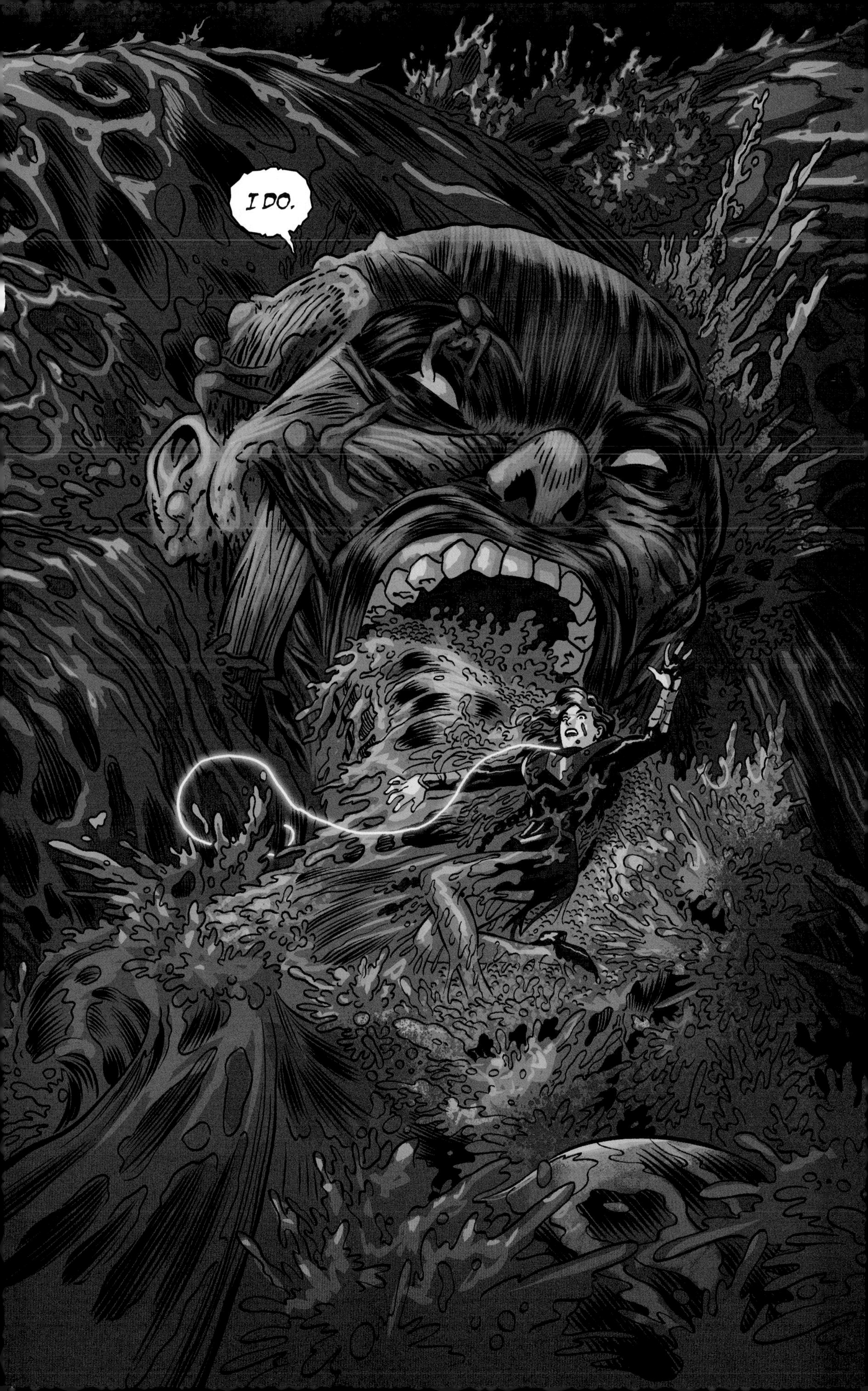
I DO.

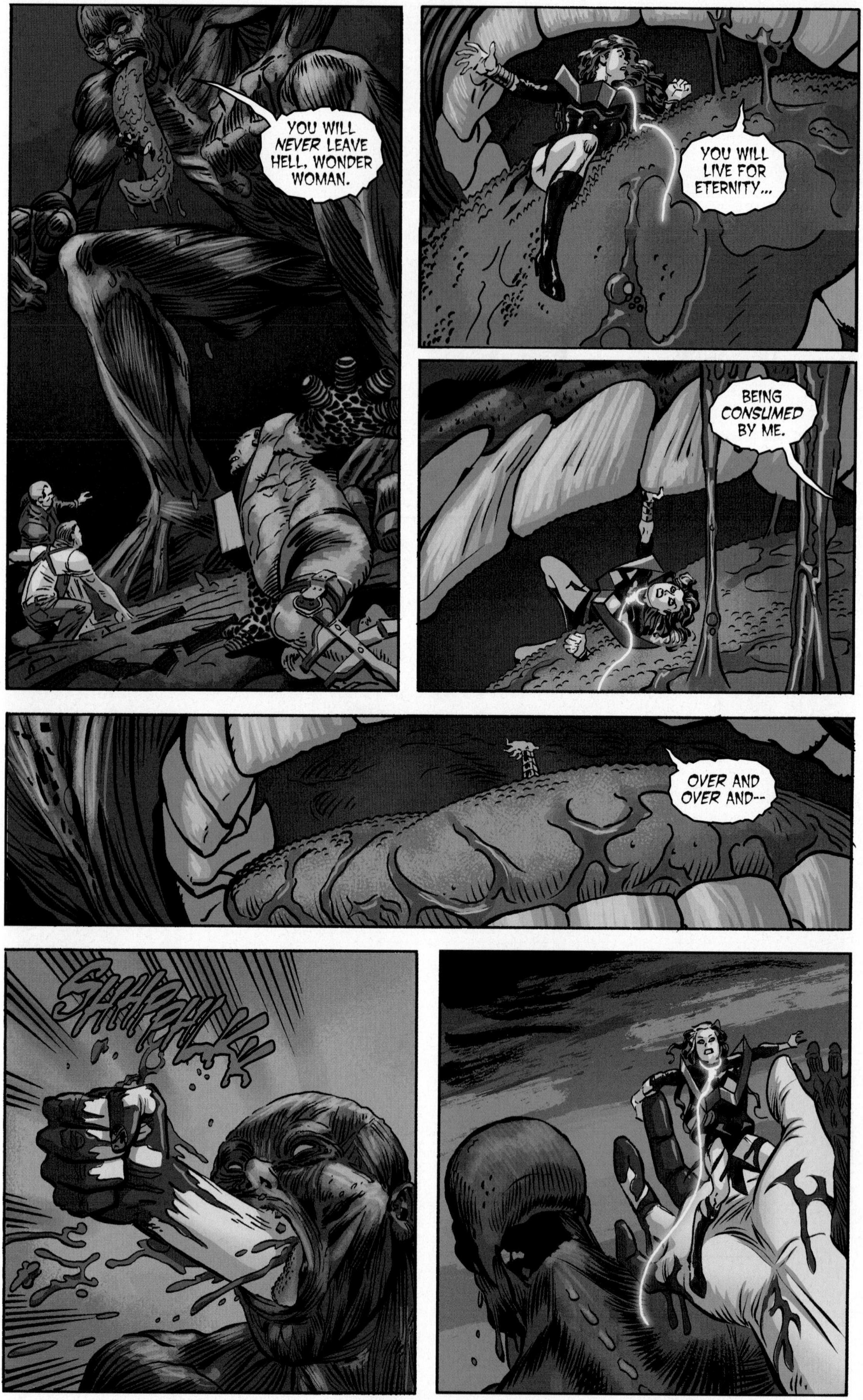
YOU WILL NEVER LEAVE HELL, WONDER WOMAN.
YOU WILL LIVE FOR ETERNITY...
BEING CONSUMED BY ME.
OVER AND OVER AND--
SHHRPHLKK!!

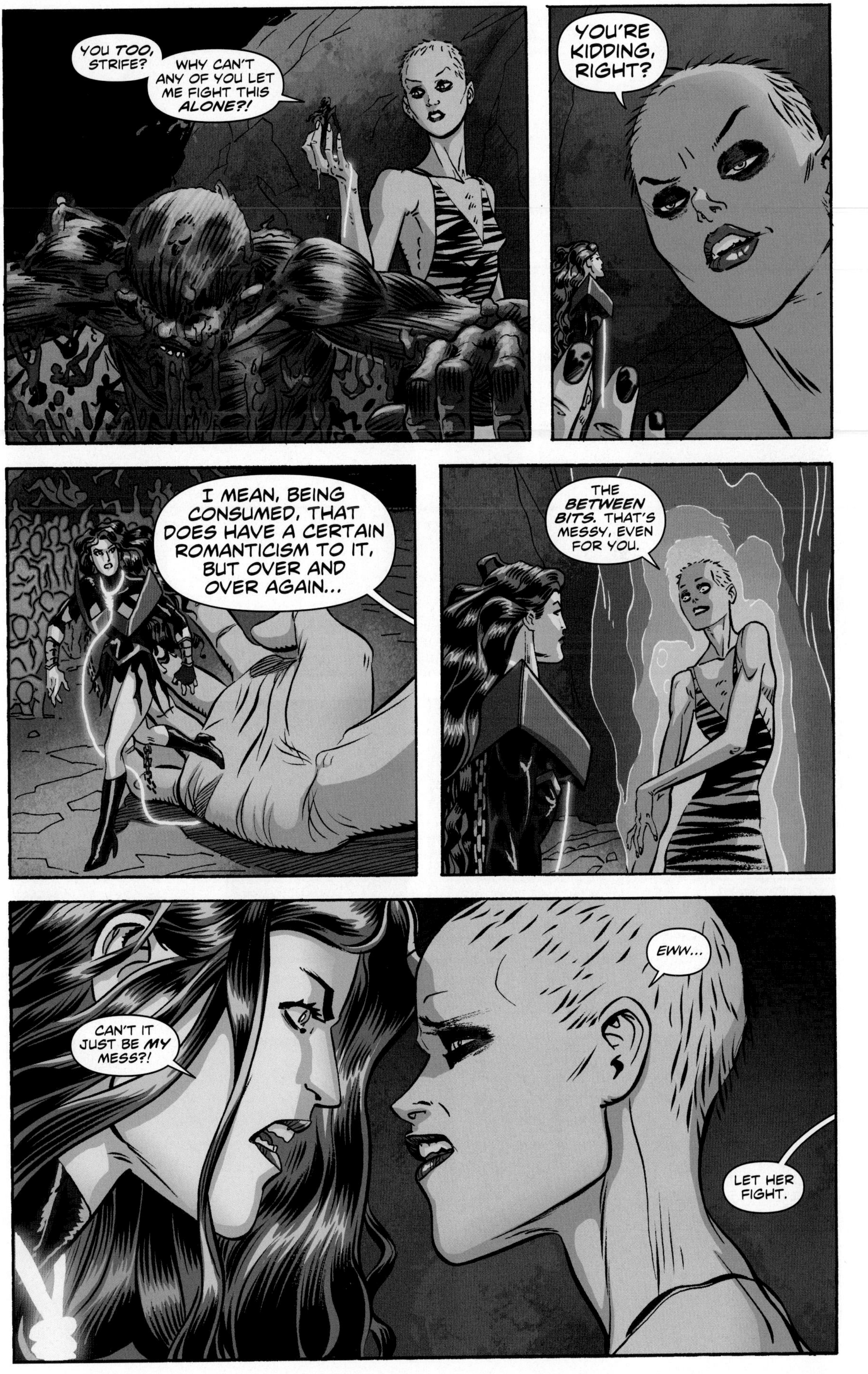
YOU TOO, STRIFE?
WHY CAN'T ANY OF YOU LET ME FIGHT THIS ALONE?!
YOU'RE KIDDING, RIGHT?
I MEAN, BEING CONSUMED, THAT DOES HAVE A CERTAIN ROMANTICISM TO IT, BUT OVER AND OVER AGAIN...
THE BETWEEN BITS. THAT'S MESSY, EVEN FOR YOU.
EWW...
CAN'T IT JUST BE MY MESS?!
LET HER FIGHT.

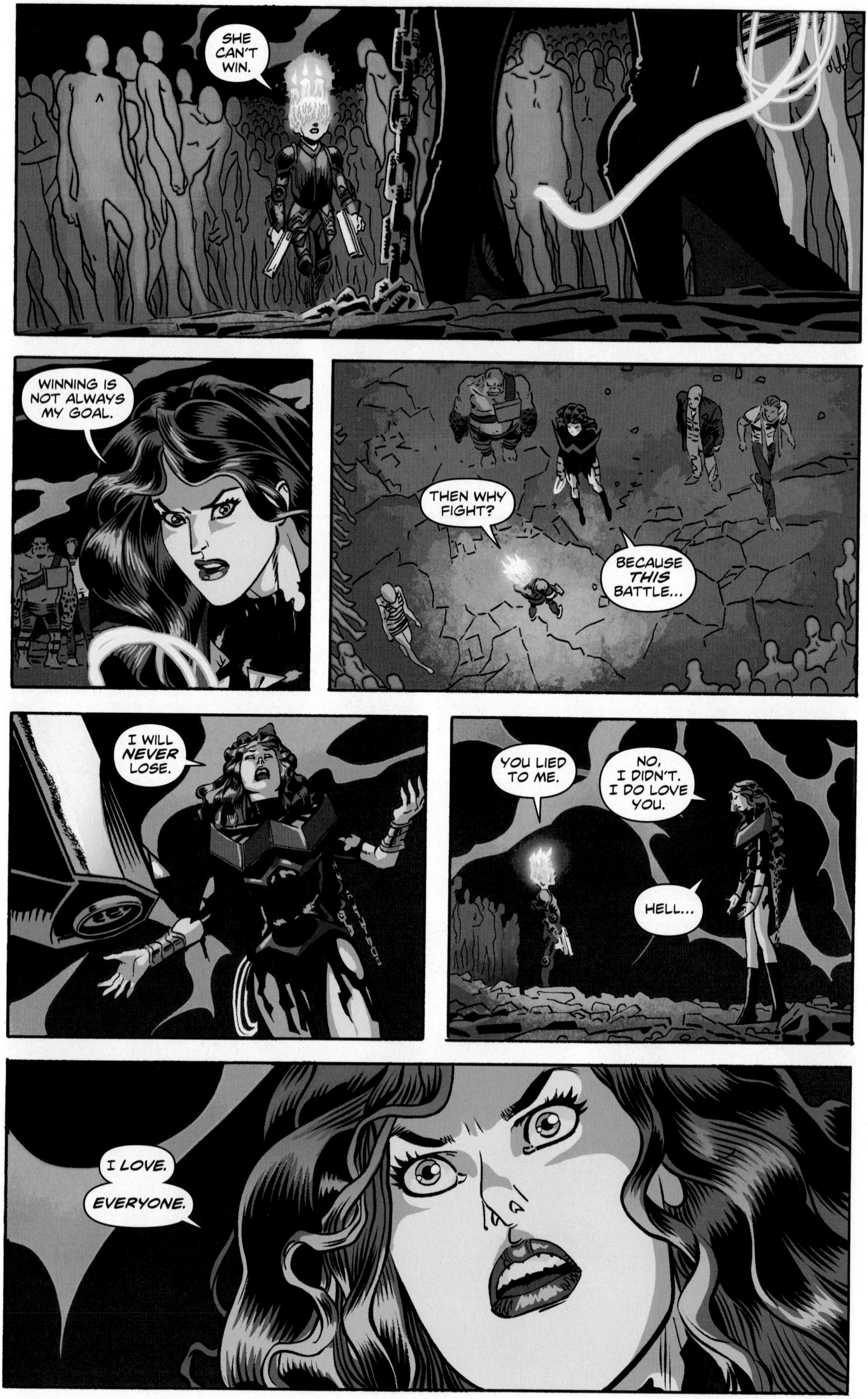
SHE CAN'T WIN.
WINNING IS NOT ALWAYS MY GOAL.
THEN WHY FIGHT?
BECAUSE THIS BATTLE...
I WILL NEVER LOSE.
YOU LIED TO ME.
NO, I DIDN'T. I DO LOVE YOU.
HELL...
I LOVE.
EVERYONE.

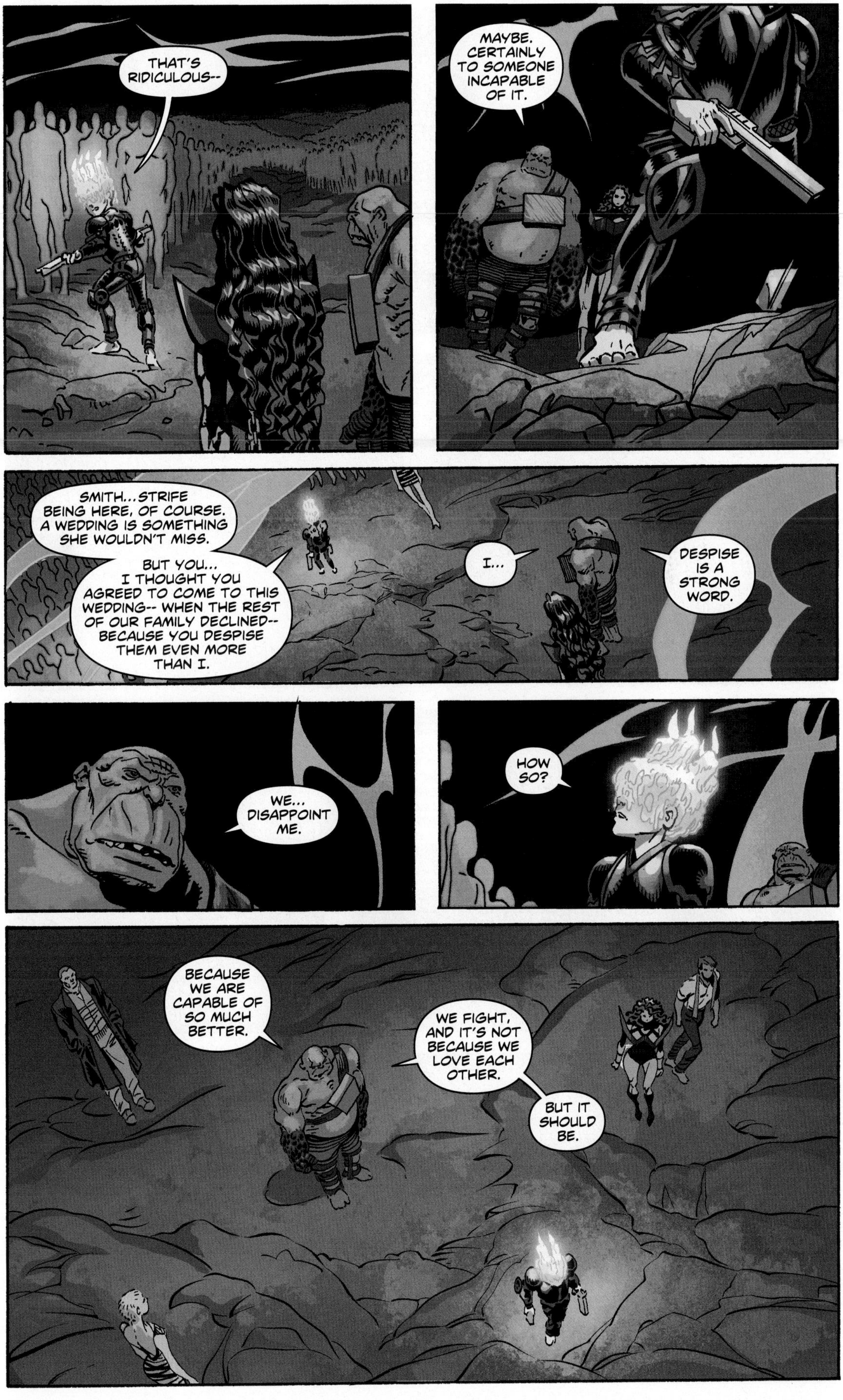
THAT'S RIDICULOUS--
MAYBE. CERTAINLY TO SOMEONE INCAPABLE OF IT.
SMITH...STRIFE BEING HERE, OF COURSE. A WEDDING IS SOMETHING SHE WOULDN'T MISS.
BUT YOU... I THOUGHT YOU AGREED TO COME TO THIS WEDDING-- WHEN THE REST OF OUR FAMILY DECLINED-- BECAUSE YOU DESPISE THEM EVEN MORE THAN I.
I...
DESPISE IS A STRONG WORD.
WE... DISAPPOINT ME.
HOW SO?
BECAUSE WE ARE CAPABLE OF SO MUCH BETTER.
WE FIGHT, AND IT'S NOT BECAUSE WE LOVE EACH OTHER.
BUT IT SHOULD BE.

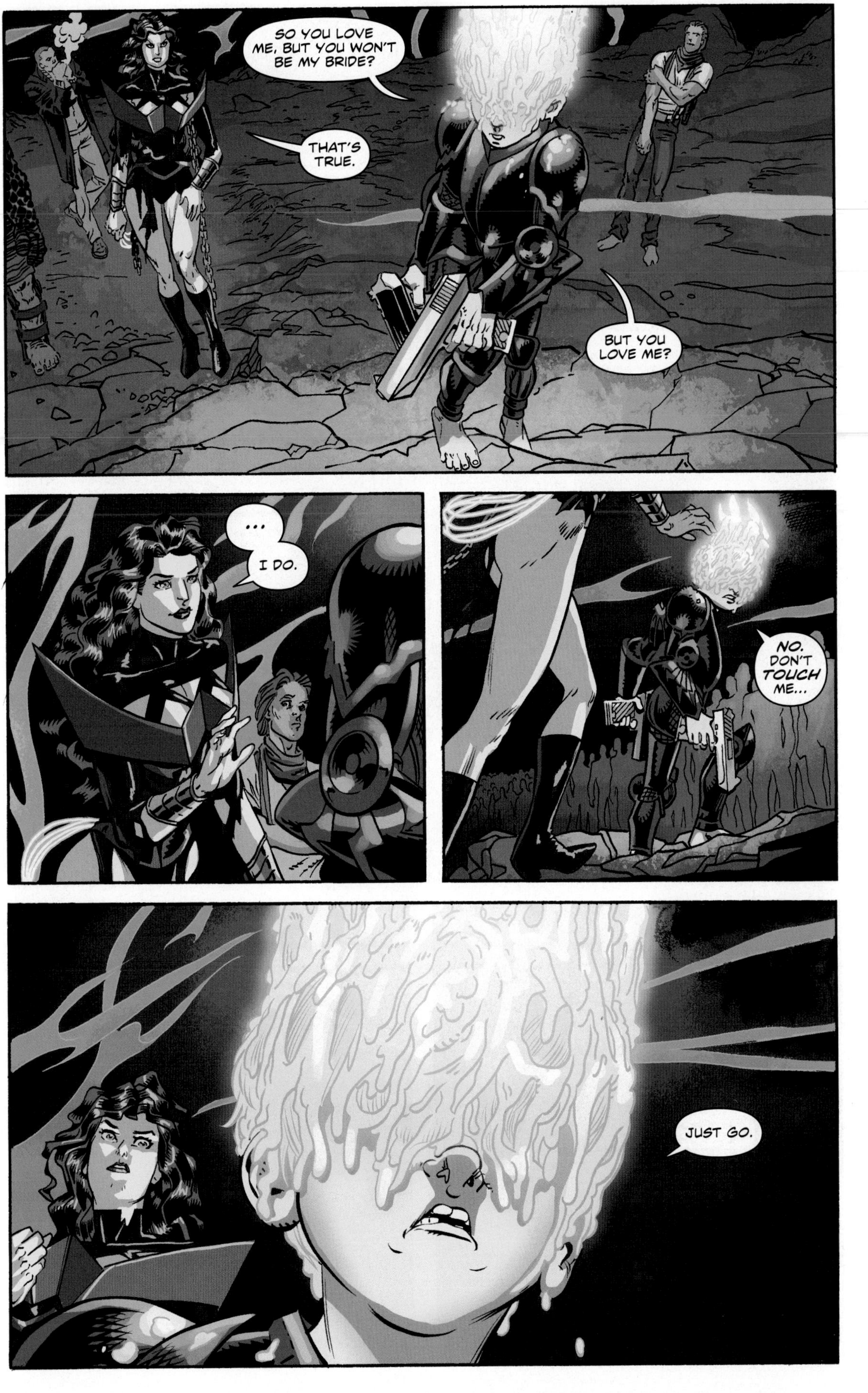
SO YOU LOVE ME, BUT YOU WON'T BE MY BRIDE?
THAT'S TRUE.
BUT YOU LOVE ME?
...
I DO.
NO. DON'T TOUCH ME...
JUST GO.

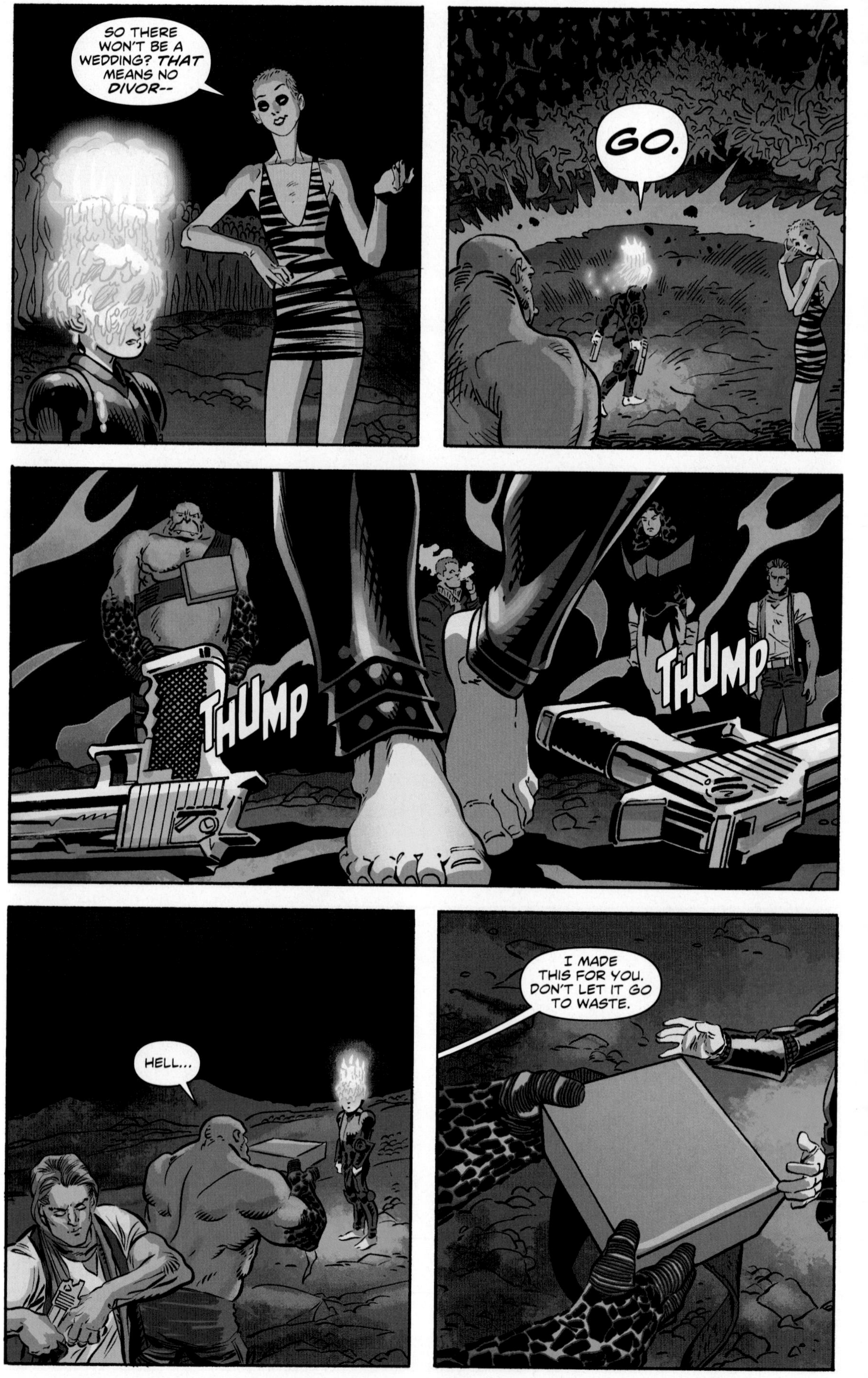
SO THERE WON'T BE A WEDDING? *THAT* MEANS NO *DIVOR--*
GO.
THUMP
THUMP
HELL...
I MADE THIS FOR YOU. DON'T LET IT GO TO WASTE.

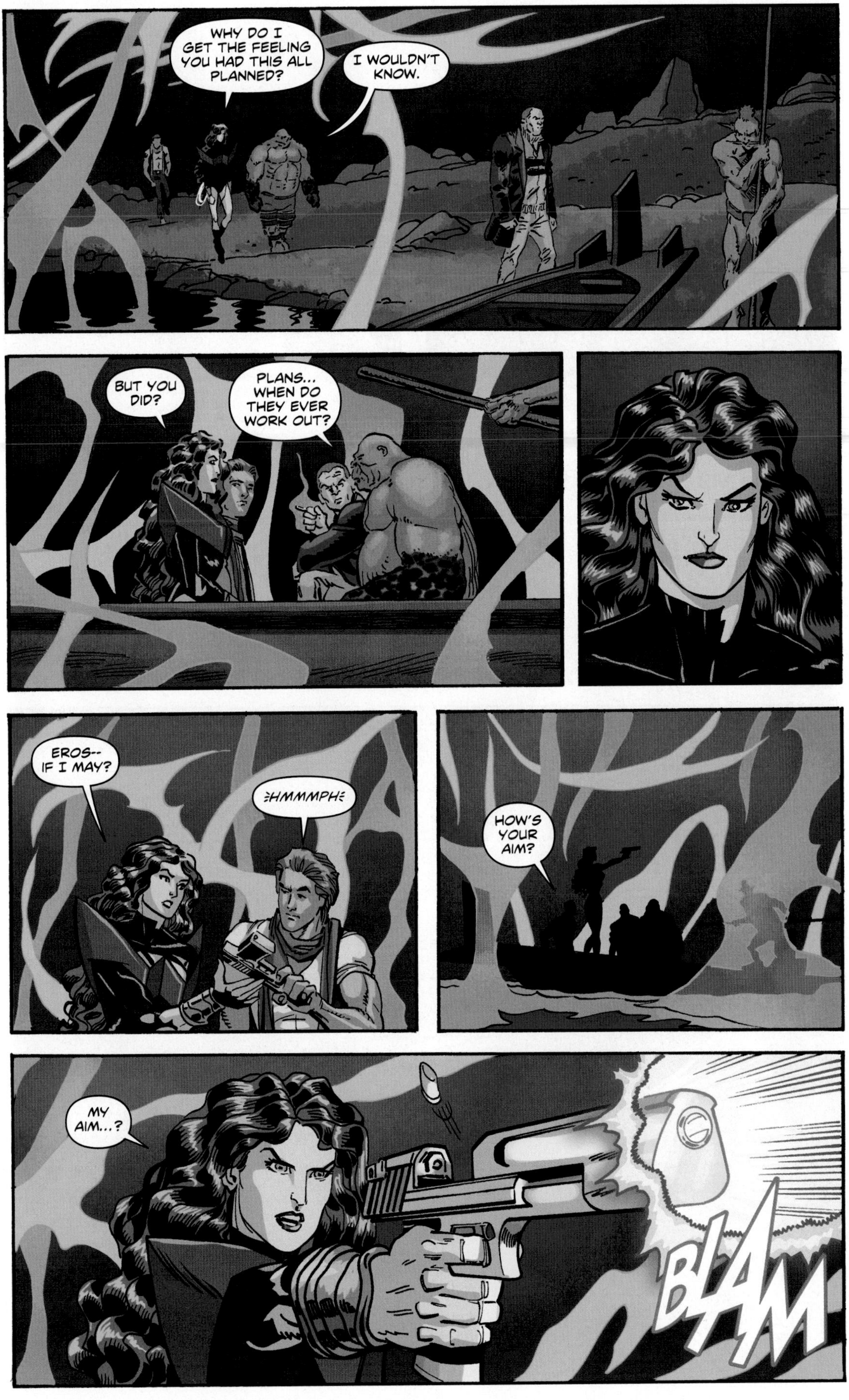
WHY DO I GET THE FEELING YOU HAD THIS ALL PLANNED?
I WOULDN'T KNOW.
BUT YOU DID?
PLANS... WHEN DO THEY EVER WORK OUT?
EROS-- IF I MAY?
HMMMPH
HOW'S YOUR AIM?
MY AIM...?
BLAM

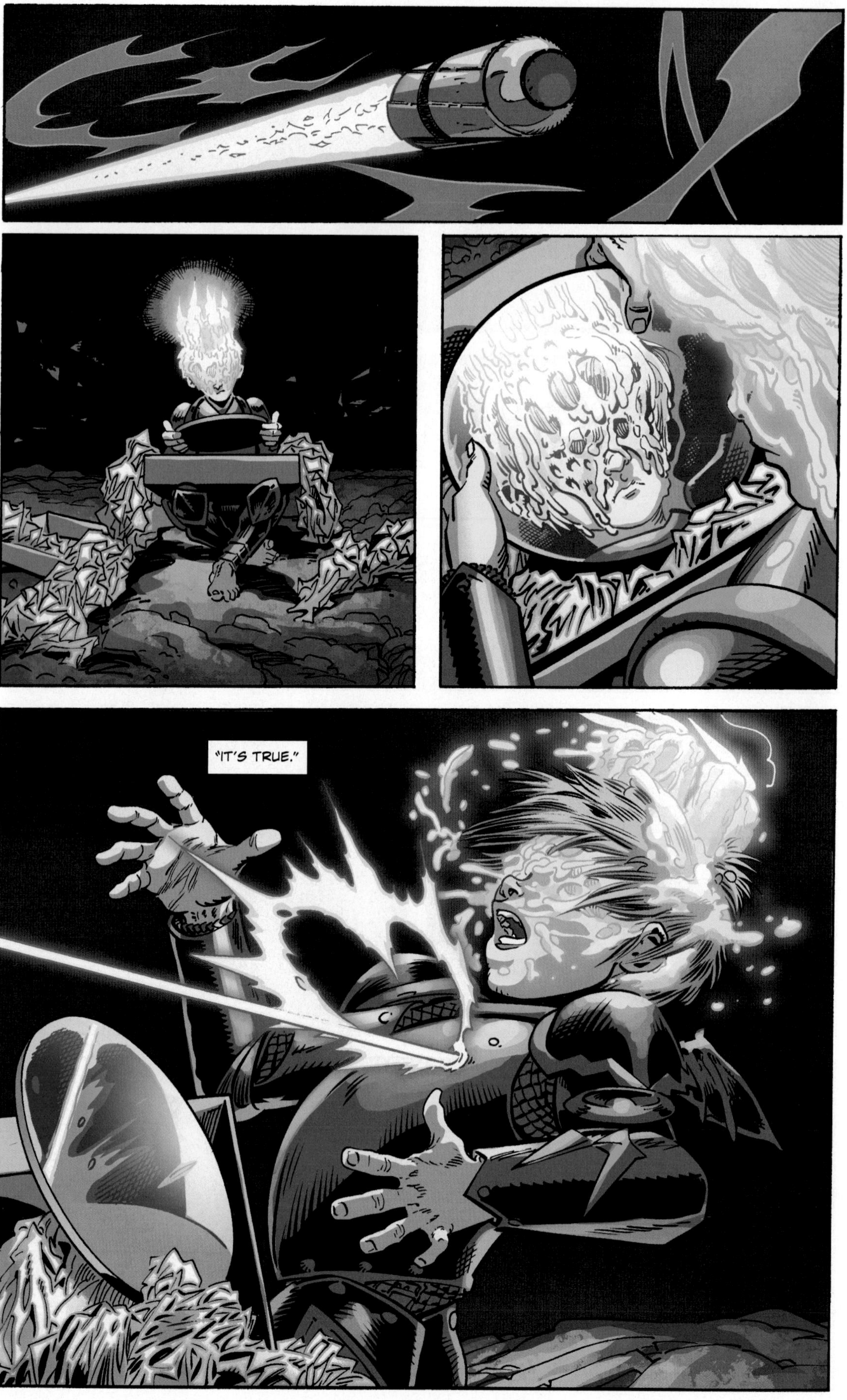
"IT'S TRUE."

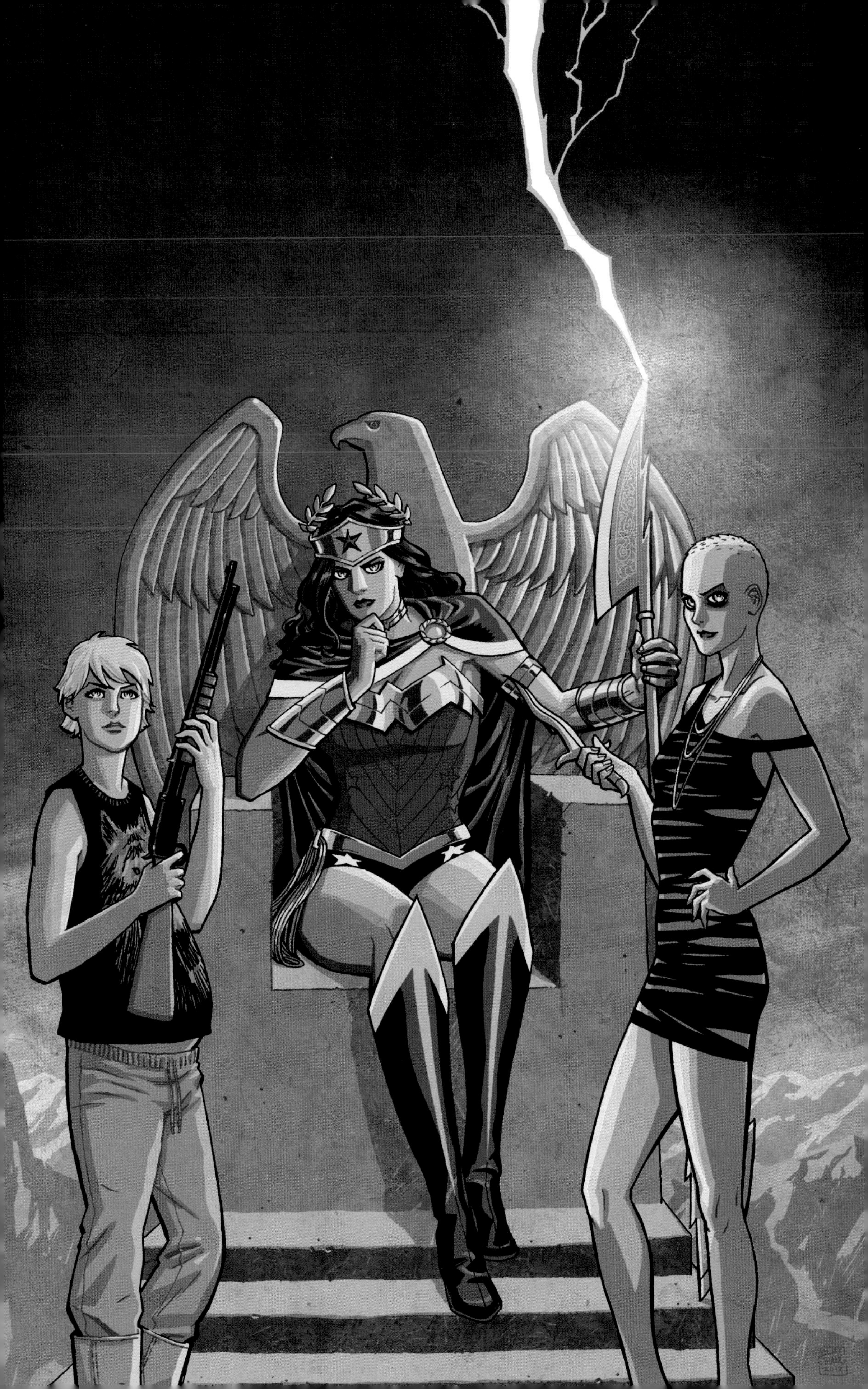

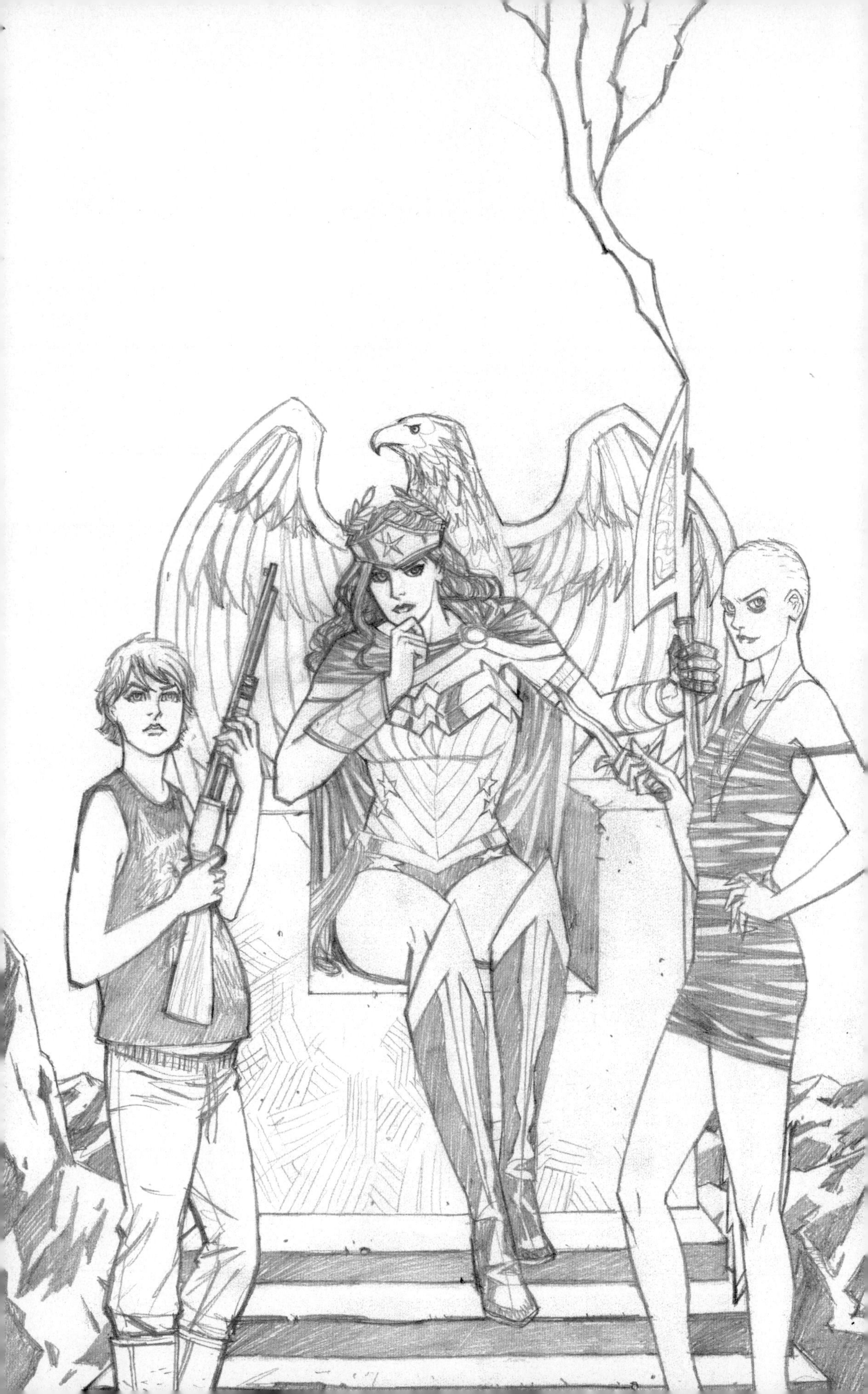

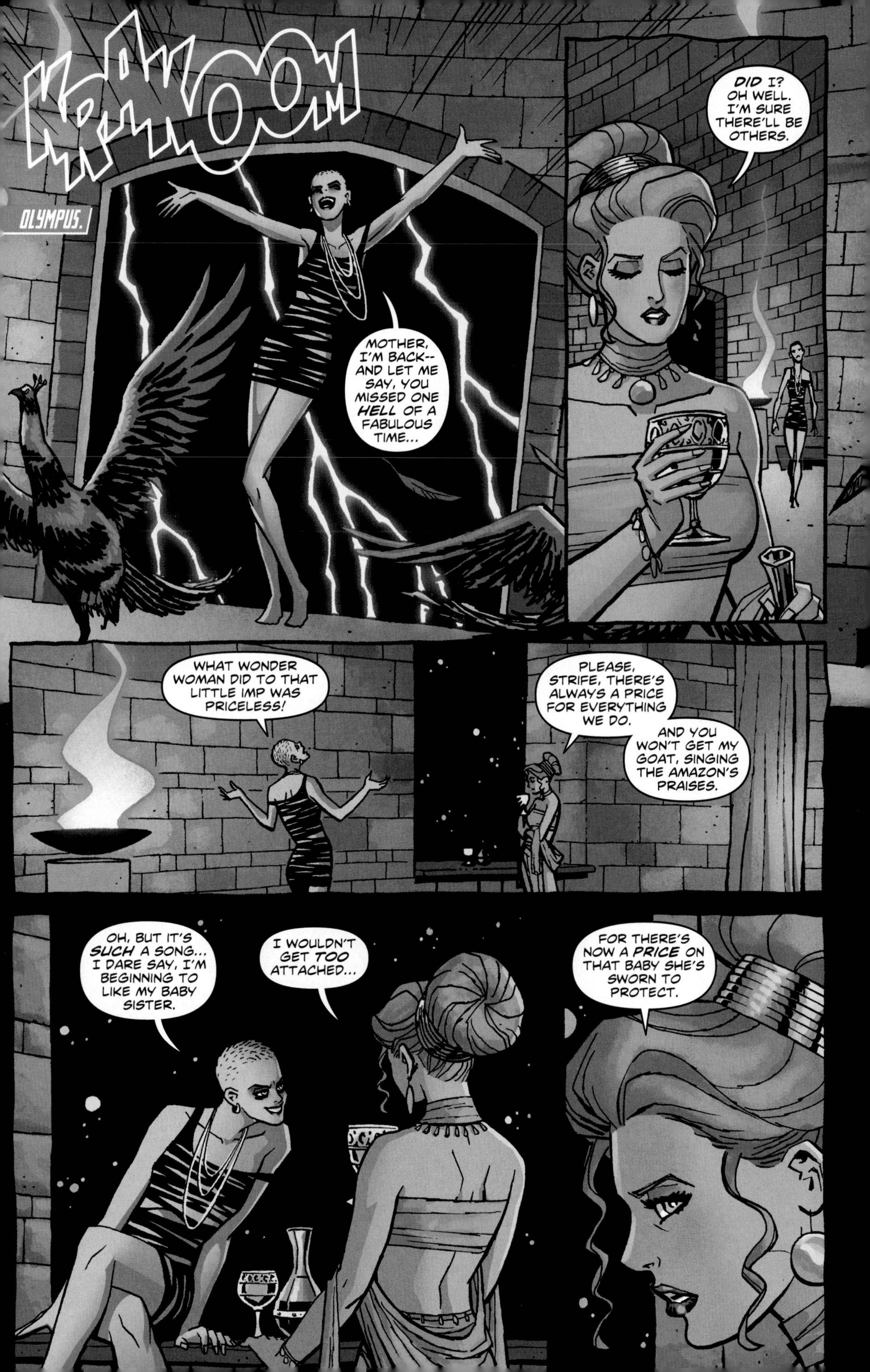
KRAKOOM
OLYMPUS.
MOTHER, I'M BACK-- AND LET ME SAY, YOU MISSED ONE HELL OF A FABULOUS TIME...
DID I? OH WELL. I'M SURE THERE'LL BE OTHERS.
WHAT WONDER WOMAN DID TO THAT LITTLE IMP WAS PRICELESS!
PLEASE, STRIFE, THERE'S ALWAYS A PRICE FOR EVERYTHING WE DO.
AND YOU WON'T GET MY GOAT, SINGING THE AMAZON'S PRAISES.
OH, BUT IT'S SUCH A SONG... I DARE SAY, I'M BEGINNING TO LIKE MY BABY SISTER.
I WOULDN'T GET TOO ATTACHED...
FOR THERE'S NOW A PRICE ON THAT BABY SHE'S SWORN TO PROTECT.

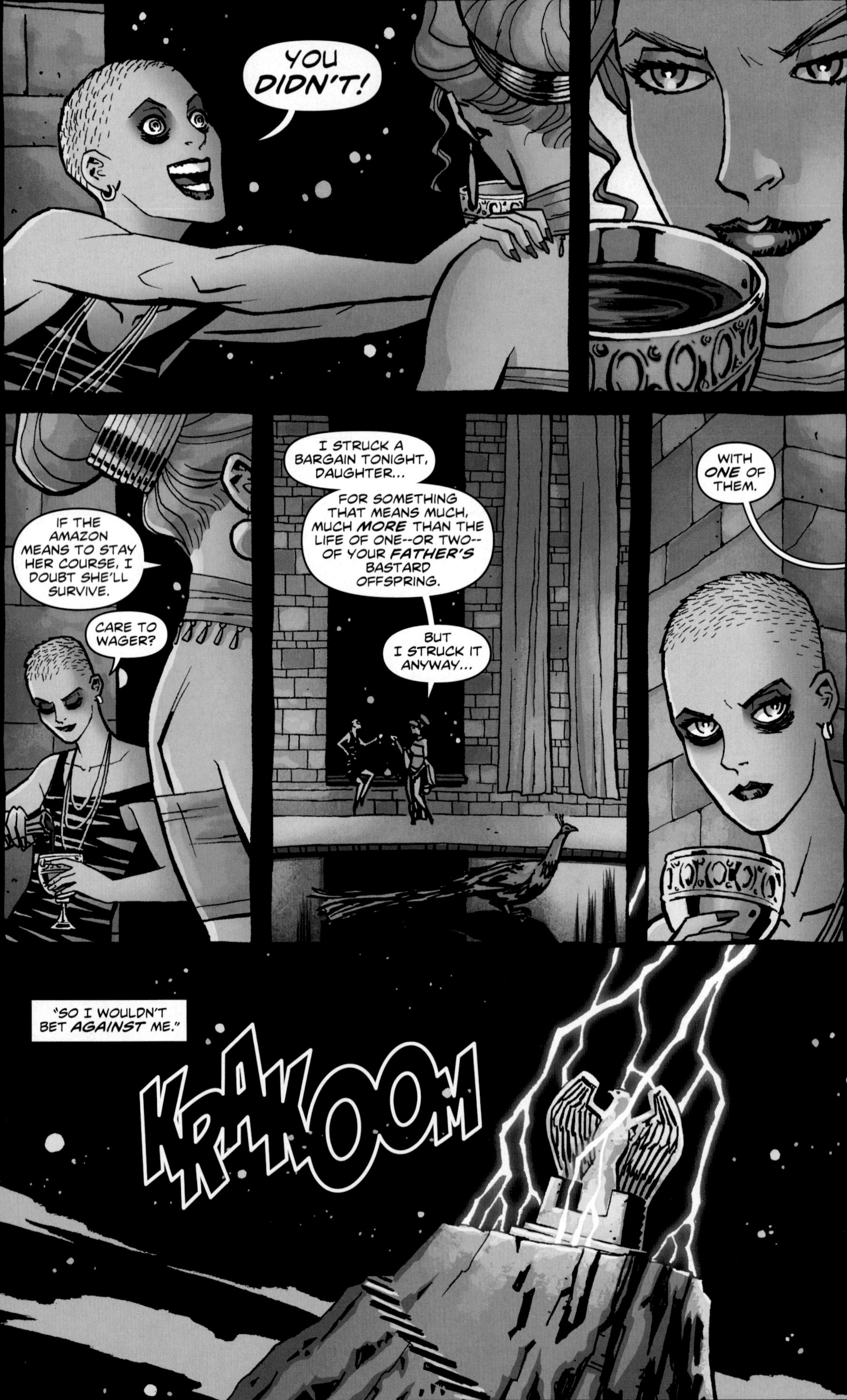

YOU DIDN'T!
IF THE AMAZON MEANS TO STAY HER COURSE, I DOUBT SHE'LL SURVIVE.
CARE TO WAGER?
I STRUCK A BARGAIN TONIGHT, DAUGHTER...
FOR SOMETHING THAT MEANS MUCH, MUCH MORE THAN THE LIFE OF ONE--OR TWO--OF YOUR FATHER'S BASTARD OFFSPRING.
BUT I STRUCK IT ANYWAY...
WITH ONE OF THEM.
"SO I WOULDN'T BET AGAINST ME."
KRAKOOM

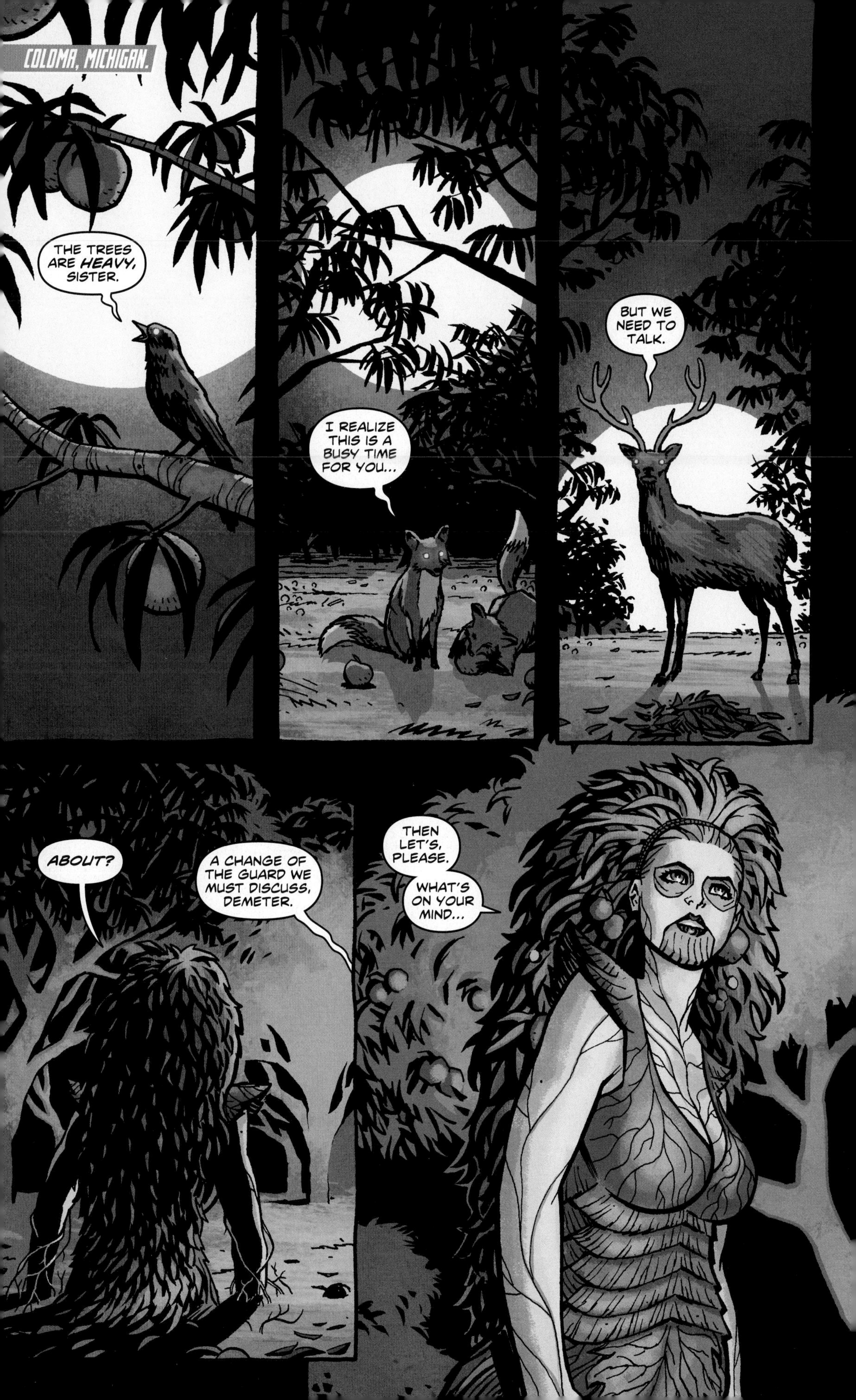
COLOMA, MICHIGAN.
THE TREES ARE HEAVY, SISTER.
I REALIZE THIS IS A BUSY TIME FOR YOU...
BUT WE NEED TO TALK.
ABOUT?
A CHANGE OF THE GUARD WE MUST DISCUSS, DEMETER.
THEN LET'S, PLEASE.
WHAT'S ON YOUR MIND...

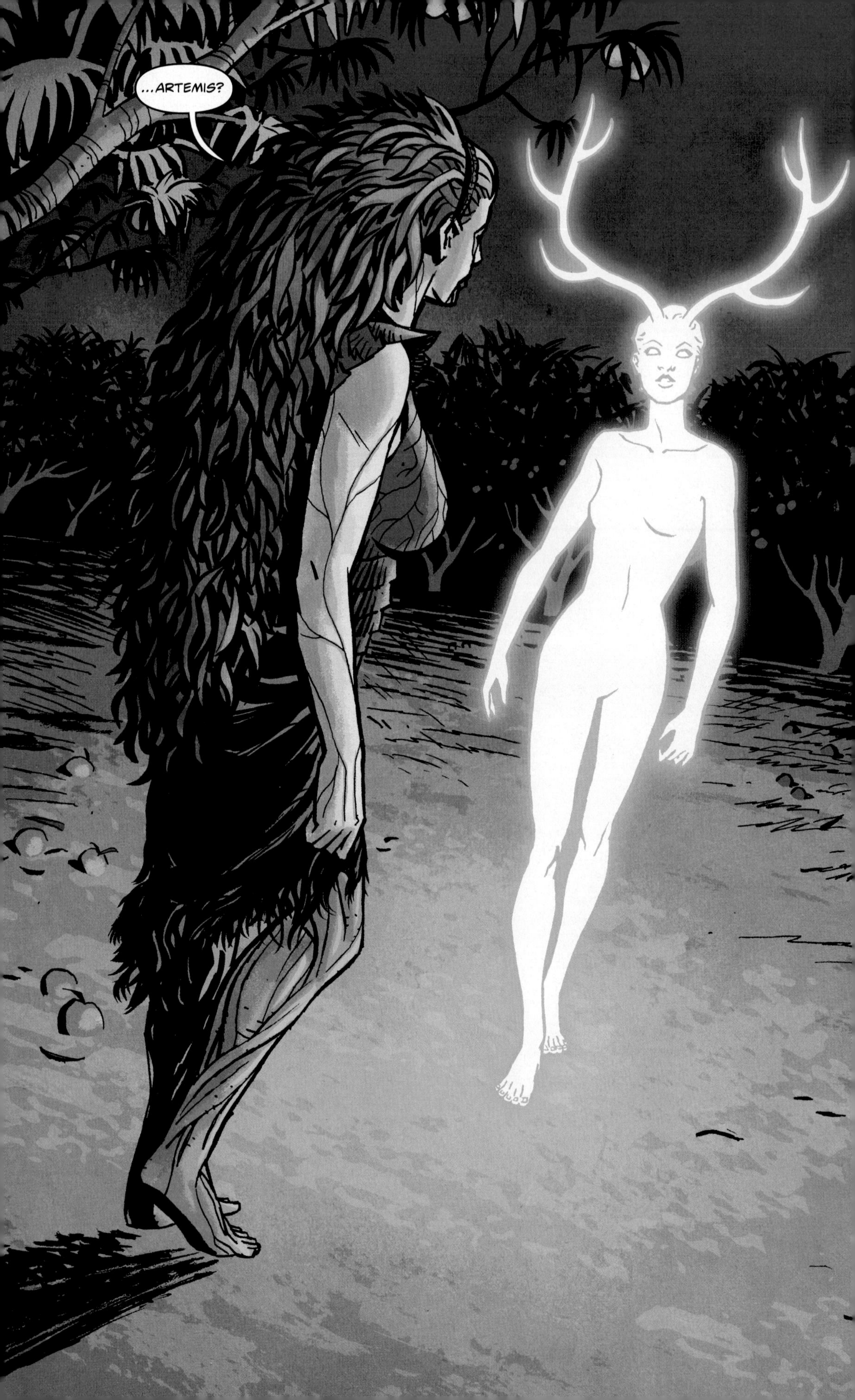
...ARTEMIS?

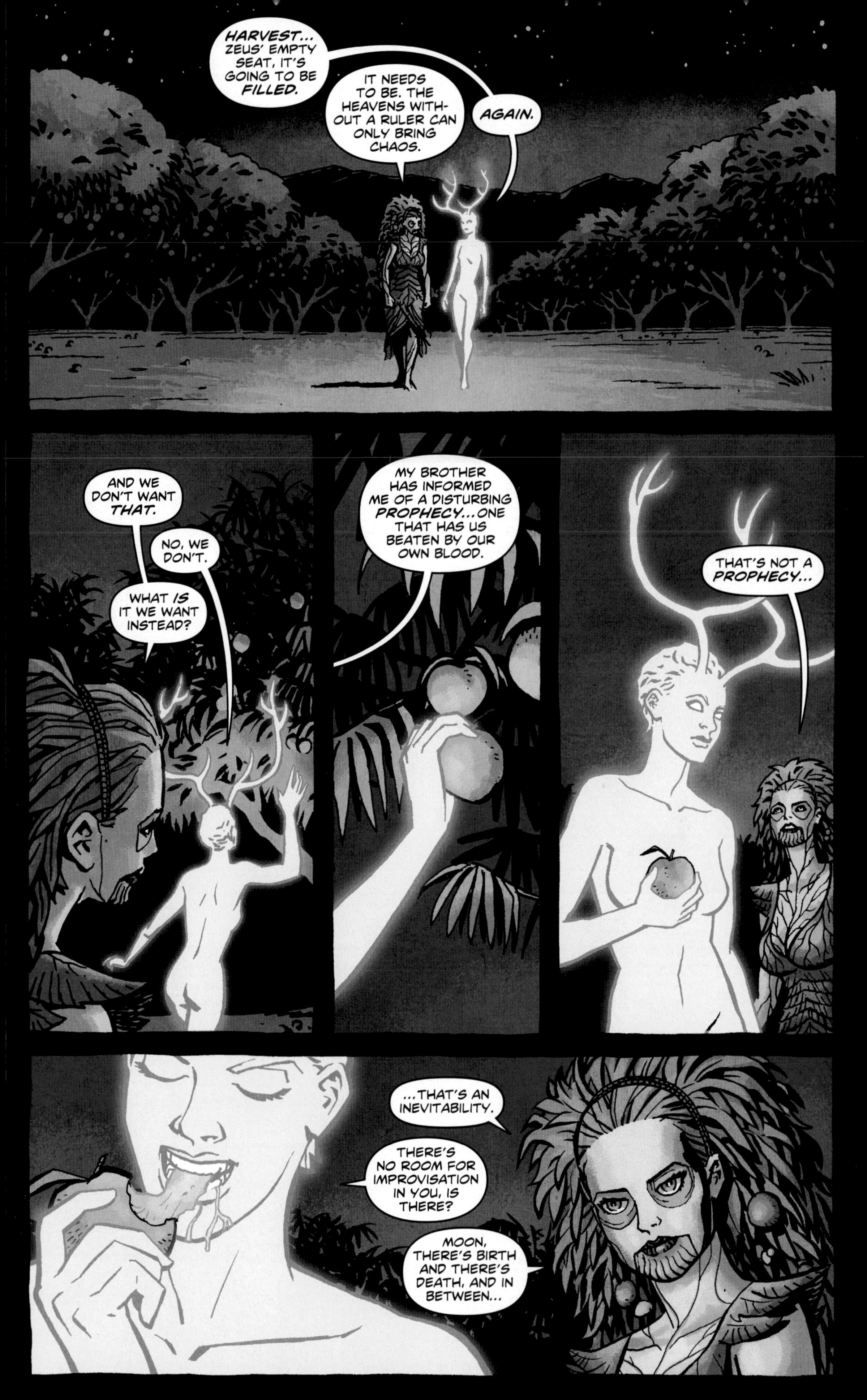
HARVEST... ZEUS' EMPTY SEAT, IT'S GOING TO BE FILLED.
IT NEEDS TO BE. THE HEAVENS WITHOUT A RULER CAN ONLY BRING CHAOS.
AGAIN.
AND WE DON'T WANT THAT.
NO, WE DON'T.
WHAT IS IT WE WANT INSTEAD?
MY BROTHER HAS INFORMED ME OF A DISTURBING PROPHECY...ONE THAT HAS US BEATEN BY OUR OWN BLOOD.
THAT'S NOT A PROPHECY...
...THAT'S AN INEVITABILITY.
THERE'S NO ROOM FOR IMPROVISATION IN YOU, IS THERE?
MOON, THERE'S BIRTH AND THERE'S DEATH, AND IN BETWEEN...

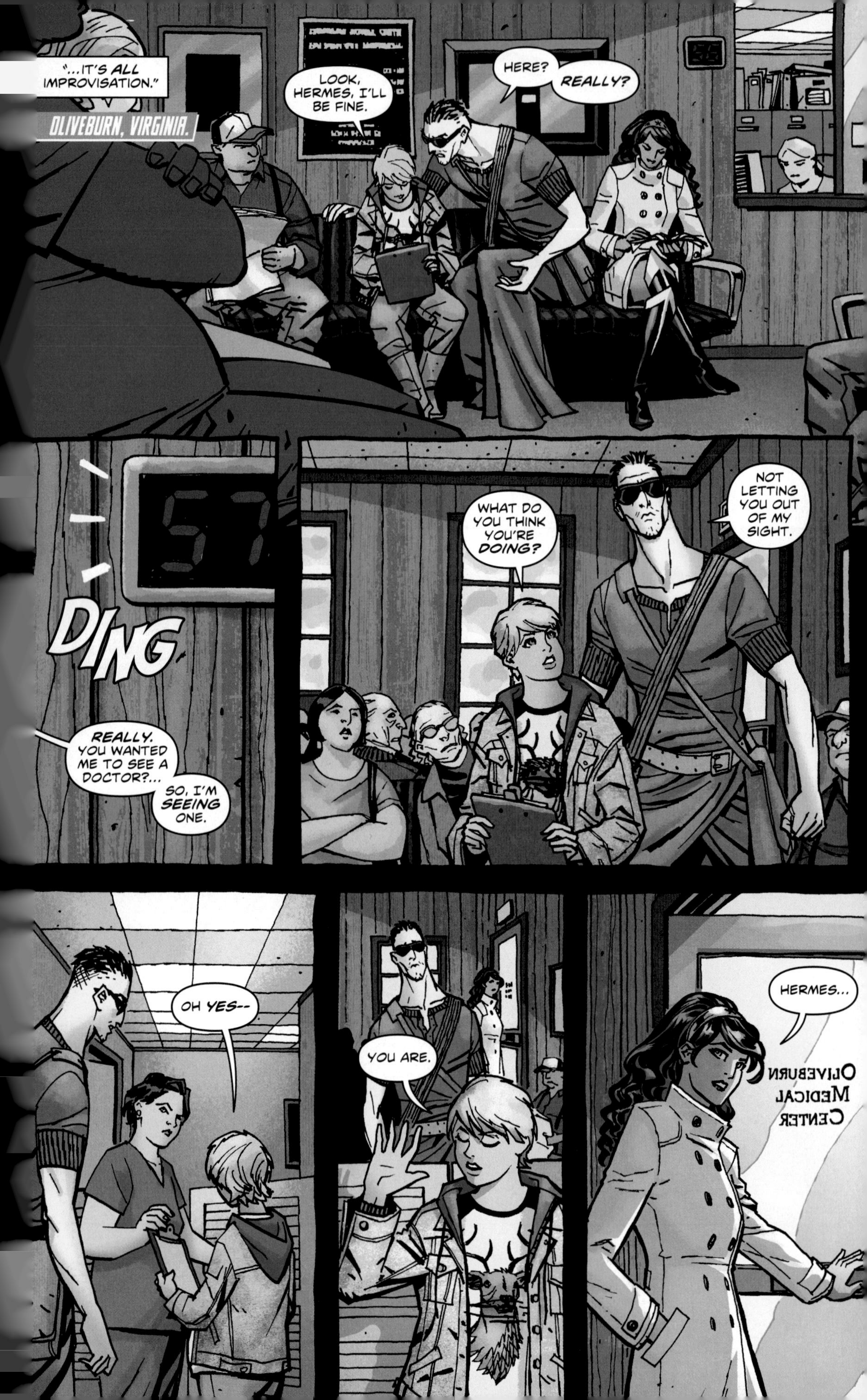

"...IT'S ALL IMPROVISATION."
OLIVEBURN, VIRGINIA.
LOOK, HERMES, I'LL BE FINE.
HERE?
REALLY?
DING
REALLY. YOU WANTED ME TO SEE A DOCTOR?...
SO, I'M SEEING ONE.
WHAT DO YOU THINK YOU'RE DOING?
NOT LETTING YOU OUT OF MY SIGHT.
OH YES--
YOU ARE.
HERMES...
OLIVEBURN MEDICAL CENTER

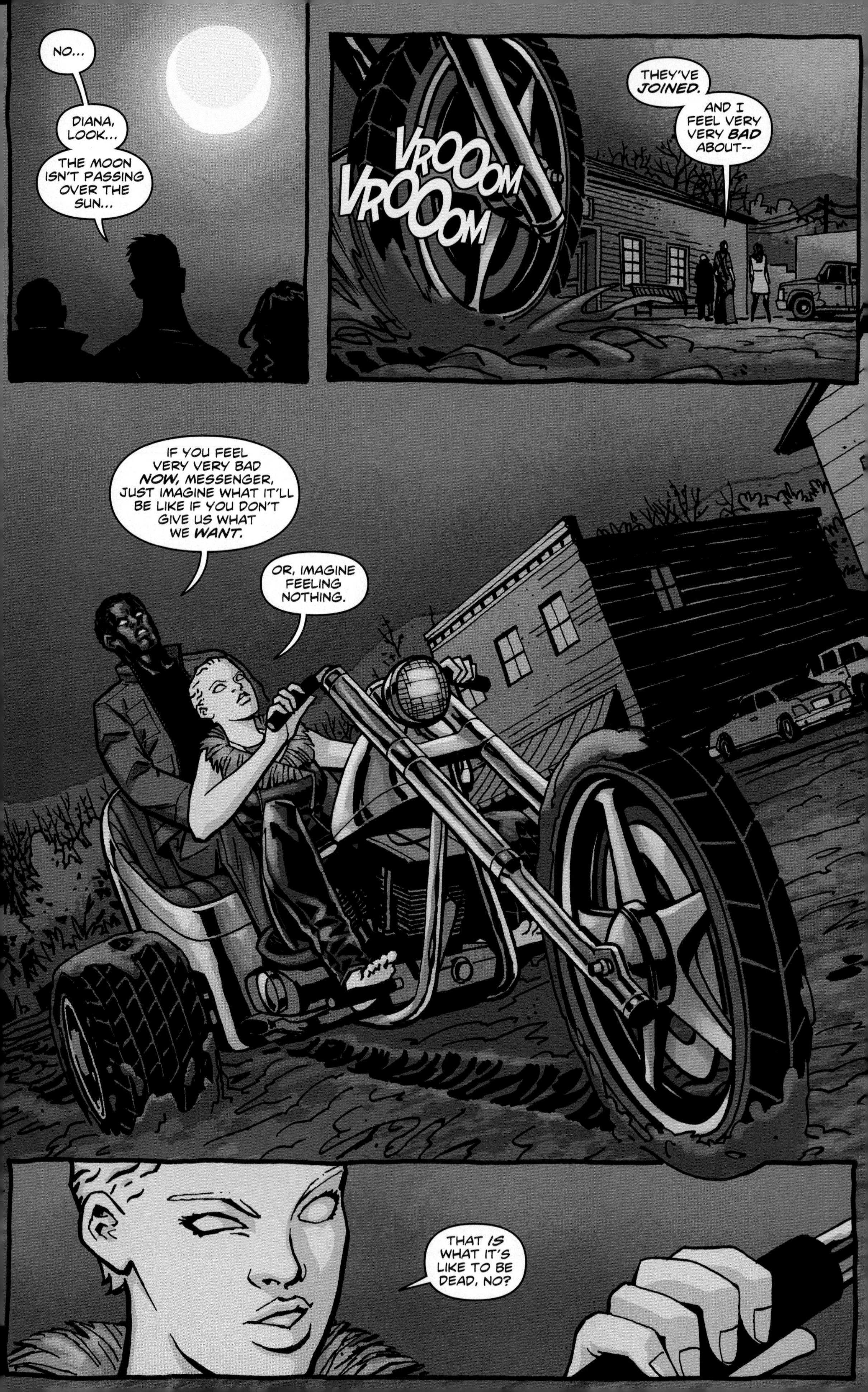

NO...
DIANA, LOOK...
THE MOON ISN'T PASSING OVER THE SUN...
VROOOM VROOOOM
THEY'VE *JOINED.*
AND I FEEL VERY VERY *BAD* ABOUT--
IF YOU FEEL VERY VERY BAD *NOW,* MESSENGER, JUST IMAGINE WHAT IT'LL BE LIKE IF YOU DON'T GIVE US WHAT WE *WANT.*
OR, IMAGINE FEELING NOTHING.
THAT *IS* WHAT IT'S LIKE TO BE DEAD, NO?

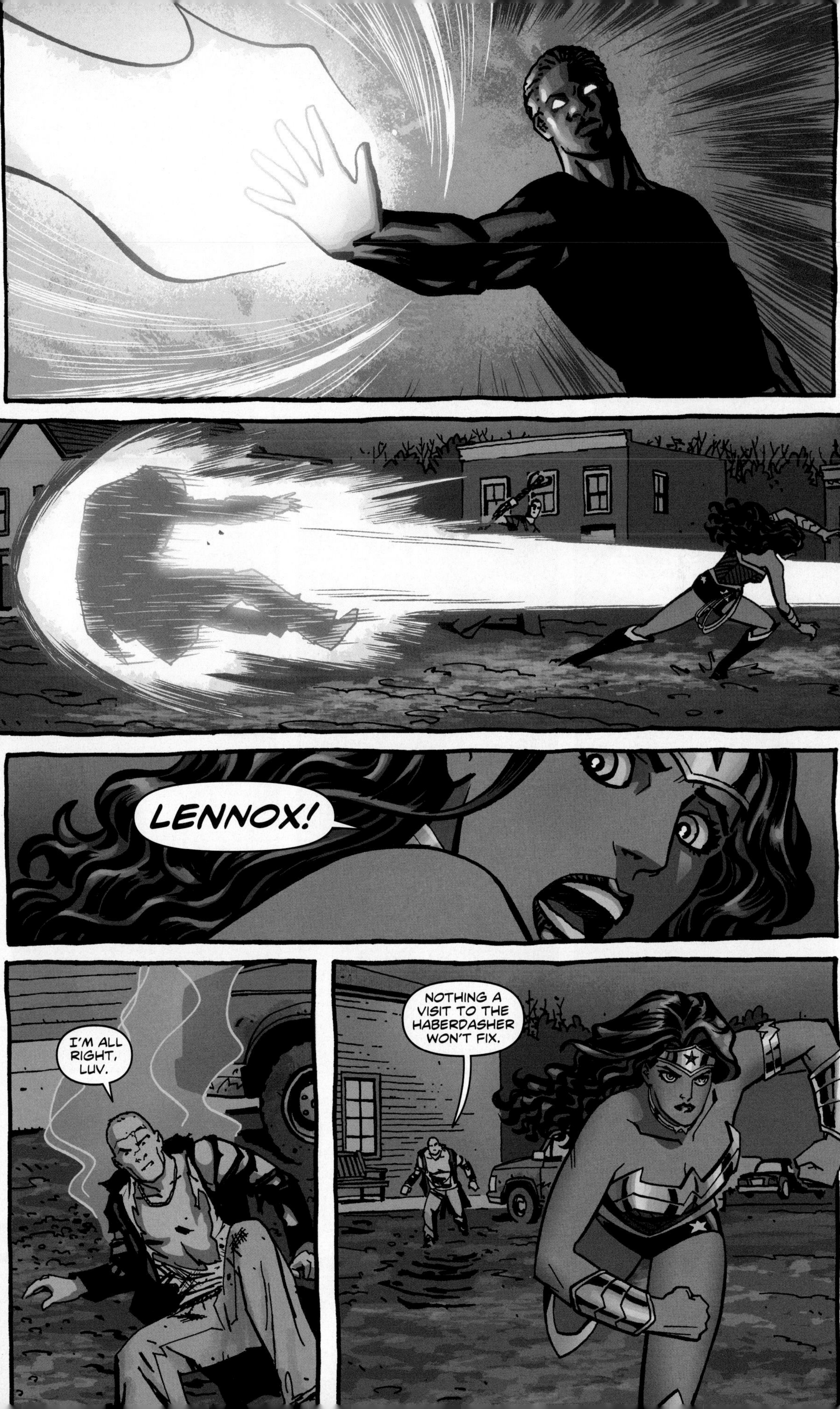
LENNOX!
I'M ALL RIGHT, LUV.
NOTHING A VISIT TO THE HABERDASHER WON'T FIX.

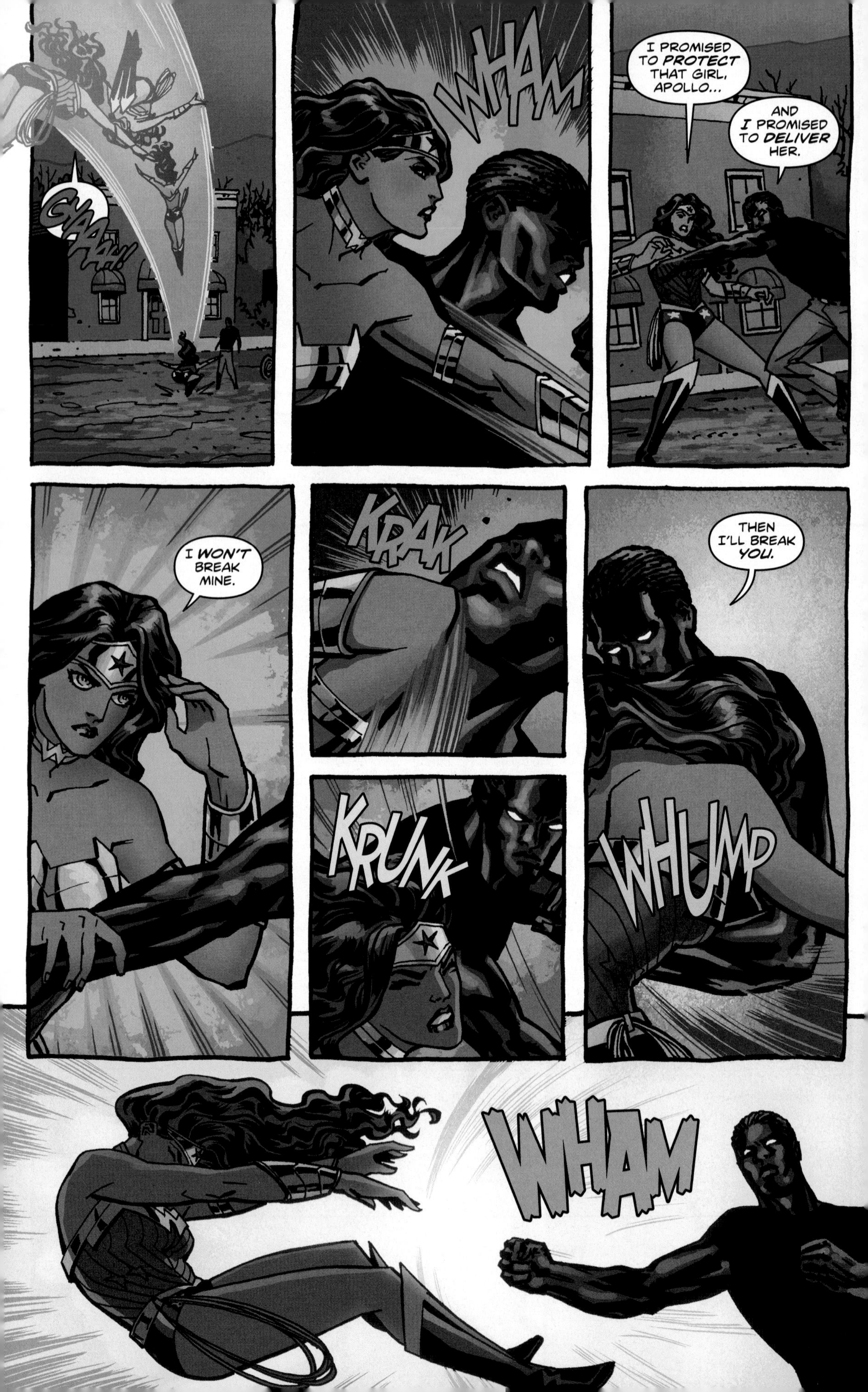
GYAAAH!
WHAM
I PROMISED TO PROTECT THAT GIRL, APOLLO...
AND I PROMISED TO DELIVER HER.
I WON'T BREAK MINE.
KRAK
KRUNK
THEN I'LL BREAK YOU.
WHUMP
WHAM

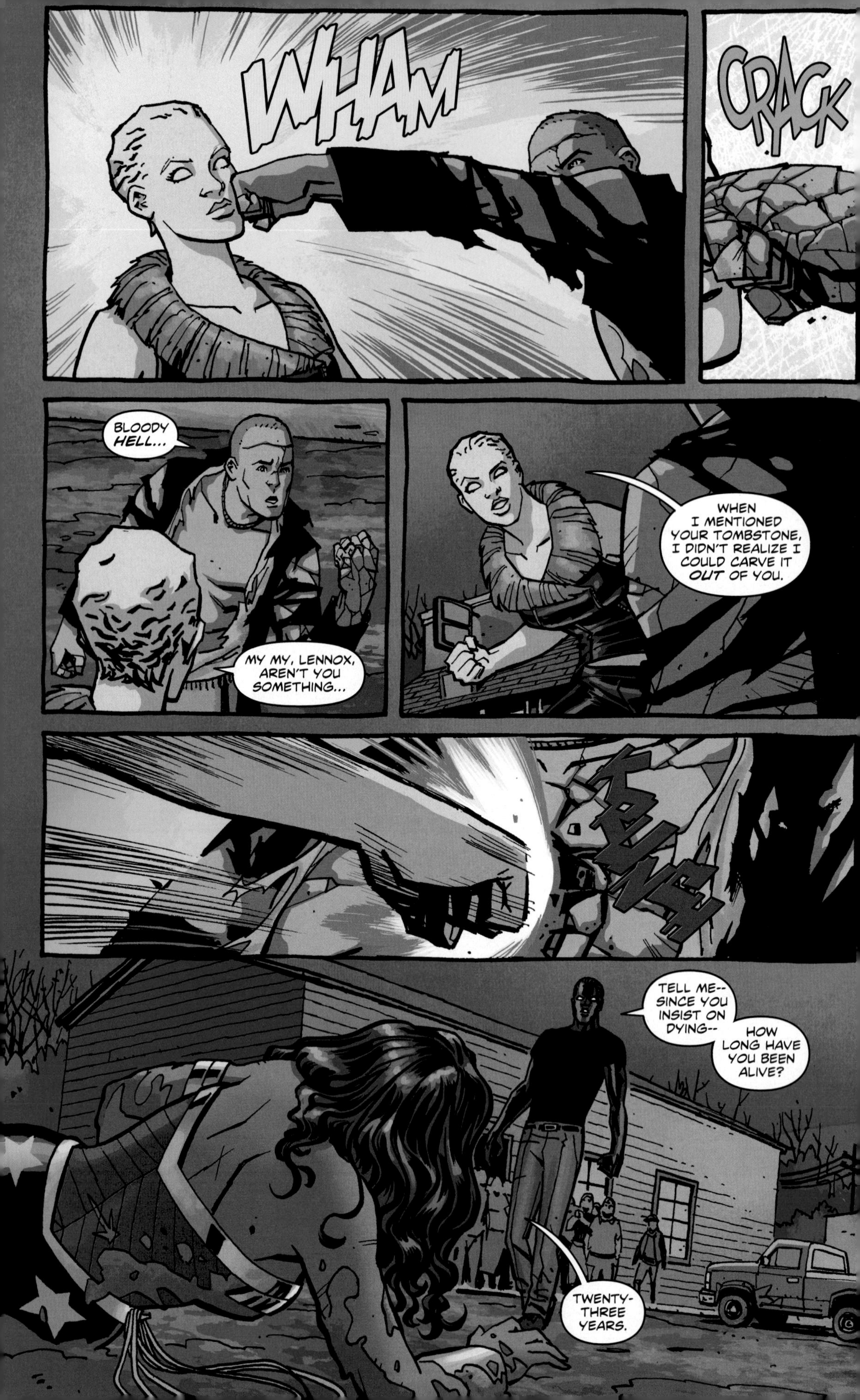
WHAM
CRACK
BLOODY HELL...
MY MY, LENNOX, AREN'T YOU SOMETHING...
WHEN I MENTIONED YOUR TOMBSTONE, I DIDN'T REALIZE I COULD CARVE IT OUT OF YOU.
KRUNCH
TELL ME-- SINCE YOU INSIST ON DYING--
HOW LONG HAVE YOU BEEN ALIVE?
TWENTY-THREE YEARS.

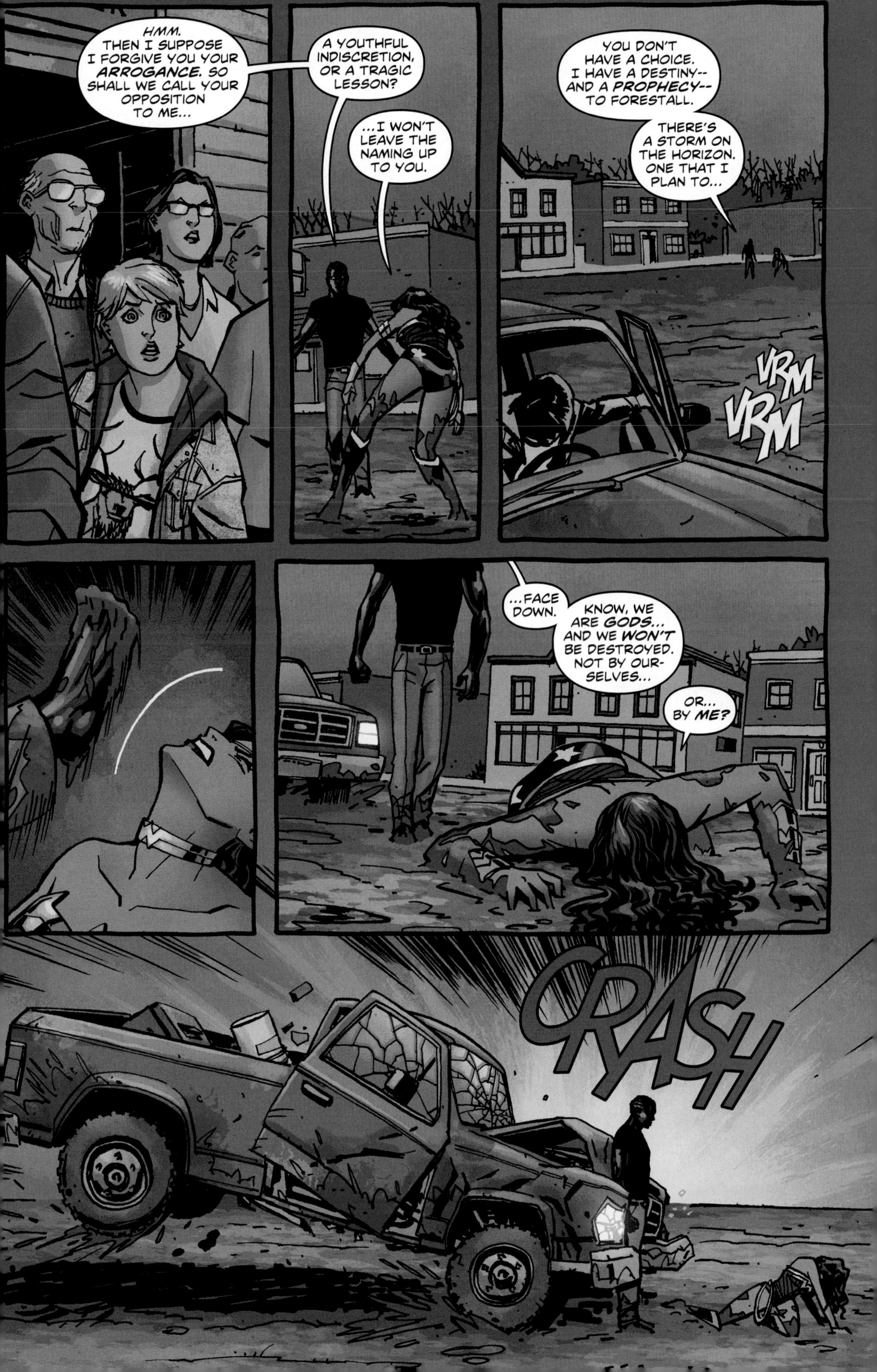
HMM. THEN I SUPPOSE I FORGIVE YOU YOUR ARROGANCE. SO SHALL WE CALL YOUR OPPOSITION TO ME...
A YOUTHFUL INDISCRETION, OR A TRAGIC LESSON?
...I WON'T LEAVE THE NAMING UP TO YOU.
YOU DON'T HAVE A CHOICE. I HAVE A DESTINY-- AND A PROPHECY-- TO FORESTALL.
THERE'S A STORM ON THE HORIZON. ONE THAT I PLAN TO...
VRM VRM
...FACE DOWN.
KNOW, WE ARE GODS... AND WE WON'T BE DESTROYED. NOT BY OURSELVES...
OR... BY ME?
CRASH

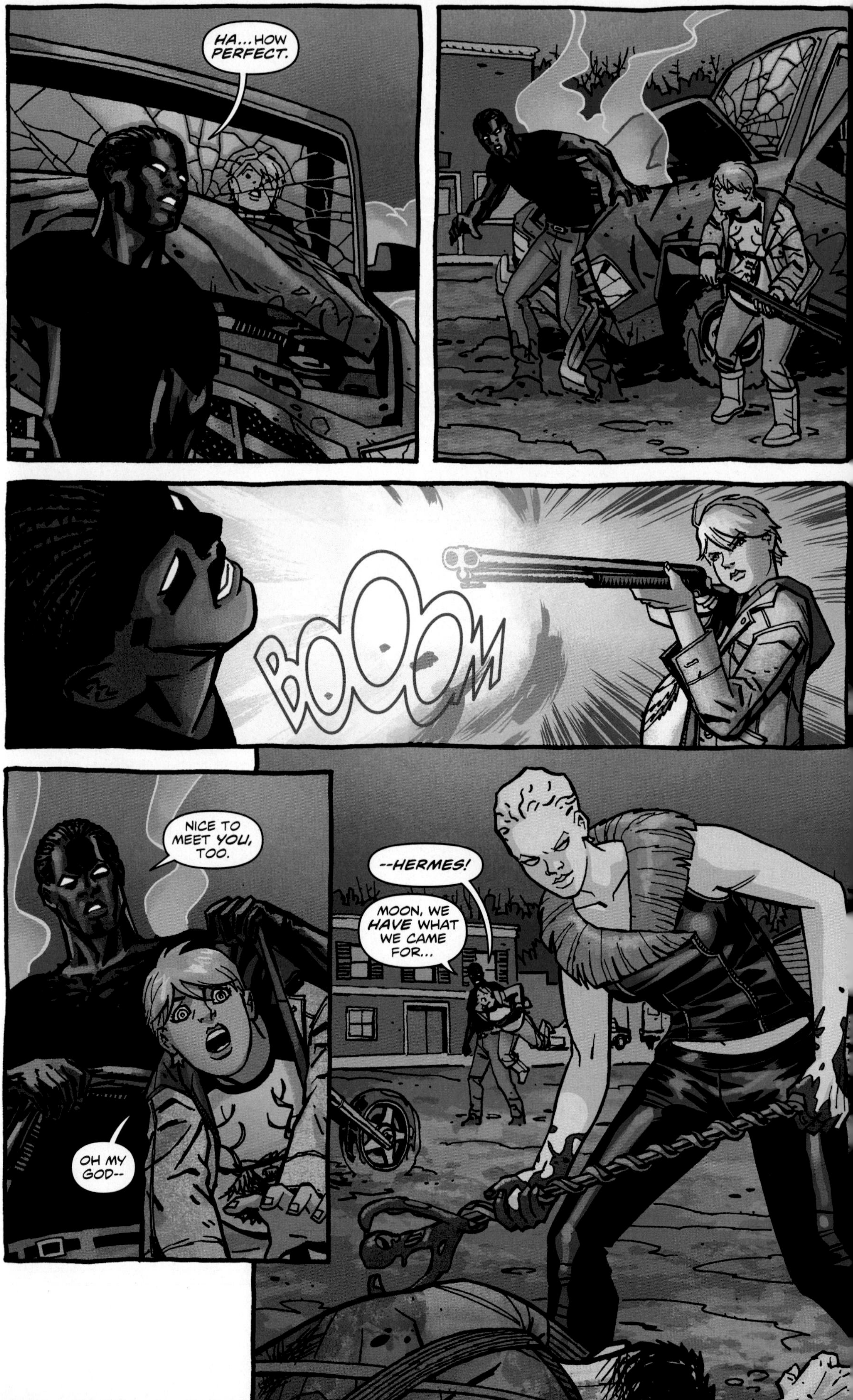
HA... HOW PERFECT.
BOOOOM
NICE TO MEET YOU, TOO.
OH MY GOD--
--HERMES!
MOON, WE HAVE WHAT WE CAME FOR...

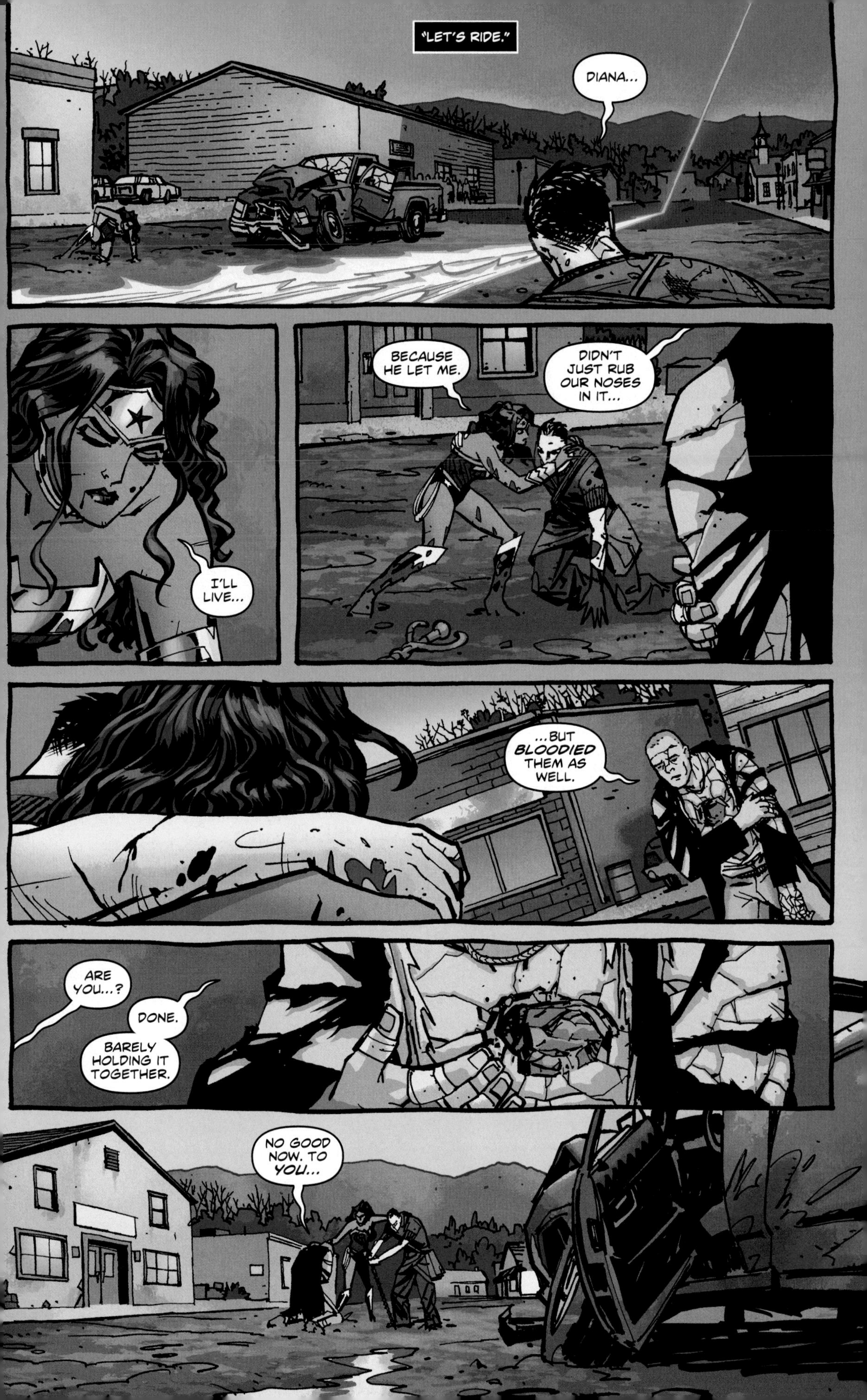
"LET'S RIDE."
DIANA...
I'LL LIVE...
BECAUSE HE LET ME.
DIDN'T JUST RUB OUR NOSES IN IT...
...BUT BLOODIED THEM AS WELL.
ARE YOU...?
DONE.
BARELY HOLDING IT TOGETHER.
NO GOOD NOW. TO YOU...

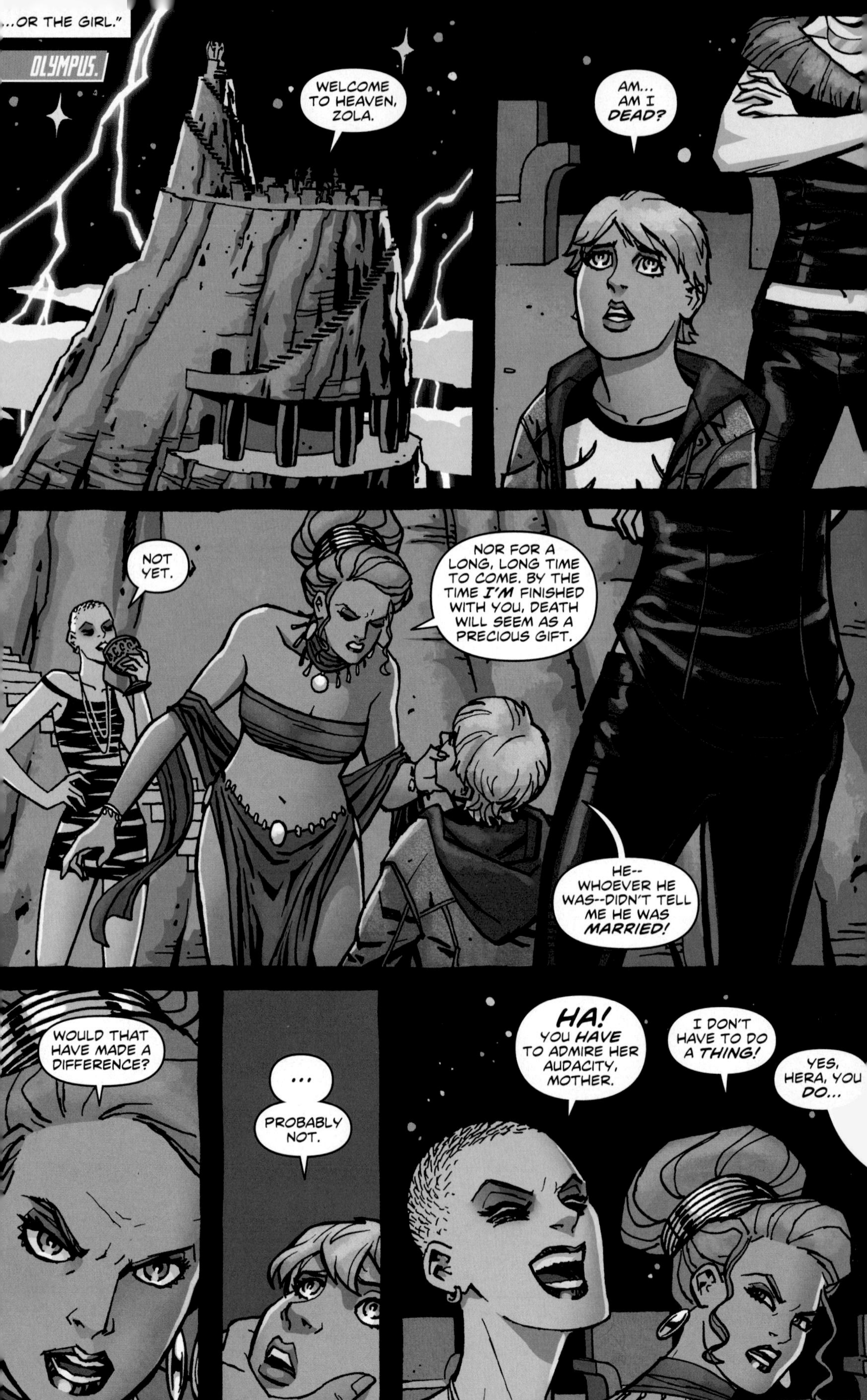
...OR THE GIRL."
OLYMPUS.
WELCOME TO HEAVEN, ZOLA.
AM... AM I DEAD?
NOT YET.
NOR FOR A LONG, LONG TIME TO COME. BY THE TIME I'M FINISHED WITH YOU, DEATH WILL SEEM AS A PRECIOUS GIFT.
HE-- WHOEVER HE WAS--DIDN'T TELL ME HE WAS MARRIED!
WOULD THAT HAVE MADE A DIFFERENCE?
...
PROBABLY NOT.
HA! YOU HAVE TO ADMIRE HER AUDACITY, MOTHER.
I DON'T HAVE TO DO A THING!
YES, HERA, YOU DO...

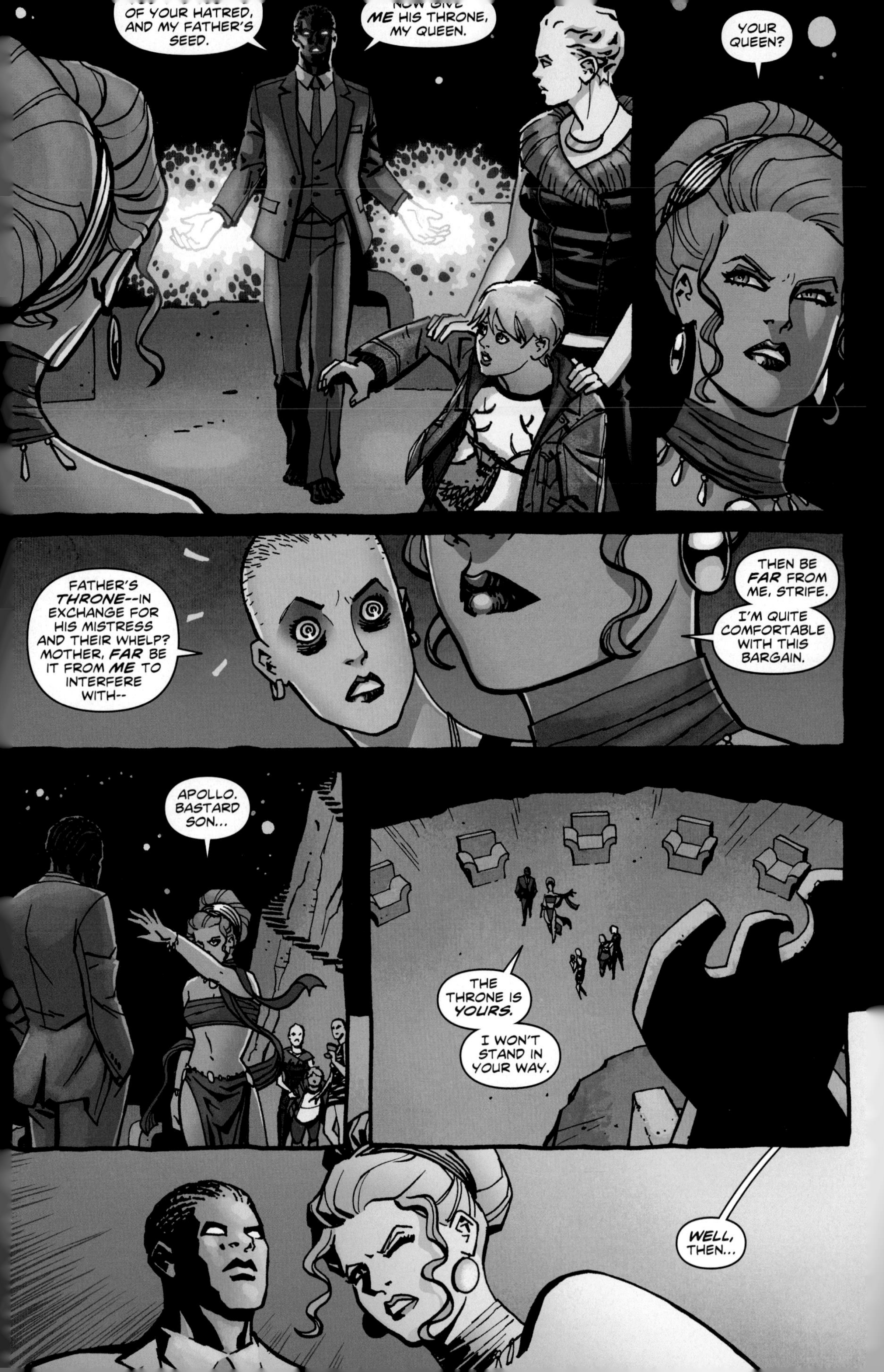

OF YOUR HATRED, AND MY FATHER'S SEED.
NOW GIVE ME HIS THRONE, MY QUEEN.
YOUR QUEEN?
FATHER'S THRONE--IN EXCHANGE FOR HIS MISTRESS AND THEIR WHELP? MOTHER, FAR BE IT FROM ME TO INTERFERE WITH--
THEN BE FAR FROM ME, STRIFE.
I'M QUITE COMFORTABLE WITH THIS BARGAIN.
APOLLO. BASTARD SON...
THE THRONE IS YOURS.
I WON'T STAND IN YOUR WAY.
WELL, THEN...

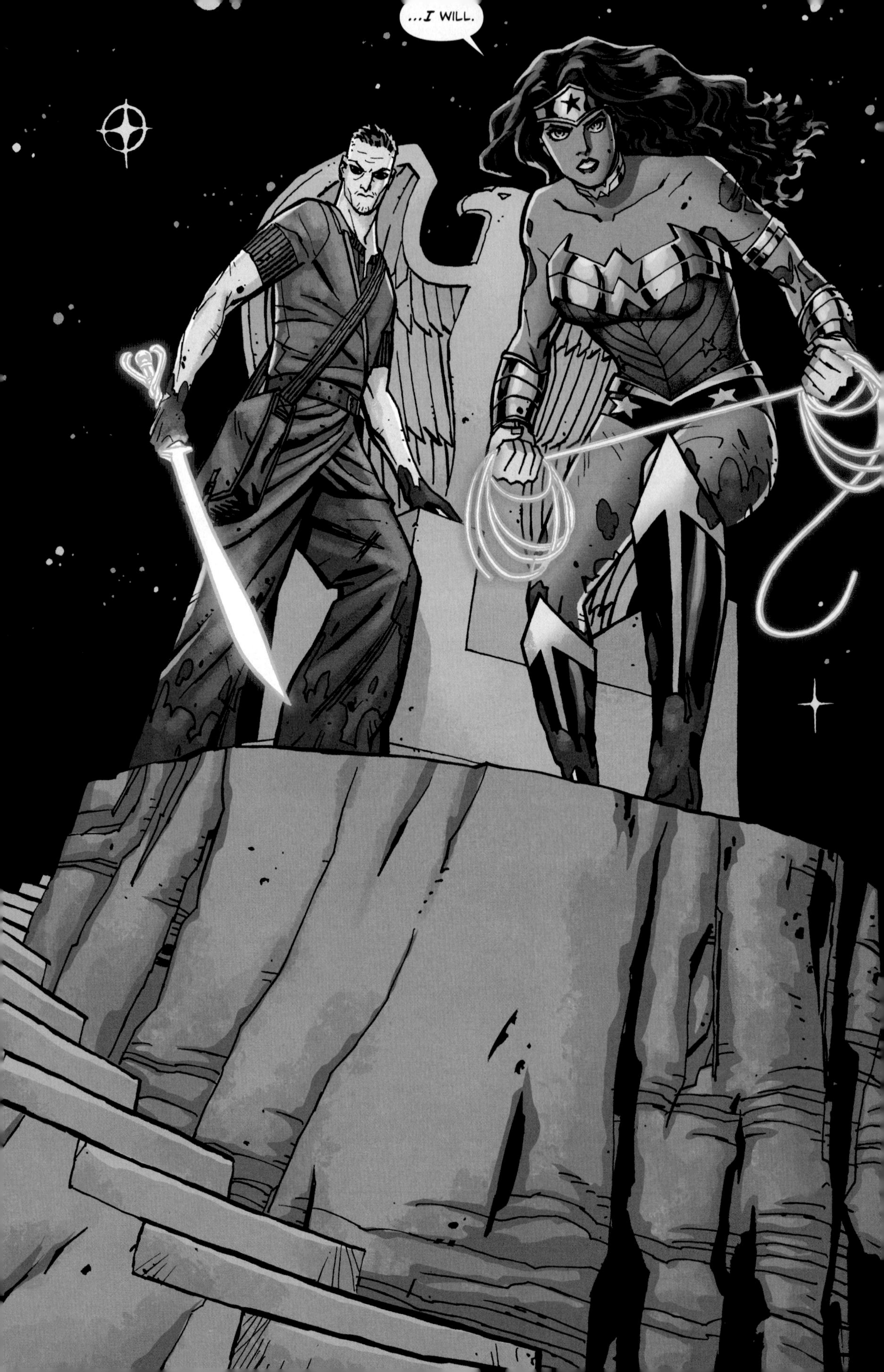
...I WILL.

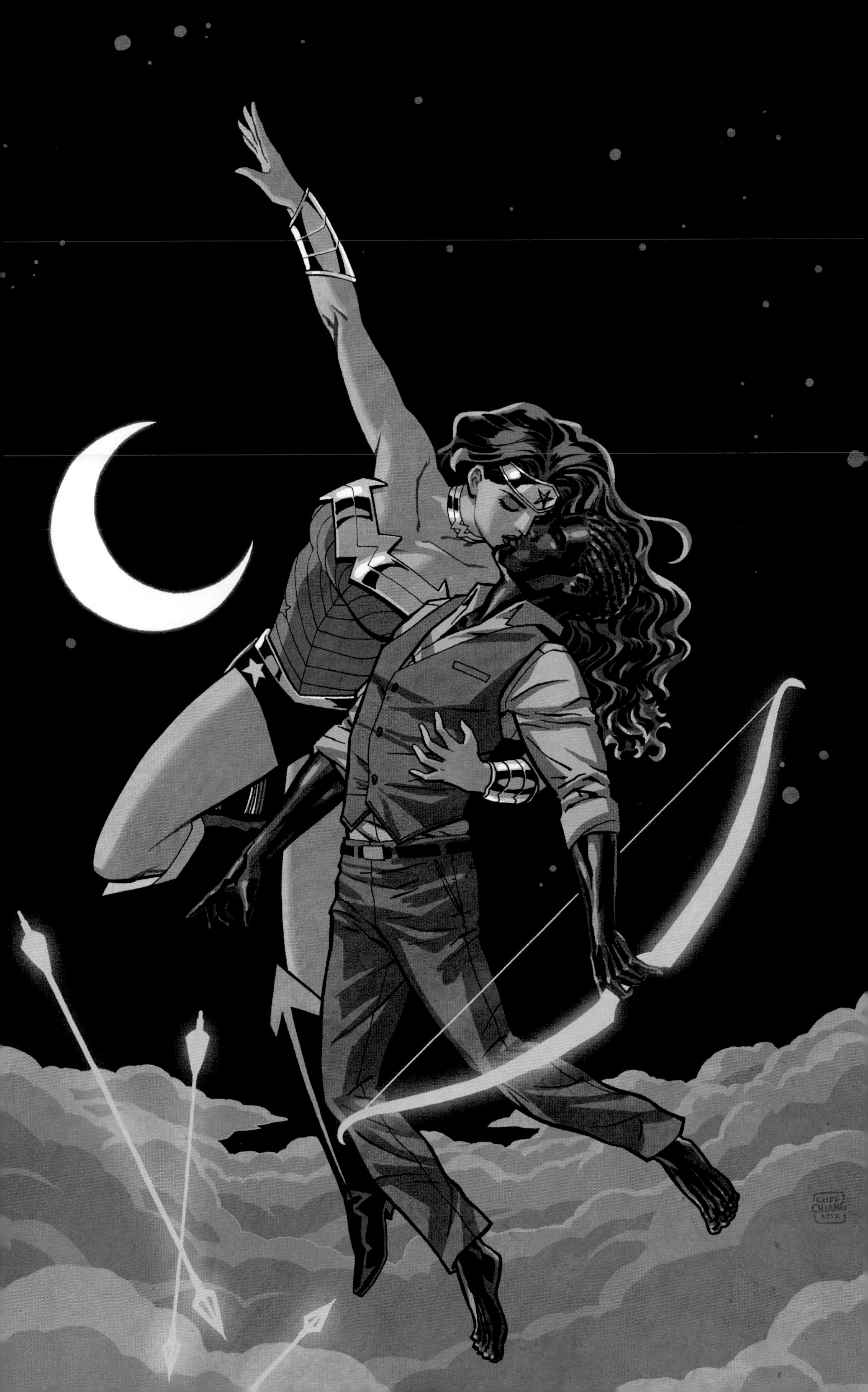
CLIFF CHIANG 2012

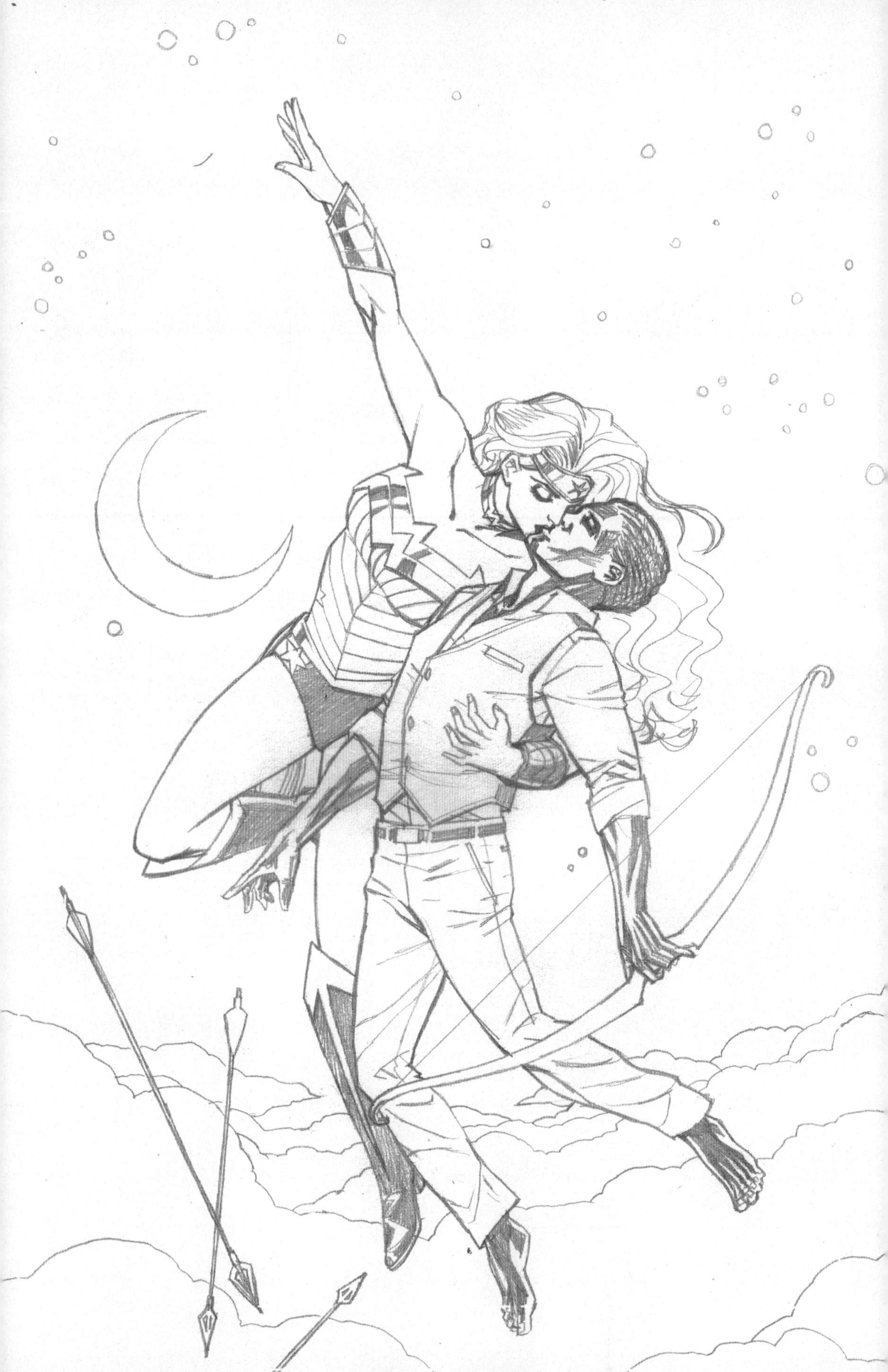

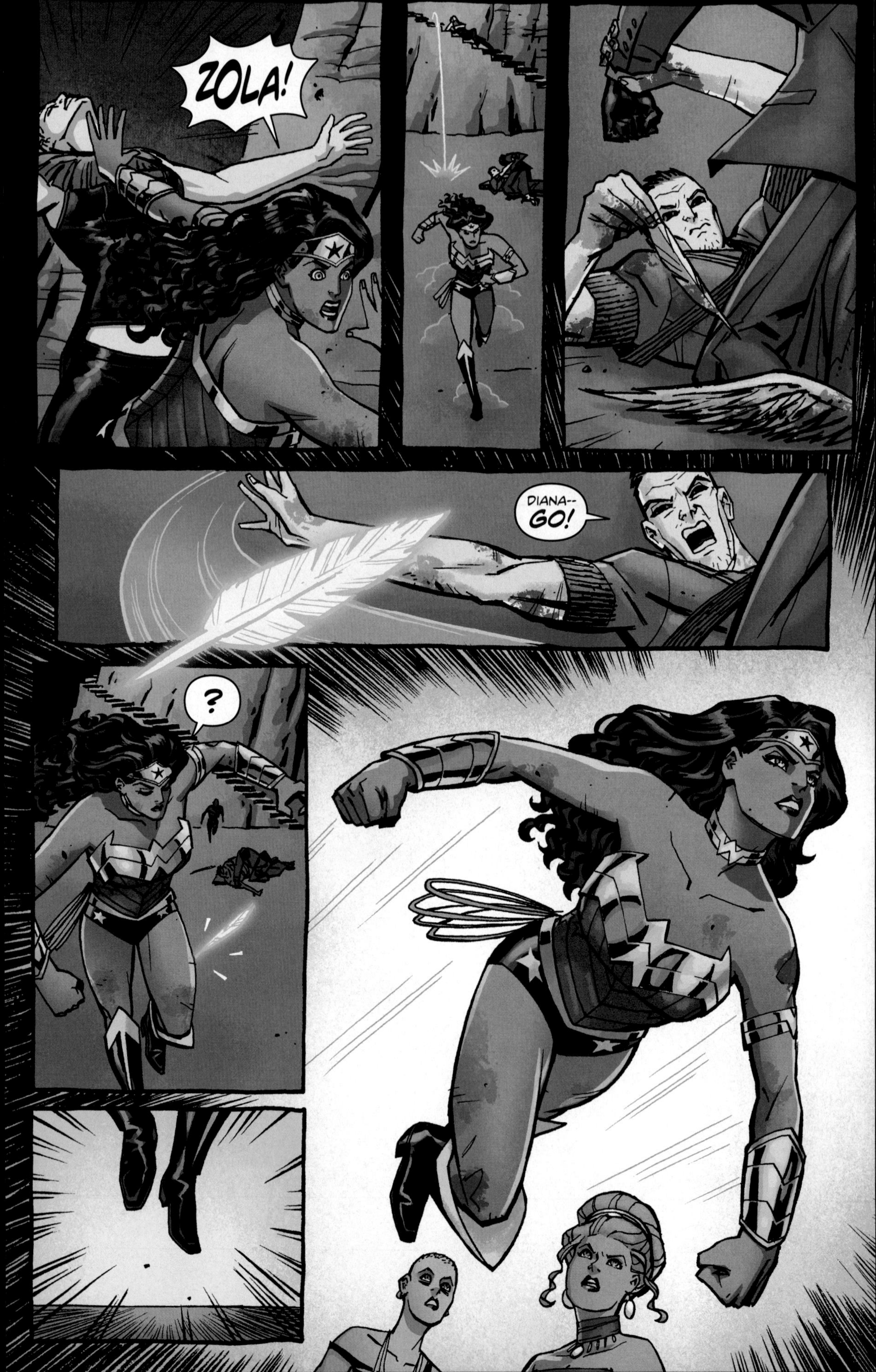
ZOLA!
DIANA--
GO!
?

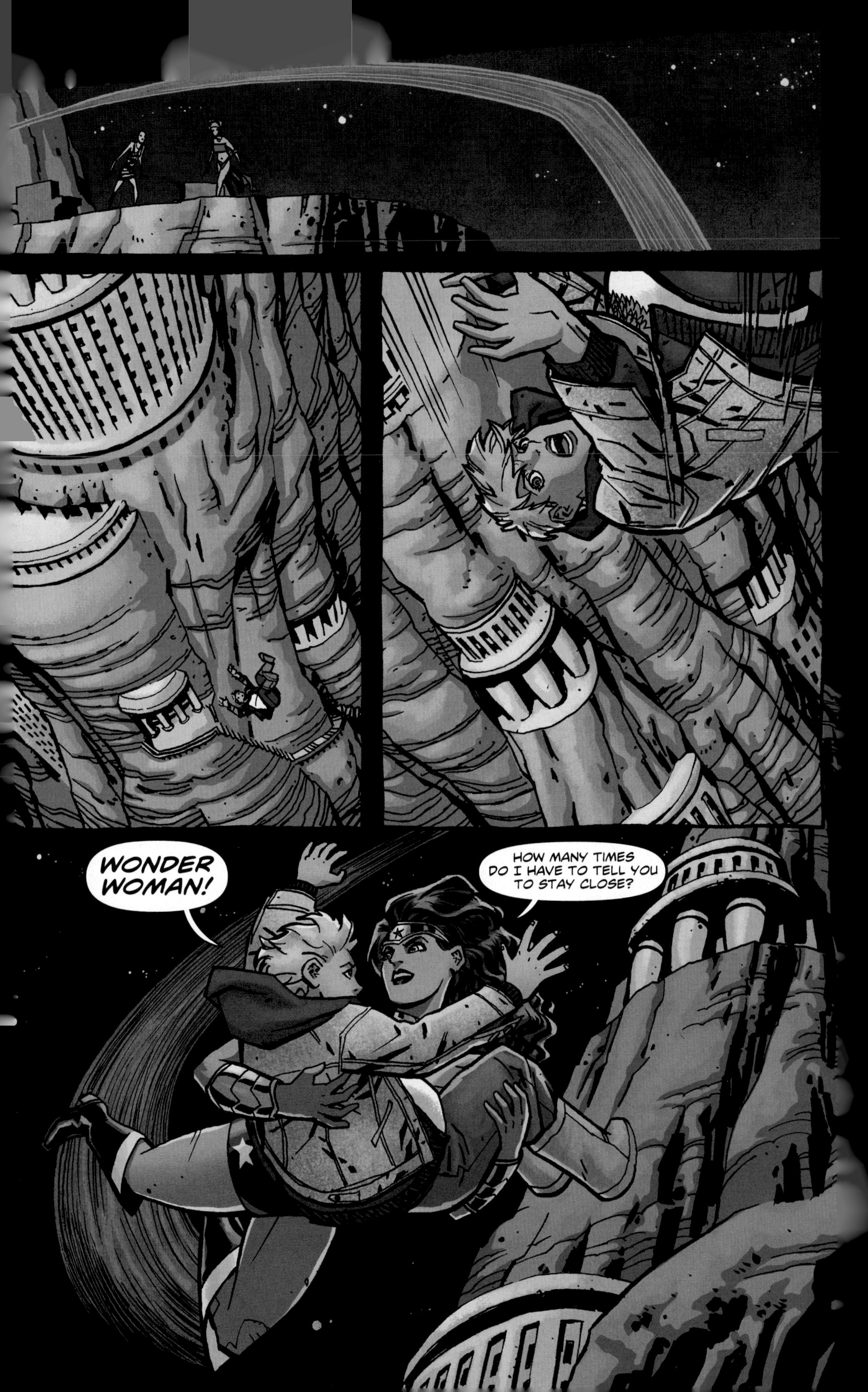
WONDER WOMAN!
HOW MANY TIMES DO I HAVE TO TELL YOU TO STAY CLOSE?

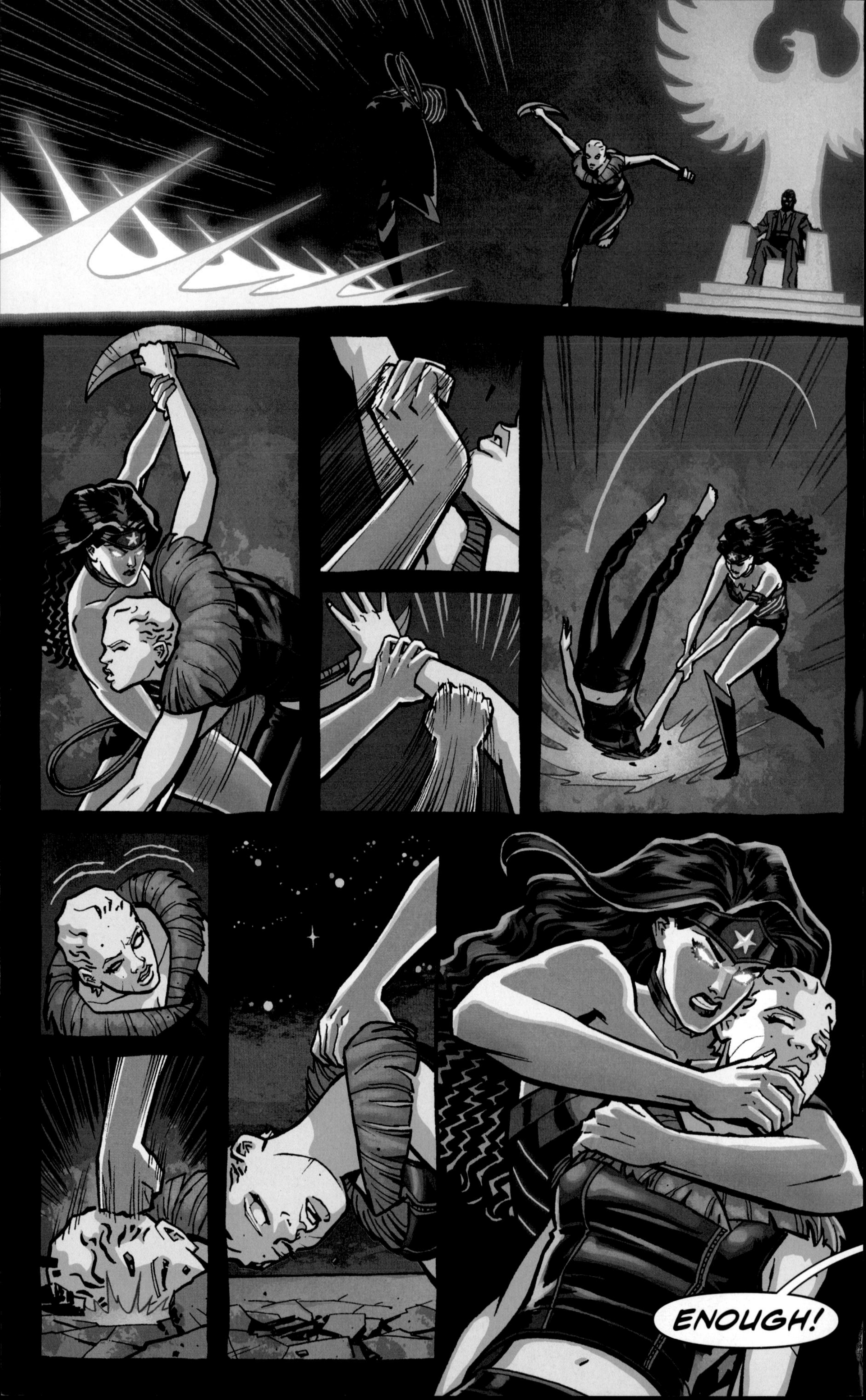
ENOUGH!

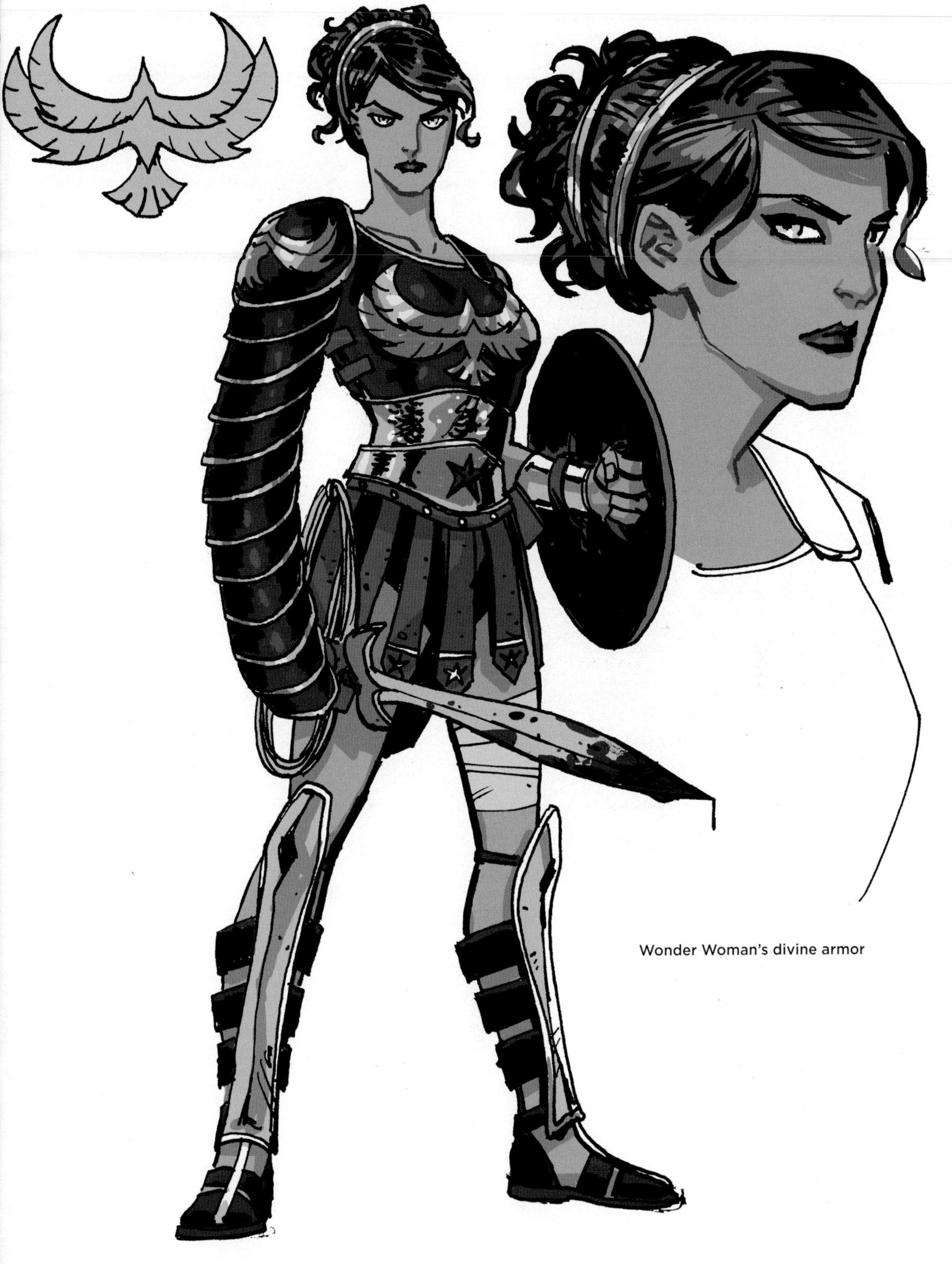

Wonder Woman's divine armor

Hephaestus

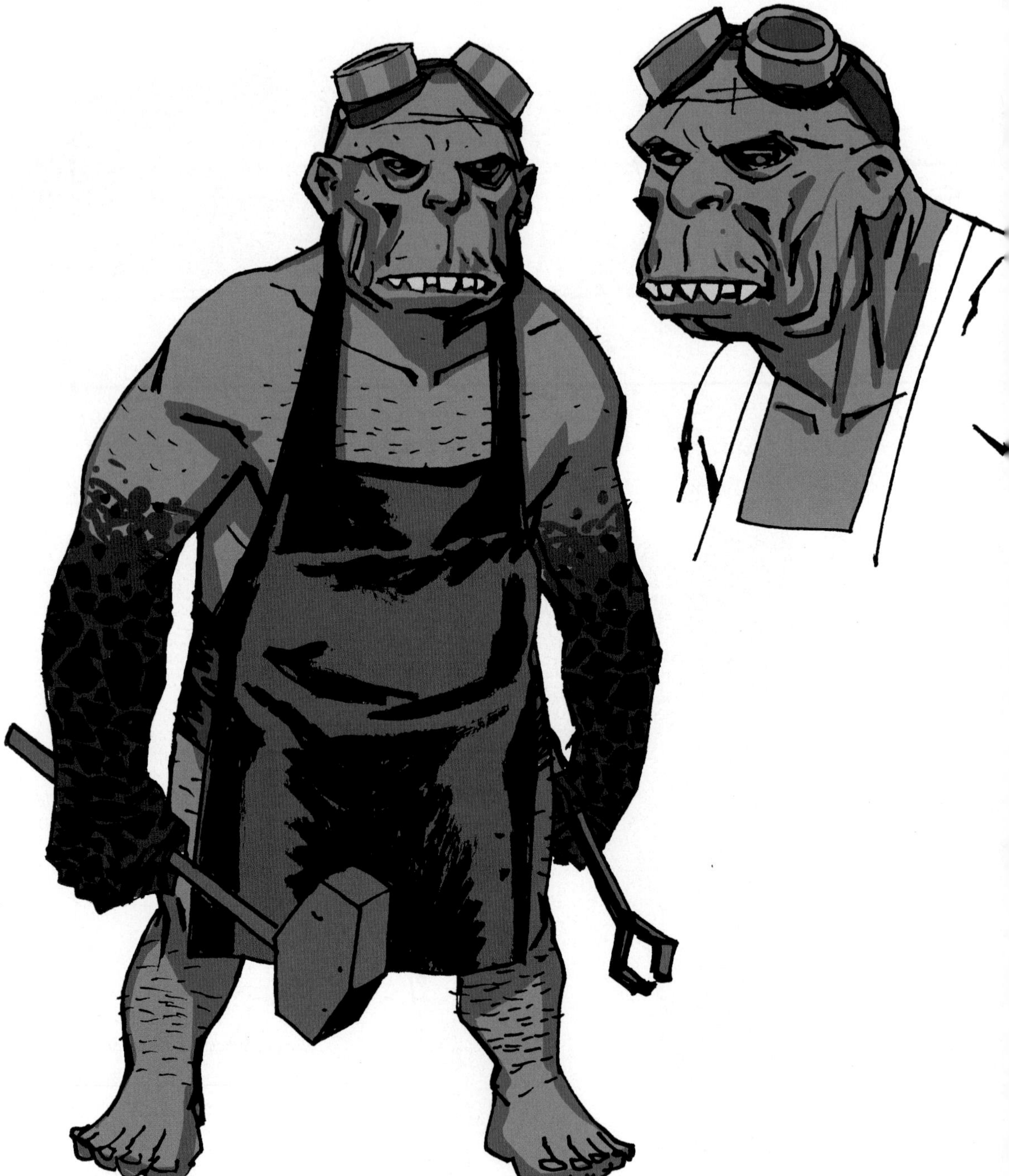

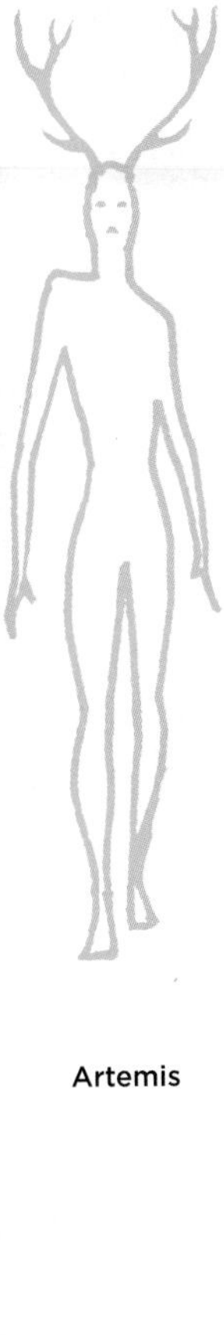

Artemis

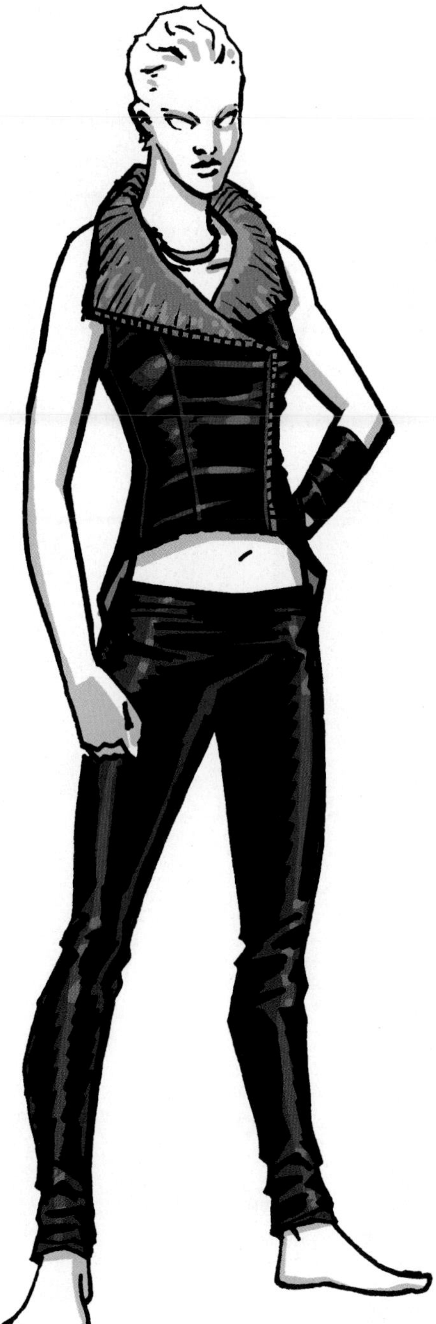

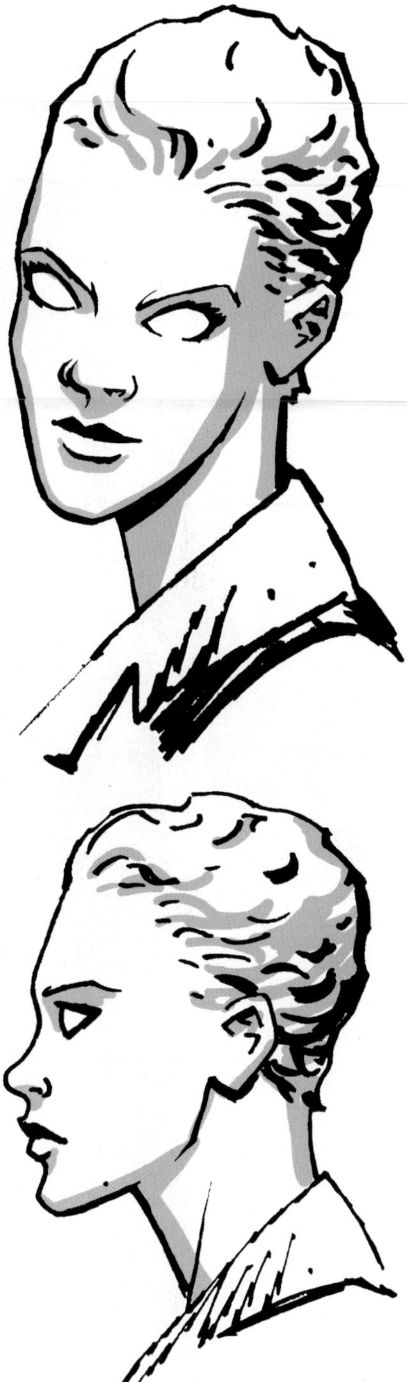

Eros

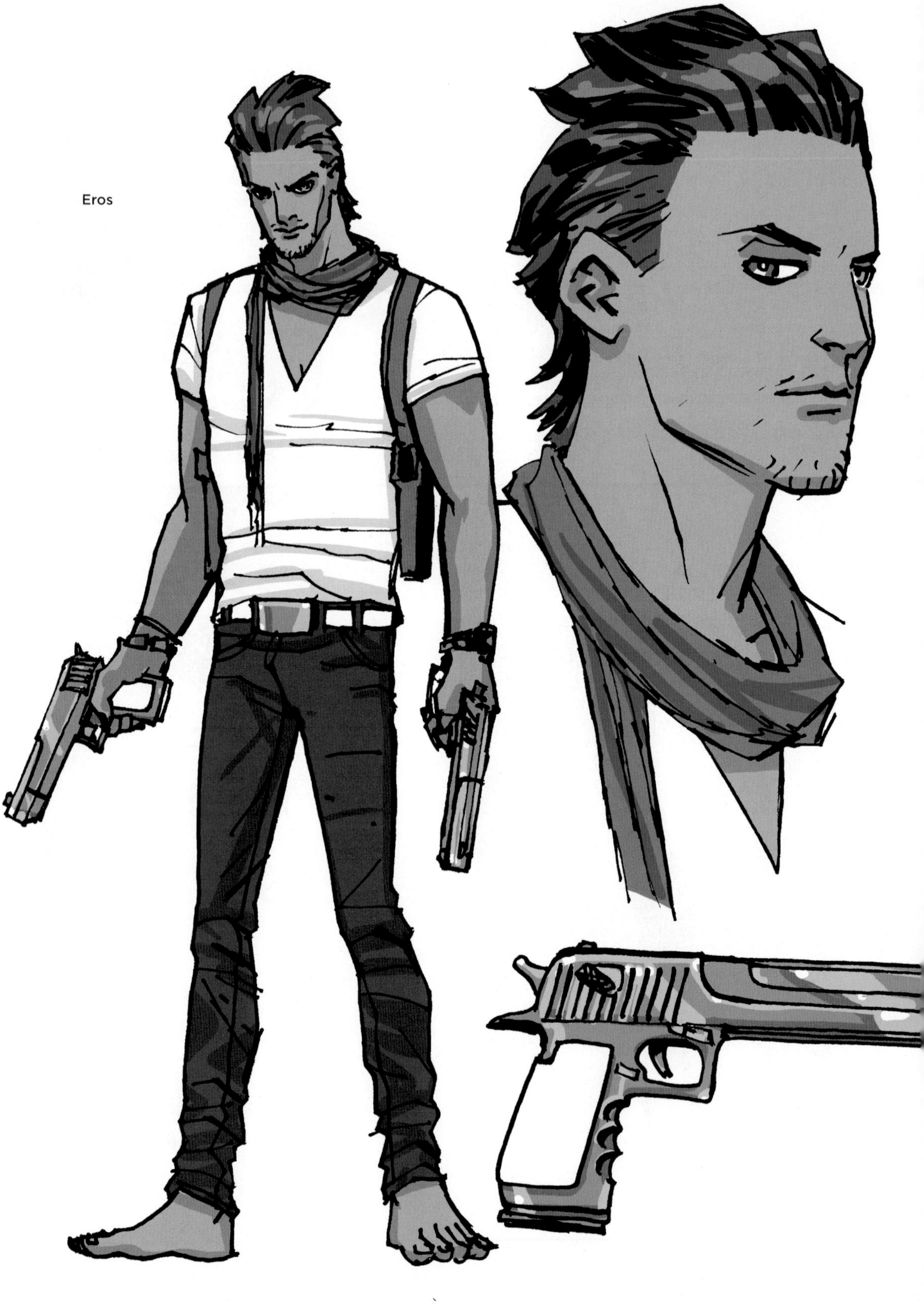

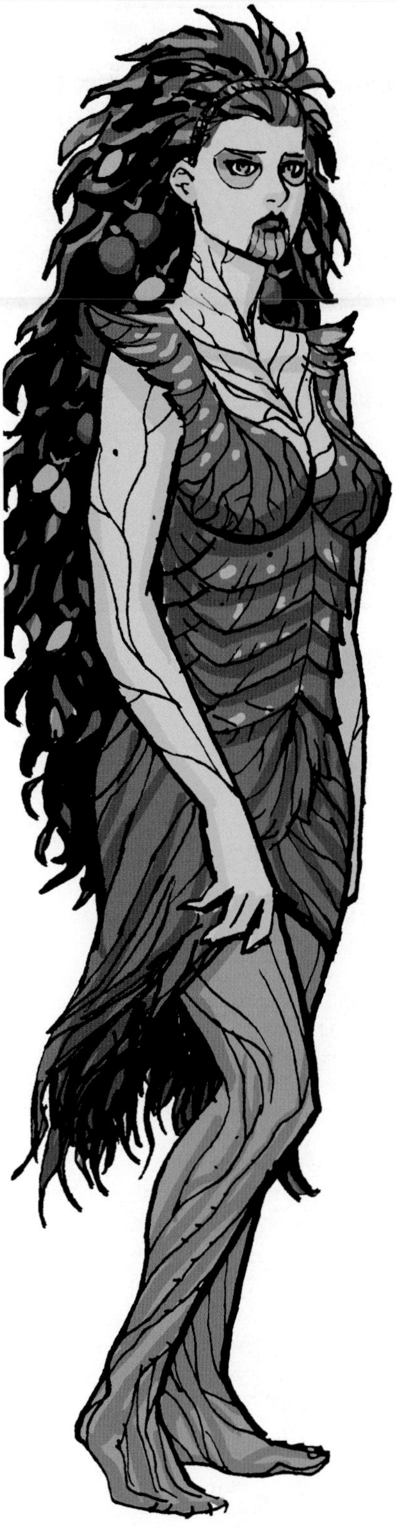

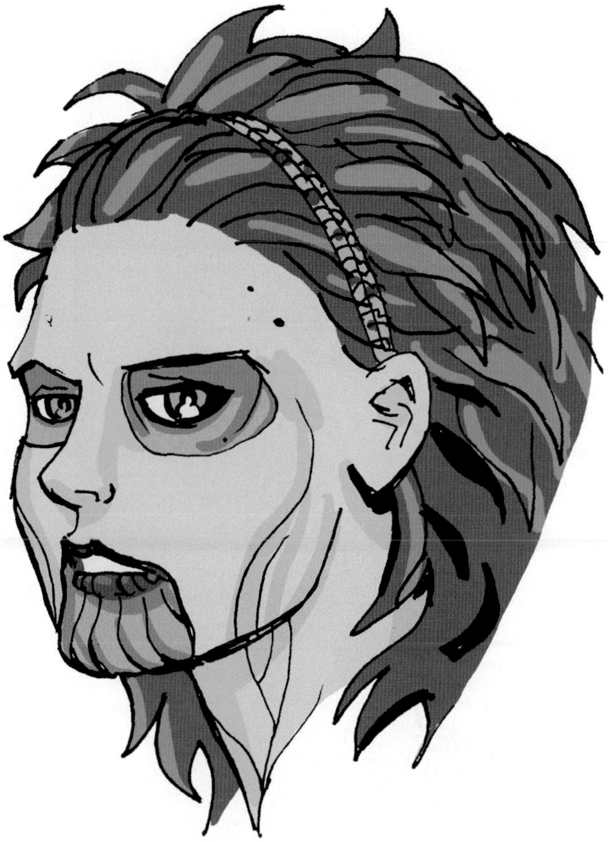

Demeter

WONDER WOMAN #7 cover sketches

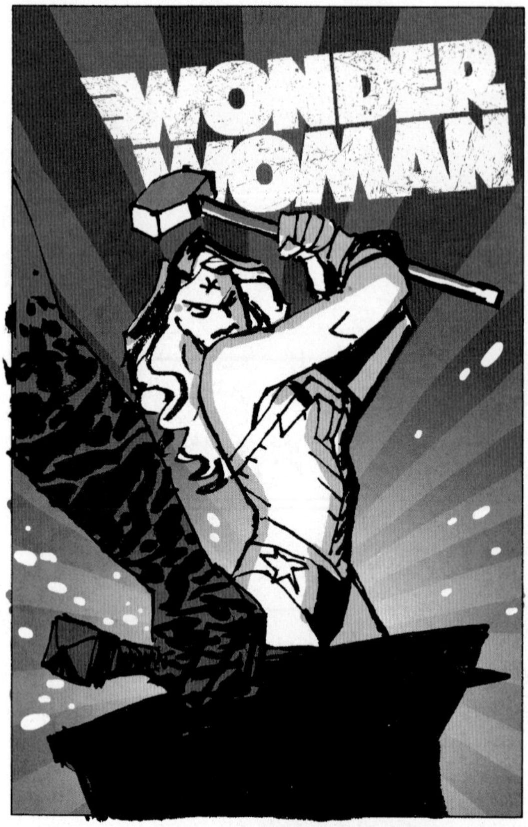
WONDER
WOMAN

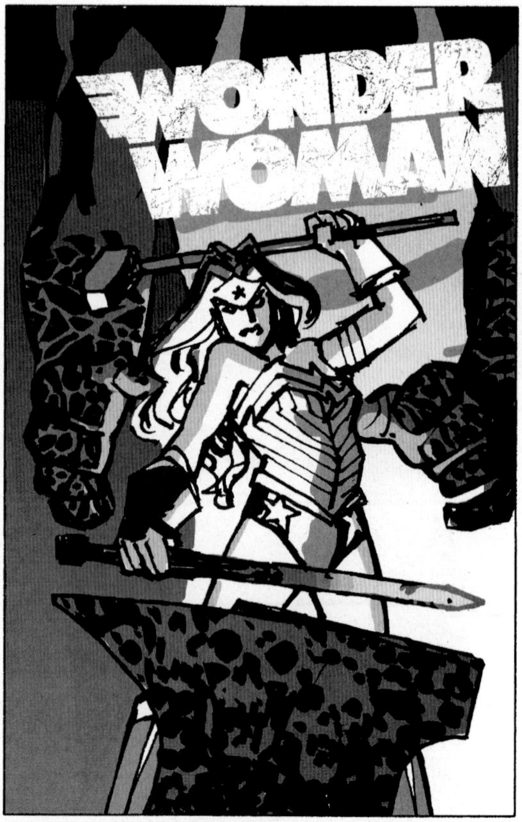
WONDER
WOMAN

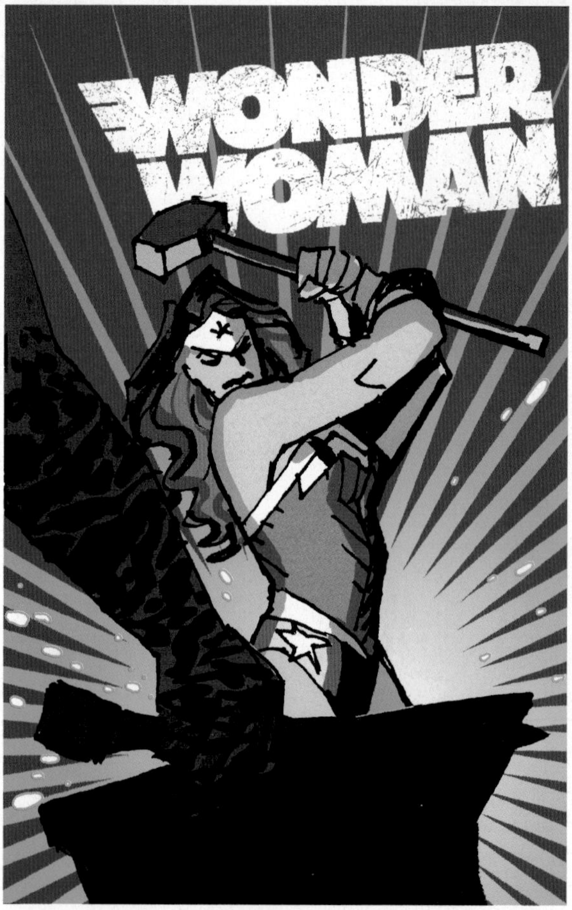
WONDER
WOMAN

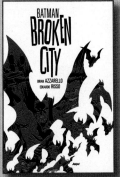

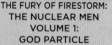
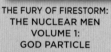